T0358271

Stretching the Qing Bureaucracy in the 1826 Sea-Transport Experiment

Monies, Markets, and Finance in East Asia, 1600–1900

Edited by

Hans Ulrich Vogel

VOLUME 12

The titles published in this series are listed at *brill.com/mmf*

Stretching the Qing Bureaucracy in the 1826 Sea-Transport Experiment

By

Jane Kate Leonard

BRILL

LEIDEN | BOSTON

The Library of Congress Cataloging-in-Publication Data is available online at http://catalog.loc.gov

Typeface for the Latin, Greek, and Cyrillic scripts: "Brill". See and download: brill.com/brill-typeface.

ISSN 2210-2876
ISBN 978-90-04-38457-6 (hardback)
ISBN 978-90-04-38458-3 (e-book)

*With Gratitude
to
Benny Leonard:
Map Maker,
Illustrator,
and
Proofreader*

∴

Contents

Acknowledgments

I would like to acknowledge with gratitude the teachers and colleagues who have supported and encouraged my scholarly work over the years: Professor Knight Biggerstaff (Cornell University), Wang Gungwu (Australian National University, Canberra), John S. Gregory (La Trobe University, Melbourne), Robert Jones and Keith Bryant (Chairpersons, History Department, The University of Akron), Huang Guosheng (Fujianshifandaxue, Fuzhou, Fujian Province). Of great assistance in the present work on the Qing sea-transport project, were Prof. Dr. Hans Ulrich Vogel (Institute of Asian and Oriental Studies, University of Tübingen), Prof. Dr. Barbara Mittler (Institute of Chinese Studies, Heidelberg University), Dr. Nanny Kim (Institute of Chinese Studies, Heidelberg University), and Robert P. Gardella (History Department, U.S. Merchant Marine Academy).

Jane Kate Leonard
June 18, 2018

Illustrations

Maps

Figures

Sea Transport Chronology

The Challenge of Innovation.
The 1826 Sea-Transport Experiment

1   The 1825 Grand Canal Crisis

When intense storms and disastrous flooding in early 1825 destroyed the Grand Canal at its junction with the Yellow River and brought strategic government grain shipping to a halt, the Daoguang Emperor (1821–1851), his trusted inner court advisers, and key provincial officials in the eight-province canal zone successfully crafted and carried out a bold new plan in 1826 to ship nearly 1.6 million *shi* of premium-grade tax grain from the Jiangnan jurisdictions of Susongchangtaizhen by sea from Shanghai to the northern port of Tianjin, then onward by canal to the capital granaries.[1] Sea transport had never been used during the Qing dynasty; there were no provisions in the administrative code for doing so; nonetheless, a plan was formulated by the end of 1825 and implemented the following spring. How was the Qing leadership able to carry out such a plan so quickly and in the face of great difficulties in doing so, given the spare, thinly spread character of imperial government, the foundational limits to its expansion at the sub-county level, and its stingy allocation of fiscal resources? Simply put, who among the bureaucratic officials charged with grain-transport tasks would shoulder these extra responsibilities? Whose fixed budget would be raided to cover the costs?

There were no easy answers to these questions! Although sea transport promised speed and economy, the scope of the plan was mind-boggling for its sheer scale and organizational complexity. The plan would require the coordination of grain transfers from the Jiangnan anchorages to merchant fleets in Shanghai for transport by sea to Tianjin where the grain would then be transferred back to Zhili grain-transport authorities for final canal shipment to the capital granaries. And as if this weren't enough, the Qing leadership simultaneously undertook a dramatic overhaul of the hydraulic system at the Grand Canal–Yellow River junction, in order to restore and thus save grain transport on the canal. The overhaul relied on a newly constructed pound lock in the Clear Passage (*qingkou*) of the junction, in order to cross grain fleets from the Southern Canal head (*yunkou*) into the Yellow River—a departure from

---

[1] P 00087–88 (5.8.9); also found in JSHY 1:54–55 (5.8.9). See abbreviations in References.

© KONINKLIJKE BRILL NV, LEIDEN, 2019 | DOI:10.1163/9789004384583_002

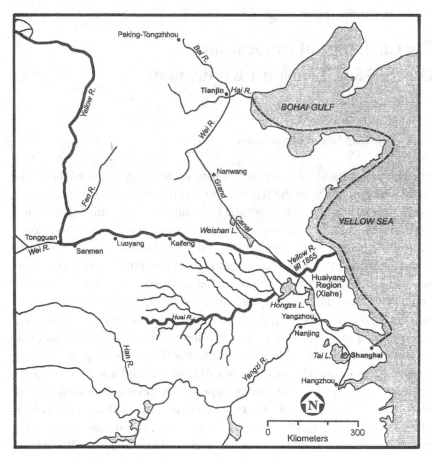

MAP 1   Grand Canal and northeast coastal route

the traditional use of the inflow of Hongze lake water into the junction.[2] This change represented an important improvement to existing hydraulic practice that enabled the Qing to perpetuate grain transport on the canal.

Both changes were seen as safeguarding government grain supply of the capital—its civilian and military bureaucracies, its grain markets, and the northern tier of interior China from Shandong to the northwest borderlands. At the time, the far more radical of the two was sea transport, which was referred to as a "temporary expedient" that enabled the dynasty to re-engineer the junction facilities in a fundamental way by 1827, and, therefore, establish a permanent second leg of a new two-pronged, or dual, approach to capital grain

---

2   See maps and explanations, Leonard 1996, pp. xix–xx, 36–49.

supply that would guarantee the shipment of southern tax grain, or tribute (*caoliang*), in the future when periodic disasters closed down the canal.

The disaster in 1825 was not unexpected. The hydraulic system at the canal-river junction, never completely reliable at the best of times, had teetered on the verge of collapse since the late eighteenth century, finally succumbing to centuries of unrelenting siltation that penetrated and clogged these fragile junction passageways and raised the bed of the Yellow River so high that the river and its massive dikes towered over the surrounding canal and communities nearby, threatening the survival of both. Qing officials had whispered of an impending collapse of this part of the canal ever since the 1770s, and they waited in trepidation for the event, even as they labored to shore up existing facilities.[3] Officials in the Jiaqing reign (1796–1820), murmured about the possibility of using sea transport, but, as Ruan Yuan had observed, officials were too frightened to raise the issue openly,[4] and Yinghe opined a decade later during the canal crisis (1825–1826), that "there had been no consensus about sea transport at that time."[5]

Prompted by a series of devastating floods in 1803, 1808, 1813, and 1819, followed by alarming memorial reports from officials in the eight canal-zone provinces, the Jiaqing Emperor undertook a sweeping review of the fiscal, staffing, and technological needs of the canal-transport system in northern Jiangsu. This review sparked important reforms in the funding and management of canal-river work that included the upward adjustment of fixed prices for labor and materials stipulated in the regulatory guidelines—prices that had tripled since the Yongzheng (1723–1735) and early Qianlong reigns (1736–1795).[6] It also sparked much needed reconstruction of the main dikes and dike revetments[7] on the Yellow River as well as the junction facilities. Even more controversial, the review authorized an increase in the appointment of low-level civil and military officials and the expansion of "irregular" staff for the three canal

---

3 HYHK [1842] 1969, maps and explanations, pp. 14–16.
4 JSWB, 48:3; Ruan served in high-level gubernatorial posts in the Lower Yangzi provinces in the Jiaqing reign, including the Grain Transport Directorate in 1812–1813. ECCP, pp. 399–402.
5 JSHY 1:8 (5.4.10).
6 Amelung 2005, pp. 293–299. Dodgen 2001, p. 30, points out that in 1748, the annual total of budget allocations for the Southern Canal Directorate was fixed at 400,000 taels, then increased to 500,000 taels. By 1806, this amount had tripled.
7 A rock, or brick, facing to protect an embankment.

directorates[8] that included expectant officials (*houbuguan*), those with purchased degrees, and extra-bureaucratic personnel.[9]

These reforms helped to stabilize the canal-river network in Henan and
northern Jiangsu during the Jiaqing reign, and they set the stage for continued technical and administrative innovations in the early Daoguang years.[10]
But these measures, of course, had enormous fiscal consequences. More construction materials, food supplies, labor, and managerial staff for the work
sites required more funds, and this in a time of fiscal shortage and monetary
instability![11] The budget categories and the prices for labor and materials for
canal-river conservancy had originally been fixed in the Yongzheng reign in
order to control expenses and to sanction the use of stalk materials for the construction of revetments. However, changes in budgetary categories and procedures, the upward adjustments of prices for labor and materials fixed in the
administrative code, and the additional costs of expanding existing hydraulic
facilities continued to be made in the Qianlong reign.[12]

To meet these rising costs at a time when the state treasury was flush, the
emperors routinely approved extra surcharges to cover the cost differential between the fixed prices stipulated in the regulatory codes and the actual market
price for labor and materials and new construction. These special subsidies,
called *jintie*, served as a kind of cost-of-living adjustment. But in the early

---

8   The three canal-river directorates included the Northern Directorate, a position held
     concurrently by the Zhili Governor-General who supervised the Northern Canal (Beihe)
     in Zhili province; the Henan-Shandong Directorate, headquartered at Jining, which su-
     pervised the Grand Canal and Yellow River (*Hedong hedao*) in these two provinces; and,
     finally, the Southern Canal Directorate, headquartered at Qingjiangpu near Huai'an pre-
     fecture, that centered mainly on the problems of the canal-riverine system in northern
     Jiangsu (Nanhe). BH 820D, pp. 399–400.

9   The additional ranked officials assigned to the canal-river directorates were generally
     assistant county (*xian*) magistrates (8a), and first- and second-class department (*zhou*)
     magistrates (6a, 7b). Dodgen 2001, pp. 30, 334–35, 172–172, notes 21–23. The sale of office
     had routinely been used in the Qing period to fund water conservancy emergencies and
     continued to serve as a particularly important funding source in the nineteenth century.
     Kaske 2008, pp. 281–308; 2010, pp. 345–397. Greater efforts were also made to appoint
     officials to high-level canal-river posts who had technical expertise in conservancy work
     even though officials and elites thought these efforts would be undermined by the sale
     of lower-level conservancy posts to "irregular" officials. See also Lufrano 2013. Extra-
     bureaucratic staff, like the Zhili grain brokers, had special technical skills that the state
     depended on. Leonard 2015, pp. 420–438.

10   The use of clay tiles, or bricks, was prompted by shortages and price increases of stalks.
     Canal officials opted for bricks because they could be produced locally and thus more
     cheaply than imported stalk supplies. Dodgen 2001, pp. 43–56.

11   Leonard 1996, pp. 36–49.

12   Amelung op. cit.

nineteenth century, when fiscal shortages and monetary pressures made these special payments untenable, the Qing leadership expanded the highly controversial practice of selling offices—a method sanctioned in the statutes for raising funds to meet the costs of river-canal projects.[13]

Yet in spite of imperial efforts in the Jiaqing and first three years of the Daoguang reigns to respond to the severe deterioration of the hydraulic network in northern Jiangsu, no major innovations were made to redesign the failing junction facilities in a fundamental way. Nor was there an attempt to expand the grain-transport system as a whole to include a sea-transport capability. The key reason was unwillingness to tamper with the imperial monopoly over grain supplies for the capital region and the strategic zone across north China from Shandong westward to Xinjiang. The grain supply for this region was a highly charged strategic issue, laden with both practical and symbolic significance for the Qing leadership, and had been so since the early reigns. If anything, the early Manchu emperors had attached even greater strategic significance to this issue than had their imperial predecessors, linking military and civilian food-grain supply to economic prosperity and social stability—goals that they considered fundamental to durable Manchu imperial rule and to the state's Confucian moral mission. The strategic importance of this issue was intensified by the Jinchuan campaigns in the southwest in the late eighteenth century.[14]

The Grand Canal served as the central artery for capital grain supply and also for the larger empire-wide grain supply network. As a consequence, the Qing emperors had, from the beginning, assiduously streamlined, monitored, and directly administered the organizationally complex Grand Canal–grain-transport system to insure the solidity of the diking infrastructure on the Yellow River and the hydraulic facilities at the canal–Yellow River junction—both essential to the yearly shipment of approximately three million *shi* of tax grain to the capital granaries in Tongzhou and Beijing. Not surprisingly, these efforts were paralleled by the empire-wide expansion of the granary infrastructure in the Kangxi (1662–1722) and Yongzheng reigns, by the linkage of local granaries to the capital supply networks, especially in the north, and by the state's monopoly of grain markets and prices in and around the capital.[15]

So important was grain supply that the Qing leadership designed a unique administrative structure for its management that reached below the county (*zhouxian*) deeply into the sub-county arena, in spite of strongly held views

---

13   Amelung op. cit.; Kaske 2008, pp. 281–308.
14   Dai 2009, pp. 189–225; Elliott 2001; Theobald 2013, pp. 27–97.
15   Cheung 2008, pp. 115–132; Perdue 2005; Will and Wong 1991, pp. 19–98.

about the foundational limits on imperial government at the department and county levels. Similarly, the Qing leadership also designed unique, but less formal, low-level bureaucratic structures to manage two equally crucial logistical tasks: the transport of monetary metals and minted coins, and of military supplies.[16]

A major change to the grain-supply system, such as the use of sea transport, was, therefore, very carefully weighed as to its consequences. Officials feared that one dangerous consequence would be labor unrest and economic dislocation in the eight-province canal zone. Because major reconstruction of the junction facilities would require the closure of the canal for a year or more, it would cause the unemployment of thousands of grain-transport troops, as well as huge numbers of private canal, porterage, and shipping laborers, particularly those connected to private lighterage organizations, that provided small craft to ship grain through silt shallows.[17] These organizations had played a pivotal role in grain transport since the early Qing period, especially in Zhili, and their role had increased dramatically in northern Jiangsu and Shandong by the mid-eighteenth century when large government grain boats found it increasingly difficult to navigate the silted junction passageways.

Another worrying question was: what would be the impact of these innovations on the existing Grain Transport Directorate, that complex bureaucratic organization that managed the yearly grain shipments to the capital, as well as on the three Grand Canal Directorates? In the long run, would sea transport, because of its speed, economy, and dependence on private shippers, undermine the use of the canal and the directorates' ability to supply grain to the capital? Would it limit the state's ability to divert tax grain to provinces adjacent to the canal experiencing food shortages, especially in the north, and also to maintain the supply lines to the military bases in the northwest borderlands? And, finally, would the vast canal-riverine diking system north of the Yangzi River be allowed to languish and deteriorate, as many of the critics of sea transport feared, subjecting the populations of Henan, Shandong, and northern Jiangsu to floods and the destruction of agricultural lands?[18]

Yet, far more daunting than all these issues were the practical obstacles to implementing a major administrative innovation, like sea transport. Simply put, sea transport was not laid out in the Qing administrative codes and

---

16   Theobald 2013; Kim 2008, 191–220; 2012; Chen 2016, 97–143.
17   Lighters (*bochuan*) were small, shallow-draft boats that could navigate silt shallows on
       the Grand Canal and smaller riverine waterways; they differed slightly in design from
       province to province.
18   CHC 10, pt. 1, 1978, pp. 119–128; Dodgen 2001, pp. 145–159.

sanctioned by years of administrative practice. By every measure, it would be a huge undertaking, requiring great organizational and managerial skill, fiscal resources, and, as well, the creation of a new *ad hoc* sea-transport agency, which would constitute an extension of the sub-county grain-transport bureaucracy. However, given the spare, thinly spread character of imperial government, the foundational limits to its expansion, and its stingy allocation of fiscal resources, who was going to do the work and how was it to be funded?

Now, at last in early 1825, after the destruction of the junction, the day of reckoning had arrived, and it was apparent to all but the most stubbornly conservative that there were no quick fixes left—only fundamental redesign of the junction passageways (if it could be done at all) and the temporary use of sea transport while the overhaul took place. The time was right for change—change that only the emperor and Banner elites had the political clout to undertake. Which is precisely what they did!

Leading the charge in the capital were the Daoguang Emperor and Yinghe, his Grand Secretary and special Supervising Minister and President of the Board of Revenue, who drove the decisional process that led to the imperial decision (5.8.9) to use sea transport in 1826.[19] They then pushed Qishan and Nayancheng, the Governors-General of Jiangsu and Zhili provinces, respectively, to complete the concrete planning and reconciliation of the competing interests of the two provinces. Qishan bore the heaviest burdens, directing the investigation, planning, and implementation of sea transport from his temporary residence at Qingjiangpu, while he simultaneously pushed the stalled 1825-grain shipments through the junction and redesigned the junction hydraulic network to guarantee the passage of grain fleets in the future. In contrast to Qishan's design of the sea-transport innovation, Nayancheng, the seasoned Governor-General and concurrent Northern Canal Director, adjusted long-established Zhili grain-transport practices to accommodate the sea-transport plan, but resisted changes that undermined the prerogatives of Zhili transport and granary officials to levy excessive fees. Yet, even these two highly skilled Banner-elite administrators struggled to build an operational plan with no prior regulatory blueprint in the administrative code to guide them.

Empire-wide policy discussions on sea transport had raged during the first six months of 1825.[20] Throughout this period, although the Daoguang Emperor and his allies were already poised for action, they nonetheless played their cards carefully and waited as the canal crisis deepened from the third to the fifth months when it became crystal clear that there was no alternative to

---

19 JSHY 1:4–14b (5.4.10); 1:16–22 (5.5.22).
20 Leonard 1996, pp. 227–243.

fundamental changes to government grain transport. However, before they committed themselves to sea transport, they wanted the answers to two practical questions. Could the junction hydraulic facilities, in fact, be restored? And was there a pool of private ocean shippers for hire in Shanghai willing to transport "southern" grain along the northeast coastal route to Tianjin in the spring of 1826?

To answer these questions, the emperor appointed the trusted Qishan to the post of Liangjiang Governor-General in the late fifth month, who, after one month on the job, completed fact-finding assessments of the damage to the junction hydraulic network and the availability of Shanghai merchant vessels for hire. He cautiously affirmed the feasibility of a program for canal redesign at the junction and the use of sea transport in 1826.[21] The emperor then immediately issued a public edict authorizing sea transport of Jiangnan tax grain in 1826.[22] But this was just the beginning—the easy part. The really hard work lay ahead and relied on key officials in the canal zone to devise a workable plan and to build the administrative infrastructure to carry it out.

To do so, the Qing leadership would have to mobilize every layer of imperial government from the Daoguang Emperor, himself, the Grand Council, and Board of Revenue at the top, down to the lowest levels of the permanent structures of territorial administration—the county—in the eight-province canal zone and also, not least in significance, down to the lowest levels of the Grain Transport Administration, a hybrid agency that the Qing had created to reach below county government to the docks, dikes, canal anchorages, and granaries in the canal zone. This specialty organization was headed by a gubernatorial-level grain-transport director (caoyunzongdu) who supervised a special military organization (caopiao), a legacy of the Ming weisuo system, whose officers and troop-laborers operated the grain-transport fleets during each yearly grain shipment cycle.[23] He was assisted by three canal-river directors and their military organizations (hepiao), who maintained water conservancy works on the Grand Canal–Yellow River network to facilitate grain transport. Additionally, each of these directorates also relied on legions of private laborers.

The grain transport director, it must be remembered, did not operate on his own but depended heavily on, and closely coordinated his work with, regular provincial, or "territorial," officials as well as those special "functional" officials in the canal-zone provinces who were charged with specific grain-transport tasks and who included grain intendants, sub-prefects, department and county

---

21   JSHY 1:32–37 (5.6.22).

22   P 00087–88 (5.8.9).

23   BH, 834; Hinton 1970, pp. 1–15; Leonard 1996, pp. 36–49; Kelley 1986, pp. 11–91.

magistrates, and the all-important "assistant" magistrates, or *chengcui* (ranks 5a to 8a) and their "miscellaneous" aides (*zuoza*; ranks 8 and 9), as well as those of comparable rank in the military.[24] Some of the *chengcui* held permanent positions in what were termed "difficult" jurisdictions where gubernatorial officials had the prerogative to assign such officials to emergency tasks or crises situations. Others were temporary appointees, or "irregular," officials that included expectants and those with purchased brevet ranks and/or degrees.[25]

Both the territorial and functional officials relied utterly on the lowly assistant officials (both civil and military) to oversee grain-transport work at the sub-county level.[26] They served as a bureaucratic bridge between the permanent provincial bureaucracy and the sub-county agencies and private organizations that performed critical grain-transport tasks.[27] They bore responsibility for "keeping the books," for fiscal accounting and reporting up the chain of command to intendants, provincial treasurers, and the central boards, and for directing work on the grain fleets and/or canal-riverine work sites. They oversaw the hybrid network of bureaucratic and extra-bureaucratic personnel that included the lowest levels of ranked and unranked officials, "irregular" officials (expectants), sub-bureaucratic functionaries, but, most importantly, they also monitored a pool of highly skilled extra-bureaucratic personnel. The last were essential to grain-transport logistics because they possessed the expertise and resources for the performance of specialized grain-transport tasks, such as grain brokerage, inspection, measurement, transfer, storage, porterage, and lighterage shipping—specific expertise and resources that "generalist" Confucian officials generally lacked.

Taken together, the assistants projected Qing authority into the sub-county arena and imposed vital organizational and fiscal discipline over bureaucratic and non-bureaucratic personnel that included hundreds of thousands of canal, shipping, and porterage laborers. They should be seen as low-level trouble-shooters or crisis managers, analogous in some ways to imperial commissioners at the top levels of imperial government, but they were arguably

---

24   BH, 849–858.

25   Guy 2010, pp. 47–78, 109–110, 144–145, 3523–63; Kaske 2008, pp. 281–308.

26   On the grain fleets, the key assistant was the fleet escort officer (*yayun guan*). Kelley 1986, pp. 38–41.

27   Guy 2010, op. cit. The pool of low-level *chengcui* managers for certain "difficult" jurisdictions was often filled by officials who had been directly appointed or temporarily assigned by provincial governors. Their numbers were increased by the temporary appointment of "irregular," or expectant, officials during periods of canal-river emergencies as noted above. Many of the latter had purchased titles and degrees that had been sold during emergencies. Kaske 2008, pp. 281–308; 2015, pp. 345–397; Dodgen 2001, pp. 34–41.

vastly more important to disciplined day-to-day management at the local level, which enabled the Qing state to partially overcome the structural limits of bureaucratic government.[28]

The same hybrid pattern of governance was also true of Qing management of two other key logistical networks, the one for emergency military supply and the other for the transport of monetary metals and minted coins, both of which also placed unique and onerous burdens on imperial government at the county and sub-county level. For military supply, the Qing also patched together an organization that centered on permanent county officials, the officials that staffed the network of communication posts throughout the empire, and the temporary extension of such posts into war zones, such as northwest Sichuan during the Second Jinchuan Rebellion (1771–1776) in the late eighteenth century.[29]

The *ad hoc* hybrid character of monetary metal transport is even more apparent. This logistical network was created after the dynasty's decision to develop an indigenous supply of monetary metals for the production of copper cash in the 1740s—a decision that sparked the development of treacherous overland and riverine routes from Yunnan, Sichuan, and Guizhou in southwest China to the metal storage depots on the upper Yangzi River, near Chongqing, then down through the Yangzi Gorges to canal and riverine routes to the capital and provincial mints. Yunnan provincial governors and treasurers created and directed the transport process, but the actual transport expeditions were led by a parade of specially appointed officials who traveled with each expedition and faced incredibly challenging geographical and bureaucratic obstacles as they shepherded loads of monetary metals to their various destinations.[30]

In each of these three strategic logistical systems created by the Qing—grain transport, military supply, and the transport of monetary metals and coins— the flexible use of assistants enabled the dynasty to perform these vital logistical tasks that would otherwise have been impossible, given the tissue-thin spread of imperial government across interior China.[31] Yet, even though these officials played a key role in the supervision and management of the dynasty's strategic logistical networks, they did not, at least technically speaking, extend the *permanent* structure of the Qing bureaucratic state at the sub-county level.

---

28   Antony and Leonard 2002, pp. 1–26; Antony 2002, pp. 27–59.
29   See the important work by Theobald 2013.
30   Kim 2008, pp. 191–220.
31   The evolution of such special managerial posts, sometimes conscripted, sometimes ranked, in the Shanghai region goes back to the Song period. Elvin 1977, pp. 444–470.

Like their Ming predecessors, the Qing dynasty held the line on the expansion of bureaucratic government to a spare 1,200 to 1,300 counties to govern a population, in the early nineteenth century, of approximately 350 million people—roughly the same number of counties that had governed a much smaller population of about 50 million a millennium earlier in the Tang dynasty (CE 618–907). When the Qing leadership perceived a need to adjust its span of control in order to cope with special fiscal or security problems in discrete parts of the empire, their practice was to form transitional independent sub-prefectures or independent departments, and if and when they created a new county jurisdiction in one locale, they typically eliminated a less important one in another.[32] Yet, realistically, beneath this bare-bones bureaucratic superstructure, especially in the case of important logistical tasks, like grain transport, the transport of monetary metals, and military supply, the Qing did, in fact, create informal hybrid governing structures at the sub-county level, directed by ranked assistant officials who managed the work of countless sub- and extra-bureaucratic personnel, the latter of whom the Board of Revenue described as "quasi" bureaucratic when they were hired to perform government jobs.[33]

Because of their vital importance, all three of these sprawling logistical networks were the core of the Qing state's strategic sphere of responsibilities (*guoji*) that centered directly on the political security of the empire, in contrast to the people's productive sphere that centered on the economic work essential to the livelihoods (*minsheng*) and social well-being of ordinary people in the sub-county community. The former sought to fund the core, but limited, functions of the state "under the six boards," while the latter hummed along at the sub-county level, seemingly independent and apart, protected by the thinly spread fabric of imperial government. In many respects, this pattern of imperial government might be characterized as a form of indirect rule.

However, while the state's strategic sphere and the people's productive sphere were conceptually separate, there was a great deal of overlap between the two, especially in the performance of key logistical tasks, that was affirmed by custom, administrative statute, and the practical need to work alongside ordinary people in private organizations at the sub-county level. In other words, the state and private organizations in China's many diverse regional locales worked collaboratively on many vital governing tasks, and were "joined at the hip," so to speak. Nowhere is this clearer than in the operation of the territorially vast and logistically complex grain-transport system.

---

32   Skinner 1977, pp. 275–346; 1985, pp. 271–292.
33   JSHY 2:63 (5.12.27).

2   Tricks of the Trade

The flexible use of assistant managers was just one of many governing tricks
that the Qing government used in order to stretch, or extend, the reach of
the bureaucracy to perform vital logistical tasks crucial to the perpetuation
of the dynasty, while not technically expanding the permanent structures of
imperial government. Well-established governing tasks, like those performed
by the Grain Transport Directorate or by officials in other permanent posts in
provincial government, such as those at the circuit, prefectural, department,
and county levels, were well defined in the Qing administrative codes. But the
codes did not address problems associated with emergencies and long-term
evolutionary changes that could undermine imperial government, a fact that
the Qing leadership had recognized from the start.[34] These challenges were
neither addressed in the administrative codes, nor easily managed with the
slender bureaucratic and fiscal resources of the Qing dynasty's minimalist governing superstructure.

Since there was no solution to be found in the established codes or customary practices, these challenges required creative official problem-solving and
the resort to a range of makeshift institutional tools that minimized the addition of new non-statutory costs and eliminated the need for new permanent
official positions. These tools, or tricks, like the assistant networks, included
the flexible use of the secret decisional process in which high-ranking provincial officials used secret palace memorials to identify and propose solutions to
pressing problems, while the emperor responded with a secret edict to sanction appropriate courses of action.[35]

The tricks also included the expansion of gubernatorial prerogatives to
transfer "assistants" and temporarily appointed expectant officials to trouble
spots, and the periodic revision of the administrative codes to adjust administrative practice to cope with new governing realities.[36] They also included
the practice of concurrency—assigning new, or concurrent, responsibilities to
pre-existing official posts, an expedient that placed great burdens on sitting officials and could not be used indefinitely to meet serious emergencies, which
was clear during the sea-transport experiment!

Short-term expedients were also used, such as the appointment of imperial commissioners to trouble-shoot challenging problems, as well as the creation and temporary use of *ad hoc* managerial and fiscal bureaus (*ju*), headed

---

34   Metzger 1973, pp. 167–232; Watt 1962, pp. 11–98; Wu 1970, pp. 34–106.
35   Leonard 1988, pp. 665–699.
36   Guy 2010, pp. 352–363; Leonard 2005, pp. 27–31; 2005, pp. 449–464.

by ranked officials, to plan, manage, and disperse funds during emergencies. Finally, Qing government recruited (*zhaolai; zhaoshang*) numerous extra-bureaucratic organizations that possessed the managerial, technical, and material resources to perform skilled and unskilled work, which the official bureaucracy lacked.

Ad hoc bureaus, the reassignment of assistants, and recruitment, used in tandem, were particularly useful because they could be organized quickly to respond to emergencies, then dissolved just as quickly. They were also plastic and malleable, capable of being stretched and molded to cope with a range of new problems. Some of these bureaus that came to be regarded as necessary for the long term were, in fact, made permanent, such as the municipal bureaus in late nineteenth-century Shanghai. Others were dissolved when crises were finally resolved. Most importantly, this approach to governance was cheap and, technically speaking, did not permanently expand the structures and costs of government. There was, of course, a heavy price to pay for governing on the cheap: a downward spiral of corruption and the dilution of state control over low-level operations, but that was a price the imperial state was apparently willing to pay.

All of these tricks of the governing trade—both long-established *ad hoc* practices and temporary expedients—came into play during the planning and implementation of sea transport, an innovation for which the state had no administrative blueprint and neither the time nor resources to develop one. These tools were an essential part of the late imperial game of juggling scarce bureaucratic resources to overcome basic, systemic weaknesses in the Qing governing structure. It was not that the Qing leadership lacked the creative or practical imagination to conceptualize changes and innovations in governing practice. Ideas for such changes abounded. It was, instead, a matter of figuring out a way to implement new governing strategies with existing bureaucratic and fiscal resources. That was the key. If one could achieve that, then one could succeed. If not, even the best laid plans were doomed.

This study analyzes the bureaucratic juggling game at the height of the grain-transport crisis in 1825–1826 when the Qing leadership successfully implemented a temporary sea-transport plan while simultaneously redesigning and reconstructing the hydraulic system at the Grand Canal–Yellow River junction. It highlights the use of special *ad hoc* governing tools that enabled imperial government to extend the bureaucracy temporarily in order to create a collaborative governing network of bureaucratic and non-bureaucratic personnel to carry out this innovation. It draws on rich source materials for studying the step-by-step organization and implementation of the plan, which include imperial public and secret edicts, secret palace memorials, the Board of Revenue's special administrative code for grain transport ([*Qinding*] *Hubu caoyun quanshu*),[37] the regulatory codes of the Boards of Works and War that bear on grain transport and canal-river administration, as well as other private writings on related issues, such as the *Qinghe County Gazetteer* (1855) and the *Collected Essays on Qing Imperial Statecraft*.[38]

Particularly useful for this study is the special collection of key edicts and memorials on sea transport, *The Complete Record on Jiangsu Sea Transport*, compiled immediately after the successful completion of the plan in 1826, by Tao Zhu, Jiangsu Governor-General, and He Changling, Jiangsu Financial Commissioner—two officials at the center of sea-transport planning in Jiangnan.[39] The collection is a work of advocacy that reflects the emphases and choices of the imperial leadership—the Daoguang Emperor and his central and provincial allies—all of whom played key roles in the planning and implementation of the project because they viewed it as an essential new pillar to government grain transport, which had hitherto centered exclusively on the Grand Canal. The work documents each step in the planning and the actual ups-and-downs of implementation, and, moreover, it was clearly intended to provide a blueprint for the much-needed revision of the Board of Revenue's grain transport code, which officials had called for as early as the Jiaqing reign (1812) and which was formally authorized by the Daoguang Emperor in 1829, in order to incorporate into the code the two new grain-transport strategies (relay shipping and sea transport) created in 1825–1826. The revision was completed in 1845.[40]

This important revision of the code incorporated the new guidelines for sea transport. Because sea transport was an administrative experiment "that had never been done before," its every aspect was new and had to be spelled out in minute detail so that officials charged with implementing the plan were clear about the tasks they had to perform. Consequently, the collection contains a wealth of technical detail on low-level grain-transport tasks which are often hidden from view in the more routine discussions of grain transport in imperial edicts and memorials—tasks, such as the loading, measuring, and bagging of grain, its temporary storage in Tianjin, lighterage logistics from Tianjin to Tongzhou, and the diverse functions of extra-bureaucratic personnel, such as grain brokers. Taken together, all these sources reveal the urgency of the Qing

---

37   CYQS, 1735; 1766; 1811; 1845; 1876.
38   JSWB (1826). He Changling, ed. 120 *juan*; Qinghe [Jiangsu] *xianzhi*. 1855. Lu Yitong and Wu Tang, comps. 24 *juan*.
39   JSHY. Tao Zhu and He Changling, eds. 12 *juan*.
40   CYQS (1845), head *juan* (*juanshou*), parts 1–2: 1–8.

leadership's response to the grain-transport crisis in 1825–1826 and the creative and crafty ways they organized and funded their work.

Chapter 1 captures the severity of the Grand Canal crisis in northern Jiangsu in the spring of 1825 through the eyes of Linqing, a prestigious Manchu official and self-taught expert on canal-river problems, who served in important canal-river conservancy posts during the height of the canal crisis from 1825 to 1838. His technical writings and drawings on hydraulic techniques capture a Banner elite's long-term assessment of the destructive impact of Yellow River siltation on crucial junction hydraulic facilities that linked the Southern Canal to the Yellow River from the middle Qianlong to the Daoguang reigns. Linqing's insights provide context for the edicts and memorials written during the canal crisis and reveal why the Qing leadership felt no qualms about forging ahead with both sea transport and technical hydraulic innovations.

Chapters 2 and 3 examine the bold leadership of the Daoguang Emperor and Yinghe, his special economic adviser and President of the Board of Revenue, who together launched the policy discussions on sea transport in the spring of 1825, first in an imperial edict of 5.2.5 that called for empire-wide discussions of sea transport, followed by Yinghe's two memorials (5.4.10; 5.5.22) that spelled out a comprehensive plan to close the canal and implement sea transport in 1826 while canal reconstruction was underway. These three documents reveal that the emperor and his central Banner-elite allies embraced sea transport as a part of a fundamentally new approach to strengthening strategic capital grain supply, and their support sparked and influenced the concrete planning and successful implementation of the plan. Without imperial and Banner-elite support for these drastic changes to the grain-transport system, it is highly unlikely that either sea transport or improved lock transport through the junction would have been undertaken so successfully. That success also flowed from the unrelenting pressure that Yinghe exerted on two exceptional Banner-elite officials who managed the provincial ends of the sea-transport plan in Jiangsu and Zhili: Qishan, Governor-General of Liangjiang, and Nayancheng, Governor-General of Zhili.

Chapter 4 explores Qishan's direction of sea-transport planning in Jiangsu after his appointment as Liangjiang Governor-General late in the fifth month of 1825—when chaos reigned at the junction and canal transport had ground to a halt in a morass of silt. It reveals his assessment of chaotic conditions at the junction, his unvarnished critique of his official predecessors, and his stubborn unwillingness to embark on new plans until he had fully investigated the impasse in canal shipping at the junction, the severity of junction destruction, and the availability of private ocean-going ships in Shanghai to transport grain by sea.

Chapter 5 analyzes Qishan's bold steps, after his investigations were completed, to "stretch the bureaucracy" by creating a special *ad hoc* management bureau (*ju*) to craft the new sea-transport regulations and direct their
implementation. Staffed by specially appointed outside officials dispatched to
Shanghai and by local Suzhou-Songjiang officials (and their assistants), the bureau functioned as the core of a loose collaborative organization that included high-level supervisory officials (Jiangsu Governor Tao Zhu and Financial
Commissioner He Changling) and crucial extra-bureaucratic organizations,
the most important of which was the Shanghai Merchant Shipping Guild
(Shangguan huiguan) that provided the ships, the navigational know-how,
and skilled marine labor for grain transport along the northeast coast from
Shanghai to Tianjin.

Chapter 6 analyzes the main features of the new sea-transport regulations
for Jiangsu and the adjustments made to maritime defenses to assure the
safety of the northeastern coastal route. It centers on the reports of Tao Zhu
and Censor Xiong Yutai, who championed the recruitment of private Shanghai
merchant shippers for sea transport and the adoption of new anti-corruption
measures intended to shield merchant shippers from sub-bureaucratic extortion on the Shanghai and Tianjin docks. When paired with the reports on
Jiangsu and Shandong maritime defenses by Qishan and Wulong'a as well as
Tao Zhu's maps and assessment of the northeastern coastal route, they suggest a changed vision of the maritime frontier in which the pattern of joint
state-private collaboration in trade and port management in the southeastern coastal provinces, begun during the Kangxi reign, was extended to the
northeast coast with the transport of strategic grain supplies from Shanghai
to Tianjin. This new vision defined a single strategic maritime highway and
created a tried-and-tested administrative model for sea transport in the 1860s
after the Yellow River changed course and ended two centuries of Qing grain
transport on the Grand Canal.

In contrast to Chapters 4, 5, and 6 that highlight Qishan's efforts to "stretch
the bureaucracy" to implement sea transport from the five Jiangnan grain tax
jurisdictions of Susungchangtaizhen, Chapters 7 and 8 investigate the final
stage of the sea-transport planning in Zhili province where authorities did not
stretch the bureaucracy, but instead adjusted and tweaked the normative administrative practices of formally "receiving" (*shou*) the grain and arranging its
final shipment by canal to the capital granaries. Chapter 7 centers on the necessarily complex and careful organizational decisions made by Nayancheng in
Zhili, who was uniquely positioned to bring the sea-transport planners down
to earth and underscore the practical realities of Zhili grain-transport logistics. He saw no reason to change in a fundamental way the existing customary

practices that had served Zhili grain-transport and storage authorities so well over the decades in handling tax grain shipments each year from the eight canal-zone provinces. Instead, he relied on these very practices to fashion a complex and effective logistical scheme that enabled Zhili lighterage fleets to coordinate the shipment of huge amounts of "delayed" 1825 grain stored in Zhili canal-side granaries, sea-transported grain, the new 1826 shipments arriving by canal, and beans and wheat arriving from Manchuria.

Nayancheng insisted that these bureaucratic procedures in Zhili were grounded in the technical expertise and experience of Zhili grain-transport and granary officials, as well as skilled extra-bureaucratic personnel, such as the quasi-official grain brokers. He agreed only to important supervisory measures to minimize the opportunity for what was termed "excessive" extortion of merchant shippers at the Tianjin docks and corrupt manipulation of lighterage fleets from the Tianjin docks to the capital granaries at Tongzhou. He remained confident that the existing practices were essential to the sea-transport plan in Zhili. His logistical skill and his insights into bureaucratic operations played a crucial role in the success of the final stage of the sea-transport experiment.

Chapter 8 centers on the Granary Vice President Bai Chun who was more resistant to change than Nayancheng and who expressed the interests of the Granary superintendency, its two Granary sub-prefects stationed at the granary office at the Stone Dam in Tongzhou, grain brokers dispatched to inspect and guide the transfer of received grain to lighterage fleets that shipped the grain to the capital granaries from canal-side granaries, Tianjin's Northern Granary, and from the Tianjin docks. These transfers required careful supervision, policing, and accounting of grain cargoes. Because these various tasks were shouldered and shared by an array of local officials, specially assigned assistants, grain brokers, and military personnel, it was difficult to define and assign responsibility for grain loss, spoilage and theft although special efforts were made to do so. Bai Chun advocated for these personnel, emphasizing the difficulty of their jobs and the need for their fair treatment and equitable pay.

The study argues that the Banner-elite officials—Yinghe, Qishan, and Nayancheng—with imperial backing, were crucial to the implementation of the sea-transport plan because they had the necessary "insider" political authority to adjust and expand grain-transport practice to include a sea-transport capability. They were able to overcome the obstacles to administrative change and the bureaucratic and fiscal limitations of imperial government by the skillful use of tricks of the governing trade: ad hoc bureaus, assistant managers, and the recruitment of private shipping organizations, in order to create a temporary hybrid collaborative organization to carry out the plan. These three officials laid the groundwork for the revision of the grain-transport code in 1845 and the later use of sea transport after the shift of the Yellow River in the early 1850s rendered canal transport obsolete.

It also argues that the recruitment of Shanghai merchant shippers for grain transport perpetuated and expanded the early Qing tradition of collaboration with merchant organizations in the administration of the maritime customs and port management in the four southeastern provinces, begun in the Kangxi period, and applied it to sea transport of tax grain on the northeast coast.

Finally, the sea-transport experiment shows how the Qing used skilled Banner-elite leadership, the administrative code, and *ad hoc* experiments to overcome the systemic thinness of the bureaucratic governing structure and respond flexibly to crises and changing times. These tricks of the governing trade were fundamental to the success of the sea-transport effort just as they were with other important administrative innovations that enhanced the effectiveness of Qing rule. They highlight the linkage between crises, Banner-elite innovation, and the revision of the code—the process by which the Qing undertook important administrative adjustments and changes in governing practice.

CHAPTER 1

Linqing and Grand Canal Conditions in Northern Jiangsu

The 1826 sea-transport experiment took place against the backdrop of a desperate struggle to restore failing hydraulic facilities at the confluence of the Grand Canal, Hongze Lake, and the Yellow River in northern Jiangsu from 1825 to 1827 at a stage when Yellow River siltation had made it virtually impossible to restore these facilities to operational viability. The struggle led to the innovation of a bold new hydraulic scheme, called "lock transfer" (*guantang duyun*), that featured the construction of a pound lock in the middle of the Clear Passage to hold Yellow River water in order to aid the crossing of grain fleets and scour out the junction passageways. Lock transfer replaced the long-established method of releasing the relatively "clear water" (*qingshui*) from Hongze Lake that had been used since Ming times "to resist the Yellow" and carry the grain fleets into the river and onwards to the entrance of the Central Canal (*Zhonghe*). This innovation helped to prolong the life of canal transport another twenty-five years until the early 1850s when the shift of the Yellow River ended canal transport for good.

Linqing (1791–1846) recounted in great detail the story of the lock-transfer innovation and the last stages of Grand Canal operation in northern Jiangsu in his important study of late imperial changes to the hydraulic system at the Grand Canal–Yellow River junction, and his careful reporting is extremely important because it sheds light on the complexity of the hydraulic issues faced by the Qing leadership from the mid-Qianlong to early Daoguang reigns (1775–1838).[1] A highly accomplished Manchu Bannerman, turned hydraulic engineer, Linqing witnessed the crisis in canal communications first-hand while serving in key canal-river conservancy positions in Henan and Jiangsu from 1825 to 1842.[2] During these years, he emerged as a skilled administrator with practical know-how on technical aspects of canal-river management.

---

1 Linqing. [1841] 1969. *Huangyunhekou gujintushuo* (Maps and explanations of the Yellow River–Grand Canal mouth, past and present). Changpai Yuan. Reprint. Taibei: Wenhai. Hereafter cited HYHK; see also his work on water conservancy tools and techniques: *Hegongqiji tushuo* (Illustrations and explanations of water conservancy tools). 4 *juan*, n.p. Daoguang 15 [1836]. Reprint. Shanghai Commercial Press, 1937. Hereafter cited: HGQJ.

2 ECCP, pp. 506–507; QDHCZ, pp. 168–171, 178–179; Dodgen 2001, pp. 56–68, for his work in water conservancy.

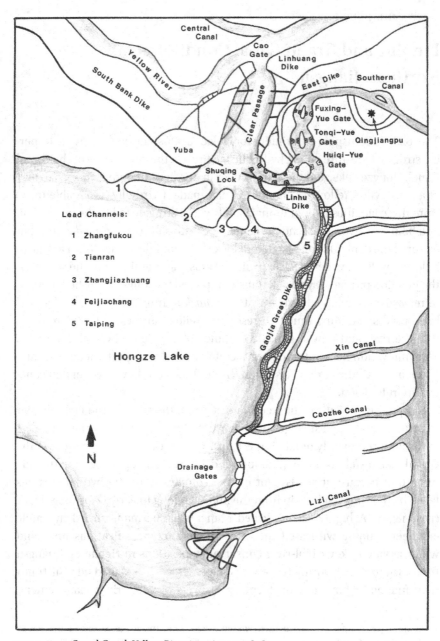

Lead Channels:

1   Zhangfukou

2   Tianran

3   Zhangjiazhuang

4   Feijiachang

5   Taiping

Hongze Lake

N

MAP 2   Grand Canal–Yellow River junction, ca. 1826

He saw first-hand how rising silt levels caused river backflows, meanders, and devastating floods that undermined the passage of government grain boats and commercial craft through the junction. His account explains and maps the elaborate changes to these facilities that were designed to guarantee grain shipments through the junction, and it documents the successful operation of the pound lock in 1827 that kept the canal operating until the early 1850s, when the Yellow River changed course, usurping the bed of the Daqing River near Jinan and exiting to the sea near Lijin in Wuding prefecture on the north of the Shandong.

FIGURE 1   Linqing (1791–1846)

A Manchu of the Bordered Yellow Banner, whose members served as bond servants in the Imperial Household, Linqing was an unlikely convert to practical water conservancy and transport issues. His family traced its ancestry to the imperial line of the Jin dynasty (1115–1234); it had aligned with Nuerhaci at the beginning of the rise of the Aisin Gioro clan. After the establishment of the Qing dynasty in 1644, Linqing's forebears continued to serve as officials, and, in contrast to many Manchus, the family also achieved marked literary success. For example, Asitan (d. 1683) who served in the Shunzhi reign (1644–1661) distinguished himself as the foremost translator of Chinese classics into Manchu and was particularly recognized for his translations and commentaries on *The Great Learning, The Doctrine of the Mean*, and the *Classic of Filial Piety*. Asitan's sons were also noted translators. Linqing's father, Tinglu (1772–1820), served as a prefect in Tai'an, Shandong province (1814–1820), and his mother, a poet, came from a family of accomplished painters. His two sons, Chongshi (1820–1878) and Chonghou (1826–1893) held important positions in Qing government in the late nineteenth century.[3]

Linqing's official career follows the appointment pattern of those singled out for high-level and challenging gubernatorial posts.[4] As a promising young *jinshi* in 1809, he first gained administrative experience in the capital, serving as a secretary in the Grand Secretariat, the Board of War, and the Office of Imperial Instruction (1810–1820). In 1821, he was appointed to the Hanlin Academy and served as one of the principal compilers of the Jiaqing Emperor's *Veritable Records*. After serving in two consecutive prefectural positions in Anhui province (Huizhou, Yingzhou) from 1822–1824, he was promoted to his first water-conservancy post, the important canal-river intendancy for the Kaiguichenxu circuit in Henan—one of three independent circuits (*hedao*) dedicated to the management of the Grand Canal–riverine network north of the Yangzi River.[5] He held this position from 1825 to 1829 during a period when

---

3   ECCP, pp. 209–211. Chonghou, it will be remembered, held the position of Superintendent of the Northern Ports from 1861 to 1870, and with the exception of Chinese members of the Burlingame mission (1867), he was the first official envoy to the West, having been sent to France to convey the Chinese apology for the events of the Tianjin Massacre (1871). Hsu 2000, pp. 269, 300, 321–323.

4   Kent Guy 2010, pp. 21–179.

5   BH, 843; Dodgen 2001, pp. 34–41; DOT, 6306, pp. 487–488; Mayers [1897] 1966, pp. 189, 280. The Zhili river intendant was called the Yunding *hedao* and his office was located in the Gu'an, a county capital in Shuntian prefecture south of Beijing located on the Yunding River; the Shandong intendant was called the Shandong canal-river intendant and was headquartered in Jining department in southwest Shandong province; the office of the Henan river intendant, the Kaiguichenxu *hedao* was located in Kaifeng prefecture. These officials held the rank of 4a.

Yellow River backflows from the lower reaches of the river peaked and repeat-edly damaged the dikes and revetments upriver as far west as Kaifeng.

After serving briefly in two high-level provincial posts, first as treasurer of Guizhou province (1832–1833) and then as Governor of Hubei (1833), Linqing was appointed to the challenging directorship of the Southern Canal–River Administration (Nanhe *hedu*), headquartered at Qingjiangpu, from 1833 to 1842, after the re-engineering of junction infrastructure and the successful implementation of lock transport. During his tenure, he often received high imperial praise for his mastery of hydraulic technology and skilled administra-tive management of conservancy work and disaster relief.[6]

His career came to an abrupt halt in 1842, however, when he was removed from office for being absent from Qingjiangpu when the Yellow River burst its dikes in Taoyuan county in northern Jiangsu[7] on August 22, 1842—at the precise moment when he was directing the construction of defenses along the north bank of the Yangzi River during the Anglo-Chinese War (1839–1844). He was promptly stripped of rank and titles and was, at first, denied the chance to help with the repair work at the Taoyuan breach although he later was dis-patched to nearby Zhongmou (Henan) to direct repair work and flood relief. He was replaced by the currently serving Huaiyang Intendant, Pan Xi'en—an official whose views on canal-river management were similar to his own.[8]

During his career, Linqing was uniquely positioned to observe and evalu-ate the fiscal, managerial, and technological challenges that faced the Grand Canal–Yellow River Directorates during the Jiaqing and Daoguang reigns.[9] He also served at a time when the Qing leadership, officials, and literati felt growing concern about the persistence of old and newly emerging practical problems facing imperial government in the wake of the Heshen affair (1798–1799), demographic pressures, the rise of unrest and rebellion, fiscal shortages, and troubling instability in the monetary system.[10] These problems prompted dedicated officials, like Linqing, to focus increasingly on the practical needs of governance and on small-scale administrative adjustments to make the Qing

---

6   Dodgen 2001, pp. 56–68.
7   As a result of this flood, the Yellow River's course to the sea was blocked and a new north-ward course was not yet coherent, leaving the Grand Canal from Huai'an to Taoyuan dry. Dodgen 2001, pp. 58–116.
8   Dodgen 2001, pp. 110; 202, note 12. ECCP, pp. 506–507. See also Polachek 1992.
9   Amelung 2005, pp. 294–300; Dodgen 2001, pp. 28–34.
10   Lin 1991, pp. 1–35; Marks 1991, pp. 64–116; Vogel 1987, pp. 1–52; Wang 1979, pp. 425–452; 1992, pp. 35–68.

bureaucratic apparatus work better—the "statecraft" (*jingshi*) approach to governance in the early nineteenth century.[11]

The canal-river administration in which he served was high on the list of perceived governing problems at the time, and it was a repeated target of censorial and other official attacks for corruption and incompetence.[12] These attacks were generally leveled at low-level directorate officials, especially the increasing number of irregular officials appointed during the Jiaqing period, like expectants, those with purchased degrees, and extra-bureaucratic personnel— three important groups of marginal, temporary, and quasi-officials. These officials, in point of fact, were often very experienced in conservancy problems and shouldered the lion's share of grassroots managerial work, but they were often vilified by literati and officials, who had little actual experience with the nitty-gritty administrative work related to canal-river conservancy.[13]

In this environment of questioning reappraisal, Linqing began to focus on the challenges of canal-river conservancy, and he developed great insight into these issues during his tenure in conservancy posts in the early Daoguang reign. He traced many of the problems of the canal-river administration to the gaping divide between literati-official generalists serving in the canal-zone provinces and those all-important lower-level assistant civil and military officials, who actually did the work of managing the fiscal and technical aspects of canal-river work.[14] In essence, he maintained that the former did not know enough to make informed judgments about the fiscal and technical problems facing the three canal-river directorates. It was just such officials that Linqing targeted in his two informational works on canal-river conservancy noted above.[15] The first, published in 1836, contained vivid drawings of the devices and tools of conservancy work, such as dredgers and fascines. The second, published in 1841, spelled out and mapped the complexity of issues at the Grand Canal–Yellow River junction caused by the unrelenting process of siltation that led to the collapse of junction facilities in 1824 and the adoption of lock transport in 1827.[16]

---

11 Leonard 1984, pp. 20–24.

12 These generalizations are often echoed in scholarly works: CHC 10, pt. 1, 1978, pp. 108–162; Dodgen 2001, pp. 35, 56–68; Hu 1954–55, pp. 505–51.

13 Amelung 2005; Dodgen 2001; Antony 2002, pp. 27–59; Antony and Leonard 2002, pp. 1–10; Kaske 2008, pp. 281–308.

14 Dodgen 1991, pp. 56–68.

15 See note 1.

16 Linqing also wrote a three-part autobiography of his life and career, *Illustrated Diary of Travels* (*Hongxue yinyuan tuji*, 3 vols., Beijing: Guji.) of which the last two, covering the years from 1831 to 1841, contain information about and reflections on his experience in canal-river administration. The second part covers his life to age 40 *sui* (1831) and includes

As a Banner elite, Linqing, understood the pivotal importance of the canal-river junction to capital grain supply and the dynasty's ability to control the grain market in the capital region.[17] This government grain network, as well as the private north-south trade in other commodities, much of which was carried on grain fleets, had mandated the careful design of the hydraulic facilities at the junction to assure the passage of government and commercial craft through the Southern Canal head and the Clear Passage into the Yellow River.

As explained above, to cross the grain fleets, canal managers at the junction used the controlled release of the clear water from Hongze Lake through five lead channels (*yinhe*) into the Clear Passage.[18] The source of the relatively unsilted water was the network of rivers that entered the lake reservoir from the west through the Huai River basin. This crossing technique, as well as other water conservancy methods used in the Qing period, was based on "narrow diking" principles developed in the late Ming period by Pan Jixun (1521–1595). This approach used narrow dikes and deep dredging to increase the velocity of the Yellow River current in order to reduce the deposition of silt on the riverbed and to scour it out. When the Kangxi Emperor (1662–1722) decided to use the Grand Canal as the sole route for shipping capital grain supplies, he embarked on a major restoration of the Grand Canal under the direction of the hydraulic engineer, Jin Fu, who applied these principles to improve and expand the canal's hydraulic system, including those facilities located at the junction, and this approach was continued in the Yongzheng and early Qianlong reigns.[19]

During the early Qing years, the "power of the clear" streaming in from the lake had been sufficiently strong "to resist" the Yellow River currents because the lake and junction passages lay at a higher elevation than the river. However, over the course of the eighteenth century, siltation raised the riverbed in the lower and middle reaches so that it loomed over the surrounding terrain, and

---

information about his work as Henan river intendant; the third part covers his life to age 50 *sui* (1841), which he describes as a period of hardship from 1833–1842—the years when he served as Southern Canal director, then acting Governor-General of Liangjiang. The third part also contains a portrait of Linqing made by the noted court painter He Shikui, who had painted a portrait of the Daoguang emperor in 1824, as well as the generals and officials who helped put down the Muslim rebellion in southern Xinjiang (1822–1828). ECCP, p. 74. The first two parts were originally printed in 1839–1841. During the year he died (1846), his sons gathered all three parts together and published them in 1847–1850.

17   Cheung 2008, pp. 17–36, 37–51, 115–132.

18   From west to east: Zhangfukou (張福口), Tianran (天然), Zhangjiazhuang (張家庄), Feijiachang (裴家場), Taiping (太平). See Map 2. Leonard 1996, pp. 41–44.

19   For a comprehensive treatment of the history of Chinese hydraulics, see Needham 1971, pp. 211–378. ECCP, pp. 161–163; for an analysis of the political significance of the Kangxi and Qianlong Emperors' southern tours, see Chang 2007; 2014.

it created huge sandbanks on the shallow ocean floor at the mouth of the river that encircled and choked off the flow of the river into the sea.[20] This caused backflows, meanders, and devastating floods from the lower reaches of the river westward across northern Jiangsu (and the junction area) to the Kaifeng area in Henan province, but some of the silt build-up at the mouth of the river was swept as far south as Haimen sub-prefecture on the north bank of the Yangzi River delta and to Hangzhou Bay.[21]

Qing officials and engineers battled to keep pace with the siltation and control the rising flood waters, trying repeatedly to dredge out the riverbed at the lower reaches or to redirect the river to more low-lying rivers leading to the sea in northern Huaiyang prefecture, but these schemes were unsuccessful because of the impenetrable clay soil in the area and the hardened layers of silt that lay atop the clay. Similarly, they increased the number of drainage gates built into the sides of the Gaoyan Great Dike in order to drain excess lake water into the Grand Canal and out to sea via the Yangzi River, and they paired these efforts with the construction of ever-higher river and lake dikes. The primary purpose of all of these projects was to improve and stabilize the junction to keep it open for grain shipments.

1   Junction Conservancy Work, 1737–1765

It was precisely this parade of initiatives that Linqing explained and illustrated in his important analysis of the engineering changes made at the junction. Written from the vantage point of the Jiaqing and Daoguang reigns when conditions were dire, his narrative highlights major turning points in junction conservancy work as canal officials gradually replaced the earlier Qing emphasis on expanding and fine-tuning junction infrastructure to one that sought primarily to safeguard, or "defend," it from the encroaching river and lake. This shift in orientation is clearly apparent in the first stage of conservancy work during the early Qianlong years from 1737 to 1765 when Southern Canal directors, led by Gao Bin (1683–1755), expanded and improved the locking system at the northern end of the Southern Canal, adjacent to the canal mouth (yun-kou), from one to three double lock-gates, anchored to earthen mounds in the middle of the canal head and extending the locking zone by 3.4 km.[22]

---

20   JSHY Maps, 12:7b–8b (maps). HYHK, p. 19. See also China coast scroll, British Museum, Map 162.0.3, 9340110, Section 4: Shandong and Northern Jiangsu.
21   Elvin and Su 1998, pp. 344–407.
22   HYHK, Maps, pp. 12b–13b.

The locks included the Huiji-Yue gate, originally built in 1710 in the Kangxi reign, then rebuilt in Yongzheng 10 (1732), as well as the Tongji-Yue and Fuxing-Yue gates (Map 2). Each of these, in turn, was reinforced by two stalk embankments (*caoba*), which served a fascine-like function to protect the gates in the event of floods from the lake or river. Three more semi-circular stalk dams were built immediately east of the canal mouth to protect the Southern Canal head.

This work on the Southern Canal head was designed primarily to improve the ascent of grain fleets through the locks to the Clear Passage that lay at a higher elevation than the Southern Canal. But it also allowed canal managers to fine-tune the flow of lake water into the canal in order to scour silt from the canal mouth and the lock zone, and also "to fill and adjust water levels" quickly in the Southern Canal as far south as Baoying and Gaoyou when levels were low. The protective stalk dams also enabled canal managers to "lock out" lake and/or Yellow River floodwaters that might damage the Southern Canal head. Finally, to protect the canal head further, canal officials undertook protective barriers and drainage projects between the Southern Canal head and the south bank of the Yellow River, building the East Dike, to the east side of the Clear Passage; they also blocked up the old bed of the canal and dug a drainage bore leading into the Yongji Canal, east of the lock zone, in order to divert any Yellow River inflows away from the canal head and to provide an evacuation conduit for dredged silt, dug from junction passages during the low-water season.[23]

Canal managers also widened each of the five lead channels that led from the lake by approximately thirteen meters to concentrate the flow of lake water through the passage and, thus, maximize its scouring effect, and they also reinforced the dikes on the north side of the lake with defensive earthen embankments (*bao*) and with brickwork placed on the inner side, or face, of these dikes. The first of these was the Linhu Dike (Linhu*di*), a structure that was 4.7 km in length, lying on the northeast side of the lake and east of the canal mouth. This dike was later extended westward to the East-West lock gates separating the lake from the Clear Passage for a total of 9.4 km. Protective brick reinforcements (7.1 km) were also placed on the inner side (*tishen*) of the lake dike that lay west of the Clear Passage, which, according to Linqing, "provided a defensive encirclement" of the canal mouth and Clear Passage in the event of floods from the lake.

It was, however, the threatening rise of the Yellow River that conservancy officials feared the most in this period. To cope with it, they devised a scheme to redirect the flow of the river northward, away from crucial junction passageways. They repositioned the canal mouth and Clear Passage 240 meters to

---

23   HYHK, Maps, pp. 12–13b.

the south and constructed five raft-like weirs, called "wooden dragons" (*mu-long*), on the south bank of the Yellow River immediately west of the junction. These structures jutted out into the river, deflecting the river flow away from the junction.[24] These initiatives, Linqing asserted, enabled government grain fleets to pass through the junction for another 60 years until the early Daoguang period, although he acknowledged that the junction crossing "was never an easy one."[25]

2   Protecting the Junction, 1770–1784

By the second stage, from the early 1770s until 1784, the dangers posed by high water levels in the river became the chief concern of canal officials as they sought to preserve the existing junction facilities. They were terrified about the impact of floods on the junction and felt that "even when they diligently carried out their mandatory yearly repairs, they still waited in fear that the power" of the current would crash through the dikes near the junction and "pour into the Clear Passage."[26] As a consequence of these concerns, throughout 1776–1777 officials in northern Jiangsu worked out more aggressive plans to redirect the course of the river into a new bed "to avoid the place where the Yellow presently meets the Clear Passage," and guide the flow "smoothly within the river banks out to sea."

The creation of a new course included dredging a distance of 3.4 km along the north bank of the river from Tao Village (Tao*zhuang*) to Zhoujia Village (Zhoujia*zhuang*) immediately west of the Central Canal entrance (Zhonghe*kou*). Simultaneously, the south bank of the river, west of the junction, was whittled away and strengthened; the wooden-dragon weirs were repositioned southward to the newly cut south bank, leaving a north-south isoceles-shaped spit of land that elongated and protected the Clear Passage.

At the same time, canal officials made a concerted effort to protect the western side of the Clear Passage from the river by constructing "blocking embankments" (*lanba*) on its outer face and "restraining embankments" (*shushuiba*) on its inner face to counter the pressure of the Yellow River's current;

---

24   HYHK, Maps, p. 13. The norms for the construction of these structures were made by Li Bing in the early Qianlong reign, and an illustration can be found in Linqing's HGQJ 3:30a. Needham 1971, 4, pt. 3, p. 328.

25   HYHK, QL 30 (1765), map, p. 12.

26   The outer dam on the west side of the passage, called the ShunHuang*ba*, and the dike on the inner face of the passage, the Shunqing*di*, are shown on Linqing's map of the junction in Qianlong 50 (1785). HYHK QL 41 (1776), map and map explanation, pp. 14–16.

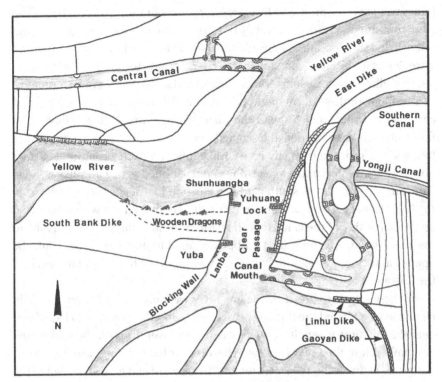

MAP 3   Protecting the Grand Canal–Yellow River junction, ca. 1776

similarly, a "blocking wall" (*lanyan*), built on the north side of the lake near Yu Embankment (Yu*ba*) served to strengthen the barrier between the lake and the river. In total, eight kilometers of such dikes and dams were constructed in this period.[27] Finally, canal engineers began to construct barrier dams *across* the Clear Passage for the first time. As a first step, they relocated the east-west lock gates that separated the lake from the Clear Passage to a site 500 meters north of the canal mouth. They also built what appears to have been additional blocking embankments as well as stalk embankments (*tusaoba*).

Linqing asserted that expectations were high that both the northeasterly diversion of the river, the strengthening of inner and outer embankments on the west side of the Clear Passage, and the construction of cross-passage barrier dams would shield the passage and turn it into "a vast and level pond" through which the clear lake water would flow in a focused way and converge with the Yellow River further to the northeast at Pengjia docks.[28] But these

27   HYHK QL 50 (1785), pp. 16b–17.
28   HYHK QL 50 (1785), p. 17b.

hopes were overly optimistic! By 1779, silt deposits in the lower reaches of the river continued to raise the level of the river, further slowing its currents and intensifying the siltation. As a result, the river dikes were built ever higher, and water levels in the lake, compared to the river, became too low and "weak to resist the Yellow," thus causing serious "delays" in the passage of grain shipments.

To cope with these developments, canal officials constructed three tamped earthen embankments to shield the Clear Passage from Yellow inflows. The first embankment extended and strengthened the western side of the passage by 2.2 km in order to intensify its weir-like function of "bending" the current northeastward. A second project in 1779 repositioned yet again the east-west dam-gates by 930 meters southward to a location that separated the lake from the Clear Passage. Two years later in 1781, a third embankment was constructed on the north side of the canal mouth, in order "to surround it" and thus shield the canal head. All three dam-embankments, Linqing explained, could be opened and closed in seasonal rotation to respond to changing water levels in the lake and river.

All these efforts to divert the Yellow River were abandoned when floods in Henan in 1784 altered the flow of the river and caused it to return to its old bed near the junction, where it "cascaded across the river dikes on the south bank and poured into the Clear Passage." This disaster led canal managers to abandon plans to divert the Yellow current northeastward and to turn instead to the construction of stronger cross-passage lock gates that could block destructive inflows from the river. First, they rebuilt the dam-gate closest to the lake and canal head, naming it the Shuqing dam-gate (Shuqing*ba*); second, they moved the old east-west version of this structure 960 meters further northward, closer to the river; finally, they built the Yuhuang lock-gate at the river entrance to the Clear Passage to serve as the first line of defense against Yellow River inflows.

Linqing judged that these various lock gates and embankments would enable canal officials to manipulate the Clear and Yellow waters to a certain extent. For example, when the river was high, the cross-passage lock gates could be closed. When the lake level was high, the Shuqing gates could release lake water into the passage. Yet he was forced to admit that after sixty years of managing the canal junction in this way, canal officials could not stem the silt build-up at the mouth of the river which "caused the lower reaches of the river to fill up and pour" southward across the dikes and into the Clear Passage. Only the west side of the Clear Passage remained fairly stable.[29] Each decade brought greater complexity to these facilities, and with it, of course, more difficult,

---

29   HYHK QL 50 (1785), p. 18.

costly, and time-consuming repair and maintenance tasks.[30] But none of this slowed the unrelenting siltation on the river bed which, Linqing asserted, lurked under the river surface, "hidden from view," raising the river bed all the way from central Henan to the sea, creating a vicious cycle of floods, meanders, and delays in grain shipments.

3   Last Ditch Efforts to Shield the Junction, 1796–1826

By the early Jiaqing reign, water levels in the lake had also risen to dangerous heights. This was partly due, according to Linqing, to the practice of routinely opening a series of six river drainage gates (*zha*) that lay west of the junction in order to divert and lower river levels. This practice allowed the seepage of the silt-laden river water into the lake, which raised the lakebed.[31] Officials, at first, mistakenly praised the utility of this tactic, which they called "draining the Yellow to aid the clear" (*jianhuang zhuqing*) because it raised lake levels and, thus, increased the "power of the clear" to carry the grain fleets through the junction. However, although this tactic did, indeed, temporarily lower river levels during emergencies, high water in the lake increased pressure on the Gaoyan Great Dike and Linhu Dike lying on the east and north sides, respectively, and clogged the lake lead channels into the Clear Passage with silt. As a result, in the early Jiaqing reign, Linqing argued, canal officials in the middle and lower reaches of the river lived in fear of the destructive power of the river currents that "tore through the river dikes and dumped massive amounts of silt into the junction channels, making them too shallow for the passage of grain fleets."[32]

Finally by Jiaqing 9 (1804), officials responsible for the canal in Northern Jiangsu and Henan, seized the initiative and carried out a comprehensive plan to mitigate the deadly impact of high water levels in both the river and lake. The plan, simply put, lengthened the Clear Passage yet again at both its north and south ends and improved the lock-gate embankments on each, thereby erecting stronger barriers against direct inflows from lake and river into the passage. On the south end, the plan returned the Shuqing lock gate to

---

30   The conservancy work undertaken during the Qianlong reign both reinforced and increased the technical complexity of the hydraulic infrastructure at the junction, which can be seen at a glance from the junction maps for 1765, 1776, and 1785. HYHK, pp. 11b–12; 14b–15, 16b–17.

31   The gates included: Maocheng (毛城), Putian (鋪天), Ranzha (然閘), Fengshan (峰山), Xiangfu (祥符), and Wurui (五瑞) gates. HYHK JQ 13 (1808), p. 19b.

32   Ibid.

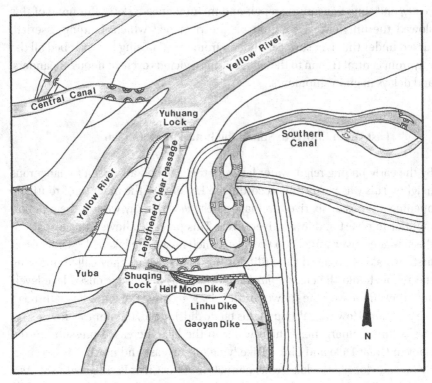

MAP 4   Junction hydraulic defenses, ca. 1808

a location south of the canal mouth so that it served as the principal barrier to
flood waters from the lake. At the north end, the plan called for the construction of a "new" Yuhuang lock-gate embankment of 1.2 km in length north of the
original Yuhuang lock-gate.[33] Interestingly, the western extension of this lock
consisted of a long, solid arc-shaped structure that functioned as a weir to redirect the current northeastward and at the same time "scour out" silt from the
gate area and "prevent flooding across the east bank" of the Clear Passage into
the Southern Canal head.[34] This structure was paired with a 960-meter extension of the gate's eastern side. These projects, Linqing explained, allowed canal
officials to seal off the gate when the Yellow River "waxes excessively." They
apparently expected this gate to be battered and weakened by high river levels
each season because they mandated maintenance procedures that included
"demolishing and rebuilding it each year."

---

33   See HYHK QL 50 (1785), pp. 16b–17, for the original placement of both gate embankments.
34   HYHK JQ 13 (1808), p. 20.

Dangerously high water levels in the lake took center stage in Jiaqing 13 (1808) after two sections of the Linhu dike on the lake's northeast side were destroyed by high winds and waves. This part of the lake dike was particularly important because, if breached, lake water would pour into the critical Southern Canal head as far south as Baoying. To guarantee the safety of this stretch of dikes, canal engineers built a semicircular "half-moon dike" (*quanyan*), shaped like an half moon, that extended out into the lake between the Linhu dike and the Shuqing lock-gate.[35] This 130-meter dike was made of "brush, sticks, and earth" to serve as a kind of fascine to absorb and dissipate the force of wind and waves off the lake. Moreover, the embankment, or causeway, that lay between the lake and the Southern Canal head and mouth was reinforced with rock fragments, which also would help to dissipate the force of the floodwaters from the lake. Canal officials also continued the sloped stacking of rock fragments on top and behind the dike's brickwork along the entire perimeter from the Gaoyan Great Dike to the Shuqing lock-gate for a distance of 340 meters.[36] From 1808 until the early Daoguang reign, floods from both the lake and river repeatedly deposited muddy silt into the Southern Canal head from Qingjiangpu to the Clear Passage and blocked the passage of government fleets. All these conservancy projects undertaken by canal officials were, however, no match for the unrelenting geologic process of siltation.

The final deadly disaster struck the junction in late Daoguang 4 (1824) when storms produced wind and waves that swept away large sections of Gaojia Great Dike on the east side of the lake. The lake water poured through and wrecked the junction passages, dissipating the "clear" water in the lake reservoir, leaving none available for carrying the grain fleets through the Clear Passage in the approaching spring of 1825. In the immediate aftermath of the disaster, panicked canal managers relied on two *ad hoc* measures: first, an often used but ineffective crossing tactic, called "borrowing the Yellow to aid transport" (*jiehuang jiyun*), throwing open the Yuhuang gate, allowing silted river water to flow in, while transport officials worked frantically to direct the tracking of grain fleets through the gate against the river back-spills. In no time, the in-flows had, of course, intensified siltation of the Clear Passage and the canal head, narrowing the Yuhuang gate opening to one-half of its original width.[37] Secondly, at the same time, canal officials raced to build tracking roads on both sides of the Clear Passage with silt dredged from the junction passageways, and then joined the two roads together into one platform-like structure just outside the

---

35   HYHK JQ 13 (1808), pp. 18b–19.
36   HYHK DG 7 (1827), map and map explanation, pp. 21b–25.
37   HYHK DG 7 (1827), p. 21b.

clogged Yuhuang gate which enabled them to position and launch the grain boats into the river.[38] They also reinforced the southwest side of the gate with two additional moveable "pincer embankments" (qiankou*ba*).

However, because the grain fleets were mired in the silted canal further south from Gaoyou to Qingjiangpu and could not reach the junction—and many more would soon be arriving from Zhejiang and the middle Yangzi provinces—officials decided to offload grain cargoes from the large government boats to smaller, shallow-draft lighters that could carry the grain with the help of trackers through the muddy canal to the junction, or use cart haulage over the river embankments (*panba*) to the south bank of the river. To facilitate transport from this point, grain-transport officials organized a costly, complicated, and time-consuming series of transfers on and off government and private lighters through Shandong and Zhili provinces to the capital granaries—a method that was called "lighterage transport to Tongzhou" (*boyunfutong*).

The following year (1826), a variation of this method, called "relay shipping" (*panba jieyun*), was used that also relied heavily on lighterage. In this plan, after lighters picked up the grain cargoes at the docks on the south bank of the river, they then ferried the grain across the river for loading onto empty government grain fleets that had returned from Tongzhou in the autumn of 1825 and had lain at anchor on the north bank of the river near the entrance to the Central Canal in order "to load and relay" the grain north in the spring of 1826. Like lighterage in 1825, this relay scheme was extremely slow, labor-intensive, and expensive, but it was significantly less expensive than the previous method because the use of government grain fleets eliminated many transaction and labor costs. In the end, Linqing commented, even though "the relay method succeeded without mishap and without wasting money on porterage labor," it was not, in the end, a "long-term solution" to the problem of controlling the Yellow at the junction.[39]

4   Qishan and the Pound Lock, 1827

According to Linqing, it was Qishan, the newly appointed Liangjiang Governor-General in 1825, who crafted a "longer-term" solution to the collapse of the junction during his two-year direction of hydraulic reconstruction—a period when Linqing witnessed first-hand the limitations of lighterage transport. After soliciting public views, Qishan and his two canal deputies, Zhang Jing and Pan

---

38   Ibid.
39   HYHK DG 7 (1827), p. 22.

Xi'en, headquartered at Qingjiangpu, modified the long-established Hongze crossing method and re-engineered the Clear Passage "to create a pound lock" (*chuangwei guantang zhifa*) that enabled the grain fleets to pass through the severely damaged junction facilities. This method was referred to as "filling the lock [with Yellow silted water] and ferrying [the grain]" (*guantang duyun*)—an "invention that had never been used before." Qishan and the canal directors built the lock and outlined the steps of the crossing procedure from late 1826 to early 1827, after the grain fleets returned to their home anchorages in 1826 and before their return to the junction with new grain shipments in the third month of 1827.

Canal managers re-engineered the Clear Passage infrastructure to include a new pound lock in the middle of the passage with lock gates at both its south and north ends. The gate at the south end near the lake was a special earthen dike-wall, called the Linqing Dike (lit., Near the Clear [lake] Dike, a reference to the lake) that shielded the Southern Canal mouth and lake entrance from silt. Paralleling this structure on the north end and lying outside the Yuhuang gate was a second barrier dike called the Linhuang dike (Near the Yellow [River]

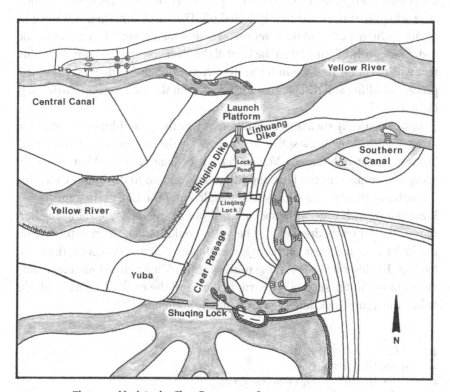

MAP 5   The pound lock in the Clear Passage, ca. 1827

Dam) that was constructed with a solid earthen core on top of two sandbars. "The water that lies between these two enclosing dikes is called the pond, or lock, water" (*tanghe*).[40]

Between these two new dikes, tracking paths on both sides of the Clear Passage were raised higher with silt dredged from the passages. The embankments on the west side of the Clear Passage were further reinforced with two new round pincer dikes (qiankou*ba*). Next, a special gate, the Cao*zha* (Straw gate), probably constructed with fascines made of straw, brush and mud, was built on the north and outer side of Yuhuang gate to serve as the new gateway for grain fleets passing into the river.[41] Finally, the interior walls of the lock were lined, or "encased" (*tao*), with wooden slabs and planks. Thus, by the end of 1826, canal officials at the junction had a newly constructed pound lock in the middle of the Clear Passage that could be used when the lake water was "too scarce and weak" to overcome the high water levels in the river.

Linqing explained that when grain fleets gathered at the Southern Canal head waiting to cross, canal officials would first block up the Cao gate and the adjacent earthen Linhuang locking dam on the north end of the lock. The grain boats were then pulled through the Linqing dam at the south end into the lock, after which that dam was tightly sealed off. Then and only then was the gate of the Linhuang dike on the river opened, at which point "river water would instantaneously fill the lock to the level of the river," raising the grain boats and readying them for passage into the river. According to Linqing, the complete process of filling and discharging the water from the lock took approximately eight days.[42]

But, realistically speaking, how different was the pound-lock crossing from using Yellow River back-spills, or "borrowing the Yellow to aid transport," Linqing rhetorically asked? Very different, he maintained! When the river water was trapped in the lock, the silt quickly settled to the bottom, clearing the water so that "not one speck of silt could enter the lake or the canal head." Presumably, each time the water drained out of the lock, the silt at the bottom of the lock was dredged out before it could harden, then deposited on the lock's east and west causeways, creating ever higher banks on the Clear Passage. He described the locking process as "building tamped-earth embankments in the water, seizing the earth to block off the river, dragging in planks to line the pound lock, and then crossing the grain boats."[43]

---

40   Ibid.
41   HYHK, DG 7 (1827), pp. 20b–21.
42   HYHK, DG 7 (1827), map explanation, p. 22.
43   Ibid.

The new method was ready for use in the early spring of 1827 when canal officials began preparing for the arrival of the grain fleets. Yet, not surprisingly, Qishan and his canal managers were, nonetheless, reluctant to try it out because they "couldn't say for sure whether or not it would work."[44] At first, they timidly followed conventional approaches for lowering the levels of the Yellow River as the spring crossing approached, which was to divert the river into the Wangying diversion channel located on the north bank of the river, east of the junction. This diversion, they hoped, would lower the river and allow them to undertake large-scale dredging of the riverbed in its lower reaches, which would, in turn, help speed the river's flow to the sea. Yet, in spite of their hopes, they were unable to direct the river current into this channel when its gate was opened in the third month of 1827 (March 27–April 26), probably because of back flows from the mouth of the river. As a result, the river was too high to use "clear" lake water for the crossing. Thus, they had "to bite the bullet" and use Qishan's new plan. There really was no alternative but to "fill the pound lock to ferry the transport." Within a month, all the southern grain fleets had passed through the junction with no delays, then proceeded to the capital granaries, followed by their timely return to their home anchorages in the autumn.

For the next twenty years, Linqing asserted, conditions at the junction "remained stable, using the method of drawing water into the pound lock." Nonetheless, canal managers were constantly on the alert for problems, such as the threat of fires that often broke out when "the hundreds of masts and sails of the grain boats filled the lock, lying close together like the teeth of a comb."[45] They also continued to fine-tune the new lock infrastructure. In 1830, an alternative channel (*tihe*) on the west side of the lock was dug in order to speed the process of filling and discharging water.[46]

Canal officials also had difficulties breaking up hardened silt that formed at the foot of Cao gate, which made the gate difficult to open and close and, thus, less effective for adjusting the flow of the river in and out of the lock—a situation that generally occurred when the lake and river levels were more-or-less equal, slowing river velocity and increasing silt deposits. To resolve this problem, two sluice gates were built on the east side of the lock. The first near Yao pond was used to drain the lock. The second, lying east of Cao gate, was used to "lead in the Yellow" (*yinhuang*) and fill the lock when the river was too high to allow the opening of the gate, itself. Five years later in 1835, one more such sluice was built to maximize the speed of filling and discharging water to and

---

44   HYHK, DG 7 (1827), pp. 22–23.
45   HYHK, DG 18 (1838), pp. 24b–25.
46   HYHK, DG 18 (1838), pp. 23b–25.

from the lock. These three sluices enabled canal engineers to "double the rate of filling and emptying the lock from one to two *cun* per hour," or from about 30 mm to about 60 mm per hour.

In 1836, the Cao gate was again rebuilt and reinforced on both sides with the Maya embankment on the inner east side of the lock and with the Crab-Pincer (*xieqian*) embankment the outer west side. A tamped earth pincer embankment was also built within the Linqing dam to reinforce it.[47] This series of on-going conservancy projects suggests that officials did not neglect hydraulic facilities at the canal-river junction in the 1830s, a point that Randall Dodgen also makes about river work in Henan during this same period.[48]

During the first ten years of using the pound lock, Linqing observed that officials and grain-transport soldiers became increasingly skilled at using the lock, and new efficiencies were achieved. Whereas at the beginning in 1827, only 400 to 500 boats could enter the lock at one time, now, ten years later, as many as 1,200 to 1,300 could be packed in each time. Nonetheless, he maintained that the mobilization of the fleets each transport cycle still required hard, disciplined work in order to assure their timely arrival at the junction before the rise of the river at the summer solstice and their return from the capital before the winter solstice when the canal froze over. But he categorically stated, "If all the grain fleets arrive on schedule and line up for the crossing with other fleets before the solstices, they never need fear that the lock itself would fail and cause delays."[49]

5   Conclusions

Linqing's painstaking assessment of conditions at the junction during the 100-year period from the early Qianlong reign to the 1840s made crystal clear to the Qing leadership that that lock transport perpetuated the use of the Grand Canal as the pivot of the empire-wide grain supply, and it also underscored the importance of using sea transport when canal disasters brought canal transport to a halt. His Banner-elite status lent credibility to his work, and it also enables modern scholars to capture a Qing elite's view of deteriorating canal conditions in northern Jiangsu, the strategic significance of canal transport, and the importance of the lock-gate innovation in junction conservancy.

---

47   HYHK, Daoguang 8 map, pp. 23b–24.
48   Dodgen 2001, pp. 42–68, 145–159.
49   HYHK DG 18 (1838), p. 25.

CHAPTER 2

Imagination at the Center: The Daoguang Emperor and Yinghe

1   The Daoguang Emperor Launches the Sea-Transport Initiative

The evolution of an actual sea-transport plan did not begin until early 1825 (5.2.5), when the Daoguang Emperor ordered high-ranking canal-zone officials to investigate the feasibility of sea transport as a concrete alternative to the faltering system of grain transport on the Grand Canal. This order gave officials the green light to explore openly an option that had not until then moved beyond whispered discussions because of what the emperor referred to as "unalterable opposition."[1] Now the issue was out in the open, and the fact that it had been raised by the emperor, suggested that he and his inner circle of Banner advisers were positively disposed to the idea if it were deemed workable.

It should not be surprising that the idea to move ahead with this option came from the Daoguang Emperor himself, being the heir to an impressive line of emperors who had expanded direct imperial involvement in governing and enhanced their ability to respond quickly and flexibly to emerging and daunting challenges and crises.[2] By the turn of the nineteenth century, these challenges intensified when imperial government was rocked by the corruption and scandal associated with the Heshen affair (1784–1799) at the very moment when the best of bureaucratic governance was required to quell the upsurge of unrest and collective violence in the interior and borderlands, as well as to manage fiscal shortages, dampen monetary instability, and respond decisively to natural disasters.[3]

When worsening conditions on the Grand Canal jeopardized the continued operation of strategic capital grain supply, both the Jiaqing and the Daoguang emperors had responded with great energy and diligence. By the time the floods had destroyed the Hongze Lake dikes and the canal–Yellow River junction in early 1825, the Daoguang emperor was in his early forties, just three years into his reign. He had witnessed the decline of imperial government in the last years of the Qianlong reign, and he had watched his father, the Jiaqing

---

1   TJ/S 00033 (5.2.5). JSHY 1:1 (5.2.5).
2   Leonard 1996, pp. 51–66. See Wu 1970 and Bartlett 1990. Huang 1994, no. 258.
3   ECCP, pp. 288–290, 574–576; CHC 10, pt. 1, pp. 1–106, 107–144.

© KONINKLIJKE BRILL NV, LEIDEN, 2019 | DOI:10.1163/9789004384583_004

道光帝朝服像

FIGURE 2   The Daoguang Emperor in court dress

Emperor, struggle to manage new and daunting problems facing bureaucratic government during his reign.[4] As a consequence, he was experienced and
ready to act decisively when disaster struck the Grand Canal.

When he called for an assessment of sea transport in the early days of the
crisis, the emperor clearly understood, and had for some time, that a new long-
term solution was required and that Yellow River backspills, which intensified

---

4   Leonard 1996, pp. 51–77.

siltation in the junction passageways, certainly could not be used indefinitely. Use of the river in this way was a short-term expedient that only caused more silt damage to the junction's hydraulic facilities. He noted that sea transport had been debated in the past—with some officials arguing for it and some against—but no consensus had emerged at that time. Yet, now after the disaster, conditions were infinitely worse and required decisive action.

The emperor made his view clear about his readiness to make changes. "If it is necessary to abandon the customary regulations for canal transport and face the dangers of sailing on the high seas, this course of action will wholly alter the old regulations and, at first glance, appears to be something that cannot possibly be done. Yet, what are the consequences of doing nothing? Tribute grain is the dynasty's main supply! How can you canal-zone officials simply sit back and do nothing to guarantee capital grain supplies? You must, of course, make preparations in advance!"[5]

Following this exhortation, the emperor discussed issues that showed his awareness and understanding of the maritime resources and navigational skills that private shippers possessed, explaining that "it might be possible to send the tax grain by sea from the Jiangsu grain jurisdictions of Susongchangtaizhen and Hangjiahu in Zhejiang province—all of which are close to the coast. If the grain were to be sent by lighters to the coast and then shipped by large sand junks (*dahaoshachuan*) that routinely sail to the northern ports of Shandong, Zhili, and Fengtian several times a year, it seems that, in fact, *the sea route is not impossible to navigate*" [author's emphasis]!

Therefore, he ordered the Liangjiang Governor-General, the Grain Transport director, the Jiangsu Governor, and the acting Zhejiang Governor "to investigate the feasibility of sea transport in your respective jurisdictions, make a comprehensive plan, and discuss it carefully without bias." He outlined five specific issues that these officials should investigate in order to determine whether or not sea transport could be carried out: (1) the hiring price of large sand junks; (2) fair treatment of these private shippers; (3) the dispatch of civilian and military personnel to guard the grain and report on accidents and losses; (4) assistance for laid-off grain-transport troops and workers; and (5) the identification of coastal ports in the south for loading grain and those in the north for unloading. If sea transport proved effective for Jiangsu and Zhejiang, then perhaps it could be expanded to include Jiangxi and Huguang grain in the future.

Even though the emperor had spoken out forcefully on sea transport early in the second month, canal-zone officials remained silent on the issue for

---

5   JSHY 1:1 (5.2.5).

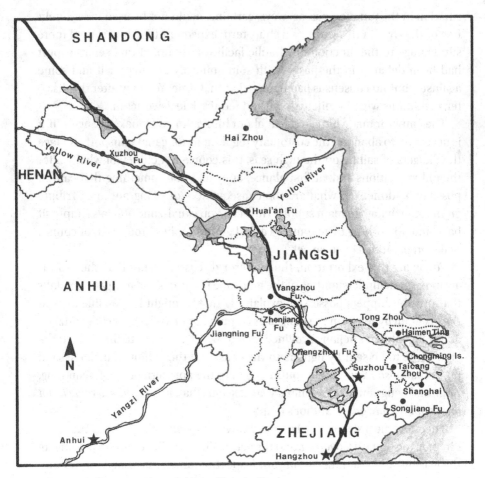

MAP 6   Jiangsu province and lower Yangzi valley

another two months (5.4.2) when finally the Liangjiang Governor-General, the canal and grain transport directors, and the former Liangjiang Governor-General, Sun Yuting, memorialized that sea transport was "too difficult to implement." And, so it must have seemed to these officials, who, at the time, were faced with the complete failure of Yellow River backspills to aid in the crossing of grain boats (as the emperor had predicted) and which had left the canal mired in mud from Yuhuang Dam to Gaoyou.[6] And, indeed, it was too difficult to contemplate as they scrambled around trying to organize relay shipping on lighters along the whole course of the canal from Gaoyu to the capital,

---

6   TJ/S 00003–6 (5.4.2); JSHY 1:3–b (5.4.2).

not to mention the need for the mobilization of armies of laborers, porters, and carts.[7]

The emperor bitterly complained that forty days had elapsed since Yuhuang Dam had been opened, and still thousands of boats had not passed through the junction. Some were either stranded in the southern canal head from Gaoyu to the junction "where silt clogs the canal ever more deeply each day," or they were waiting in the canal south of Gaoyou. Others from Huguang, Jiangxi, and Zhejiang had not even entered the canal at Guazhou! The summer solstice loomed ahead, only a month away when, "in the blink of an eye," the Yellow River would begin to rise and make it impossible to cross the fleets.[8]

At precisely this moment of turmoil at the junction, Yinghe, one of the emperor's closest advisers in the capital, proposed a bold comprehensive plan to resolve the grain-transport crisis that placed sea transport at the very heart of grain-transport institutions (5.4.10).[9]

2 Yinghe (1771–1839): Principal Architect of the Sea-Transport Plan

Yinghe was the principal architect and driver of a comprehensive plan to restore and stabilize the government grain-transport system in 1825–1826. He was uniquely positioned to mastermind this controversial plan. He had risen to prominence in 1799 after the death of the Qianlong Emperor and the fall of the Heshen clique, at a time when the succeeding Jiaqing emperor turned to officials, both Han and Banner elites, who had distanced themselves from Heshen in the declining years of the recently deceased emperor. Yinghe's father, Tebao, had remained outside the Heshen circle prior to 1799, and Yinghe had commented that he himself had probably gained favor with the new emperor because his father had declined Heshen's suggestion that Yinghe marry his daughter.[10]

Yinghe, a Manchu of the Socolo clan, was young when he passed the *jinshi* exam in 1793 at age 20. The family had served in the Imperial Household as slaves, or bond servants, before the founding of the dynasty in 1644. However, in the eighteenth and nineteenth centuries, the family's power and prestige had risen when its members began to achieve *jinshi* status, starting with Yinghe's

---

7   Leonard 1996, pp. 151–172; Leonard 2002, pp. 184–198; Leonard 2005, pp. 458–461.

8   TJ/S 0005–6 (5.4.2).

9   JSHY 1:4–4B (5.4.10).

10   ECCP, pp. 931–933; QDZJCK, 1986, 016:236 ff. See DOT 4291, p. 354, on the Imperial Household Department.

FIGURE 3   Yinghe (1771–1839)

father, Tebao, in 1737, after which they began serving in important central government posts, such as the Grand Council, Grand Secretariat, and, in addition, the Imperial Household. The family was unusual in having its members
achieve six *jinshi* degrees within four generations, ending with Yinghe's grandson, Xizhi in 1835. These included Tebao's cousin, Guanbao (1737), and Yinghe's
two sons, Kuizhao (1814) and Kuiyue (1811).

After achieving the *jinshi* degree, Yinghe entered the Hanlin Academy and
in 1795 served as a Hanlin compiler. In 1799 he was appointed sub-chancellor
of the Grand Secretariat (*neigexueshi*; 1799), and in 1802, he was appointed to
serve as the emperor's private secretary in the Imperial Study, and, thereafter, in
a series of posts that included presidencies and vice presidencies of the Boards
of Revenue, Ceremonies, and War, as well as positions in the Grand Council
and the Imperial Household, the latter of which his father had also held.

His close bonds with the emperor were reinforced in 1813 when, in his
capacity as private secretary, he had accompanied the emperor's summer

hunting party to Jehol. On its return, news of the Tianli rebel attack on the palace reached the emperor's entourage, and the emperor promptly dispatched Yinghe ahead to the capital to take command of the palace police. His swift action in rounding up the rebels and his leadership of the subsequent campaign against the rebels in Henan reinforced his ties to the emperor and led to his appointment to the Presidency of the Board of Works and Civil Office as well as to the lucrative position as Superintendent of Customs and local sales taxes levied on imports into Beijing. Throughout the Jiaqing reign, Yinghe proved himself to be a trusted adviser to the emperor and a disciplined administrator. Although he was sanctioned and demoted several times, he was quickly reinstated to various capital positions. At his fiftieth birthday in 1820, the emperor honored him for his service.

When the Daoguang Emperor succeeded to the throne in late 1820, he immediately posted Yinghe to the presidency of the Board of Revenue to tackle what he, the emperor, perceived as the urgent need for fiscal retrenchment and the problem of fiscal shortages. When the emperor assigned him to the concurrent position of Grand Secretary, Yinghe became what E-tu Sun has termed a "supervising minister" of the board—one who took general overarching responsibility for board affairs (*zongli hupu; jianli hupu*) and for pursuing the new emperor's fiscal agenda.[11] This unique post had been used to head the six boards in the early Qing period, but it was soon replaced by board presidencies, and although it was never formally entered into the *Huidian*, it continued to be used episodically for the most important boards, such as those of Civil Office, Revenue, War, and Works during emergencies when these boards' resources were strained.

This position was generally filled by trusted Manchu princes prior to the Jiaqing reign and had facilitated direct lines of communications between the emperor and his Inner Court circle with the Outer Court boards. In 1799, for example, as part of his efforts to restore Qing administrative discipline and morale after the removal of Heshen, the Jiaqing Emperor appointed Yongxing (Prince Cheng) as a supervising minister over the Board of Revenue to wind up the financial issues stemming from the military campaigns in Sichuan, and his brother Yongxuan (Prince Yi) was given a similar appointment to oversee and clean up the Board of Civil Office after the corrupting influence of Heshen.[12] Both princes were sons of the Qianlong Emperor and brothers of the Jiaqing Emperor. The emperor continued to appoint supervising ministers, but

---

11   Sun 1962–63, pp. 77–79.
12   Yongxing 1752–1823; Yongxuan 1746–1832; ECCP, pp. 962–964; Sun 1962–63, pp. 77–79.

thereafter they were generally drawn from among the Grand Secretaries, and this practice continued throughout the nineteenth century.

The Board of Revenue was arguably the most important central ministry for orchestrating the practical aspects of the imperium's fiscal, logistical, and economic tasks.[13] This included the procurement and minting of monetary copper, the stabilization of the bimetallic currency system, supervision of regional and capital granaries and treasuries, the regulation and collection of land and grain taxes, fiscal auditing, and the transport and payment of official and military salaries.[14] Key among these tasks was the management of the transport and storage of strategic capital grain reserves from the eight canal-zone provinces.

After twenty years of administrative service in many branches of the central government, including the Board of Revenue, Yinghe was a skilled and experienced official who had developed a network of ties with officials in the Inner and Outer Courts. He would have been intimately acquainted with the Board of Revenue's fiscal tasks and steeped in the precedents and problems of Qing grain-supply management and its dependence on open Grand Canal communications. Moreover, as a Banner elite, he would have shared the imperial emphasis on the strategic importance of these tasks. Similarly, he would have been familiar with the on-going practice of "recruiting" private grain traders and their distribution networks to meet the empire's grain needs during famine and military campaigns and to supply chronically grain-deficient regions, such as the southeastern coastal provinces of Fujian and Guangdong.[15]

Yinghe would also have been keenly aware of the dynasty's critical dependence on private lighterage shipping (*panbo*) of tax grain and its increasing use in northern Jiangsu near the Grand Canal–Yellow River junction in the late eighteenth century, as silt blockages threatened the continued use of large relatively deep-draft government grain junks on this sector of the canal. Finally, he would have had direct knowledge of the expansion of the Taiwan grain trade on the Fujian coast in the Jiaqing reign (1810) and the Daoguang Emperor's decision in 1824 to permit Fujian traders to ship Taiwan grain directly to Tianjin to augment capital granary supplies—all of which drew attention to the limitations of Grand Canal transport and the advantages of sea transport.[16]

---

13   Bastid 1985, pp. 51–79.
14   Cheung 2008, pp. 37–51, 115–132; Chuan and Kraus 1975; King 1965; Sun 1968, pp. 835–845; 1992, pp. 9–20; Vogel 1987, 1–52; Wang 1973, pp. 5–48ff.; Wang 1979, pp. 425–452; van Glann 1996, pp. 207–247; Will and Wong 1991, pp. 19–98; Zelin 1984, pp. 1–7.
15   Huang 2000, pp. 97–103, 166–167; Perdue and Wong 1992, pp. 1–83, 291–332; Will 1990, pp. 21–75.
16   Huang 2000, pp. 97–103, 166–167.

The sum of these experiences as well as his Banner elite status in the central administration gave Yinghe the know-how and prestige to press forward with the Daoguang Emperor's initiative to explore and implement sea transport in 1825. Yet it was precisely because of his long history of administrative leadership and disciplined fiscal work in both the Board of Revenue and the Imperial Household that contributed to his downfall in late 1826 and 1827 when he was deprived of high office and ordered out of the Imperial Study and the Imperial Household administration for offenses that, in retrospect, seem fairly trivial. The emperor was extremely displeased that year by Yinghe's request that merchants be allowed to open silver mines in the southern metropolitan district; his character was further disparaged by the accusations of a tenant that he was unfairly raising the rent on his landholdings. He was briefly assigned to the Lifanyuan, then to the military governorship of Jehol, then to Ningxia, the last of which he avoided by pleading illness. The final blow came in 1828 when it was discovered that the construction of the Daoguang Emperor's imperial tomb, for which Yinghe was personally responsible, was not up to standard. As a consequence, he and his two sons were dismissed from their posts and exiled to Heilongjiang until pardoned in 1831 when he returned to Beijing and lived in retirement until his death in 1839.

Yinghe completed a range of writings, two of which on Heilongjiang, were completed during his exile. Because of his prestige as a literati, he directed two provincial exams (Shuntian 1800; Jiangnan 1801) and two metropolitan exams (1805; 1809), and many famous scholars and officials who passed those exams called themselves his disciples, including Muzhang'a, Xu Song, and Jiao Xun. He was apparently on good terms with his contemporaries, except for the powerful Cao Zhenyong, whose proposal to raise money with the sale of offices in 1814 was vetoed by Yinghe and sparked enmity between the two that lasted into the Daoguang reign[17] and may partially account for his fall; additionally, his biographer, Fang Zhaoying, suggests that Yinghe's anti-corruption measures taken against functionaries in the Imperial Household may also have contributed to his fall—a fate shared by others who had taken similar actions, such as Songyun, Jingzheng, Xi'en, and Yiji. His energetic pursuit of the sea-transport innovation may also have soured his relationship with other Han and Banner elites, who either had a stake in the established grain-transport system, or, like the senior Mongol official, Songyun, opposed sea transport because it was not perceived to be as safe as transport on China's inland waterways. Nonetheless, Yinghe's success as a prestigious degree-bearing Banner elite in

---

17   ECCP, pp. 739–40.

the central government was critical to the adoption and implementation of the innovative sea-transport project.

3   Yinghe's First Memorial on the Comprehensive Grain-Transport Plan

Yinghe outlined his comprehensive three-part plan for fundamental changes in grain-transport practice in two key memorials, the first written early in the fourth month (5.4.10) as the canal crisis deepened and the second late in the fifth month (5.5.22) when transport through the junction had ground to a halt. They marked the beginning of a serious policy debate on sea transport, and they contain some of the regulatory features that later appeared in the final Jiangsu plan that was approved in the ninth month.

He prefaced his first memorial with a resounding endorsement of the appropriateness of change when conditions warranted it.[18] Leaving no doubt that he and the emperor's inner circle supported major changes to the faltering grain-transport system, he quoted the Song scholar-official Cheng Hao, who had asserted that "when you want to put the Way in order, you must follow the unfolding of events; and if you want to save the Way, then you must absolutely make changes. Big changes lead to big benefits; small changes lead to small benefits."[19]

This larger view of the appropriateness of change stood in sharp contrast to the two stopgap measures that junction officials had used year after year to cross the grain boats through the junction: Yellow River backspills and large-scale lighterage schemes. Debate had raged over the former from the beginning of the current crisis, with the emperor as one of its harshest critics.[20] For lack of an alternative, backspills had been initiated two weeks before the opening of the Yuhuang gates early in the second month (5.2.20),[21] and, not surprisingly, by the end of the third month (5.3.29), the junction was clogged with mud, at which point junction officials had turned in desperation to the second stopgap: a large-scale lighterage scheme called transfer, or relay, shipping.[22] This scheme required the mobilization of government and private shallow-draft lighters in Jiangsu, Shandong, and Zhili to carry the grain cargoes

---

18   JSHY 1:4–14b (5.4.10); TJ/S 0079–80 (5.4.10).

19   JSHY 1:4 (5.4.10).

20   Leonard 1996, pp. 123–134; TJ/S 00053–59 (5.5.10).

21   S 00207–00209 (5.2.7).

22   P 00191–00192 (5.1.29); TJ/S 00003–4 (5.4.2).

from mired fleets at the junction to Tongzhou, and it had been embraced because officials sought to insure the timely return of stranded grain junks to their home anchorages in the autumn in time to load the next year's (1826) tax grain, which officials feared would be delayed by the destruction of junction facilities.

Yinghe accepted the fact that lighterage was imperative for the 1,700 grain boats that had already successfully passed through the junction and entered the Shandong canal. Similarly, it was essential for the transport of grain from an additional thousand-plus craft from Jiangsu, Zhejiang, and Jiangxi-Anhui that were currently mired in mud in the Huaiyang Canal between the junction and Baoying and Gaoyou. There was simply nothing else to be done! Once again county officials adjacent to the canal in northern Jiangsu, Shandong, and Zhili would be required to hire private lighters in their respective locales to carry the grain in a series of costly and time-consuming transfers until the grain reached the capital granaries.[23]

Yinghe knew that the use of relay shipping was a gamble because the delays caused by the myriad transfers would take time and jeopardize the speedy return of the first 1,700 grain boats to their home anchorages before the canal froze over and the junction became even more damaged. To hasten the return of these grain boats, he urged that the Zhili Governor-General deploy Zhili lighters to the Zhili-Shandong border to pick up and ship their cargoes to Tongzhou. Yet, because he feared that even this step might not save enough time to guarantee their return south, he also urged, citing a precedent from Jiaqing 14 (1810), that perhaps these fleets might offload earlier in Shandong onto regular Shandong and Henan grain boats that were returning empty from their first shipment of tax grain to Tongzhou, or, alternatively, onto 300 government and 300 private lighters in and outside the "Canal of Gates," a reference to the many lock gates on the Shandong canal. And if time were short, these lighters could then transfer the grain to Zhili official lighters at the government lighterage hub at Yangcun on the Bai River section of the canal near the capital that served as the anchorage for 2,000 official lighters, for the final trip to Tongzhou. Even better, if the large-hulled, sail-driven West River boats in Shandong were recruited, they could ship the grain all the way to Tongzhou.[24]

Lighters would also be required to transport the cargoes of the craft that were mired in silt in the Gaobao section of the canal. These lighters would,

---

23   Lighters normally stayed within their own provincial jurisdiction when hired for grain transport. The difficulty of pulling, or "tracking," the lighters through the silt was also factored into the payments to lighter owners.

24   JSHY 1:6b–7 (5.4.10).

more than likely, have to be pulled through the silt to the junction—a task that would be glacially slow. Yinghe referred to alternative methods for handling the grain in stranded grain boats that had been used in the Qianlong and Jiaqing reigns,[25] such as selling the grain cheaply in jurisdictions close to the canal that were experiencing food shortages; or storing it in canal-side granaries; or waiting until the following year to send it on the regular grain fleets. However, as he pointed out, conditions in 1825 were far different from those in these earlier cases. There were no food shortages. Local storage was not an option because of the problem of grain "leakage," or smuggling. Moreover, because he did not know at the time he wrote this memorial whether or not the 1826 tax grain would be sent by sea or canal, the use of the returning fleets could not be determined in advance. Thus, none of the earlier precedents applied.

The only option for the blocked shipments in the Gaobao section of the canal, which totaled approximately one million *shi*, was more lighterage and some cart haulage over the south bank of the Yellow River to waiting lighters that would carry the grain across the river to the Central Canal entrance on the north side of the river and on to Tongzhou, using a series of lighterage transfers. While this would be extremely difficult because the silt-filled junction passages were only compensated by three miles (*li*) of roads and 20 to 90 miles (*li*) of inferior waterways, he felt, nonetheless, that it could be done. He estimated that the cost of porterage, lighterage, and the provision of strip mats to protect the grain would amount to 300,000 to 400,000 taels, based on the cost of two to three copper cash per *shi*, which was in line with earlier experience.[26]

Yinghe assumed that there were a sufficient number of lighters in Jiangsu to move these grain cargoes through the junction, noting that there were 750 government lighters presently stationed at the junction and that, fortuitously, there were an additional 460 lighters, newly built in Jiangxi and Hunan and bound for Zhili, that could be detained temporarily for use during the crisis. But once in Shandong, the loads would have to be transferred to Shandong lighters at Jining, or, depending on circumstances, as noted above, the Henan and Shandong grain fleets might be impressed into service between their first and second regular shipments to Tongzhou.[27]

Yet even though these various stopgap measures had been used in the past as large grain boats had found it increasingly difficult to navigate the silted canal, lighterage was no panacea! It was extremely time-consuming and cumbersome, filled with stops and starts, each of which required local officials to

---

25   JSHY 1.6 (5.4.10).
26   JSHY 1.6b (5.4.10).
27   JSHY 1:4b–6 (5.4.10).

recruit the necessary private craft and to work with local brokers who served as the interface with private lighterage and labor organizations for canal-side dock and shipping labor. Each of these transactions required fees, donations, gifts, and squeeze.

The hire of private lighters had other serious drawbacks. The most contentious was the resistance of local officials in jurisdictions close to the canal to hiring these craft because, although hiring costs were technically to be reimbursed by provincial authorities, they rarely were. Yinghe understood this, and he proposed that as soon as local officials determined the actual hiring price of lighters, provincial governors should then forward the necessary funds up front. Otherwise, local officials had little alternative but to coerce private shippers and commandeer their craft, which undermined the livelihood of ship owners and caused disturbances locally.[28]

The second drawback was water damage to the grain during transfers from grain boats to lighters. The off-loading process would coincide with the arrival of summer storms, which subjected the grain to water damage either when porters transferred the grain in large open baskets to waiting lighters or when the grain was shipped in smaller lighters whose open holds were vulnerable to the rain. Either way, the grain became moldy. By the time the cargoes were unloaded, the grain would be ruined. To guard against water damage, local officials were required to provide mats to cover and protect the grain, but, here again, these officials were required to advance the funds for the purchase of mats, and they were rarely reimbursed.[29] Yinghe opined that water damage could be avoided by careful, on-site supervision of grain transfers by low-level grain transport officers—hardly a corruption-free solution!

Yet there were even greater problems to come. What was to be done with the cargoes on the hundreds of grain boats that had already entered the southern section of the Huaiyang canal *but were not yet mired in mud*? And also, what about those from Jiangnan, Zhejiang, and the middle Yangzi provinces that had not yet even entered the Huaiyang Canal? How could relay shipping possibly move all these cargoes to Tongzhou before the new 1826 grain shipments arrived at the junction the following spring? For this, Yinghe boldly proposed that sea transport could be used to ship the late-arriving 1825 tax grain as well as the 1826 levies.

This is how Yinghe saw the plan working in 1825! Grain junks that had already entered the Huaiyang Canal, but were not mired in muddy silt, should

---

28   The cost of lighterage labor and food was ultimately taken from the funds allotted for the silver and rations of the grain fleets.

29   JSHY 1:7–7b (5.4.10).

turn around and exit the canal at Guazhou, cross the Yangzi, and enter the Danyang Canal at Zhenjiang. These craft should then exit the canal at the Huangpu River and proceed to Shanghai where the grain would be transferred to private sand junks for final shipment by sea to Tianjin. If the larger Jiangxi, Anhui, and Huguang grain boats could not navigate the Danyang Canal, their cargoes should be transferred to returning empty Jiangsu and Zhejiang fleets, then proceed to Shanghai for shipment to Tianjin. It hardly seems plausible that he thought this plan could be worked out in a mere two months![30]

The plan for 1826 was much more elaborate and ambitious and aimed to send part of the tax grain from Jiangnan and Zhejiang by sea while the remainder would be collected, then commuted to currency in order to pay for a thorough restoration of damaged parts of the canal north of the Yangzi River during a two-year period ending in 1827. This work would include dredging the canal from the Baogao sector of the canal, north to the junction, while restoring the dikes and junction channels, as well as repairing the Shandong water gates and the hydraulic system that fed water from the Shandong lakes into the canal.

Yinghe justified the use of sea transport by citing precedents in previous dynastic periods. For sixty years, the Yuan Dynasty had used sea transport while it completed the construction of the Grand Canal over the Shandong mountains. Similarly, it had been resumed in the early Ming period until the Huitong part of the Shandong Canal from Nanwang to Linqing was completed, and even when the Ming primarily used the canal for grain transport, many officials, such as Qiu Jun (1420–1495), believed it was still too risky to rely on the canal alone because recurrent canal blockages could choke off these supplies.[31] It was far better to have a dual system, using both canal and sea transport, just as Yinghe was advocating in 1825.

More recently during the Qing period, Yinghe asserted, officials had also begun to discuss sea transport. Xiao Zhi raised the issue in 1807, and the then renowned Governor-General of Zhejiang, Juan Yuan, had also asserted that if "there were no alternative," then the Qing leadership must divide up the tax grain, "change current practices," and send part of the southern tax grain by sea. As recently as 1824, a censor had recommended that the government buy grain on the open market and send it by sea, although the idea was rejected because provincial officials believed it would cause food shortages in Jiangnan.

Yinghe frankly acknowledged that implementing sea transport posed daunting challenges. If the government were to act quickly to change the

---

30   JSHY 1:7b (5.4.10).
31   JSHY 1:7b–8 (5.4.10); DMB 1:249–252.

longstanding practice of transporting the "state's strategic grain supplies" by canal, it would be extremely difficult to sort out the tangle of issues and write new regulations, and, even worse, it would "incite fears of the danger of wind and waves among officials and provoke widespread popular opposition."

More important than the fear of ocean sailing, Qing officials recognized that practical obstacles stood in the way of government sea transport. The state lacked the necessary capital, managerial, and skilled labor resources to carry out sea transport. Such a plan would require the construction of ocean-going ships and the establishment of a bureaucratic infrastructure of *official posts and funds.*" In other words, it would require the extension of the Qing governing structure into the sub-county arena. Yinghe pointed out that, unlike the Yuan dynasty, which could recruit people close to the government "who were experienced and knowledgeable about sea transport, to take responsibility," the Qing had no such official resources to enable them to "venture out to sea and face drowning in order to carry out sea transport." The remove from and ignorance of maritime issues were, of course, both consequences of Qing maritime policy, which had, since the 1680s, built a system of maritime trade and defense that relied heavily on merchant groups in the four southeastern coastal provinces to manage harbor, market, and customs administration—a practice that shielded Qing provincial officials from direct administration of maritime issues in coastal ports.[32]

Third, the state had no security infrastructure along the northeast coastal route to protect the grain junks, investigate accidents, or determine the liability for grain losses, in contrast to that on the canal route where low-level civil and military officials were posted along the entire length of the canal to oversee and protect the grain fleets. The final difficulty, Yinghe asserted, was the widespread official fear that the convenience and economy of sea transport would lead to the neglect of yearly water-conservancy projects on the canal-riverine system. Many officials feared that "if no effort were made for one hundred years to dredge and carry out thousands of miles of conservancy work along the canal, then the day would come when the canal will be too far gone to restore."[33]

While these various difficulties were significant, Yinghe, nonetheless, argued strongly that the advantages of sea transport far outweighed them. The resources needed for sea transport lay right at their fingertips in Shanghai. The Shanghai Merchant Guild (Shanghai *shangguan*), he explained, had abundant capital and skilled managerial and labor personnel, who had many long years

---

32   Leonard 2006, pp. 27–39.
33   JSHY 1:8–8b (5.4.10).

FIGURE 4   Sand junk

of sailing experience along the northeast coast. They possessed over 3,000 large registered sand junks, each capable of shipping 3,000 *shi* of grain, as well as smaller craft with cargo space for 1,500 *shi*. The junk owners "are rich and well-established local people (*tuzhufumin suozaoli*), who have close relationships with Tianjin customs and commercial organizations. They guarantee their cargoes; have brokers to facilitate their deals; and they are known for not cheating or quibbling with those with whom they do business."[34]

Moreover, they sailed the northeast coast several times a year, "following the winds" as far north as the Manchurian ports. Consequently, they were skilled at

---

34   JSHY 1:8b–9 (5.4.10).

navigating the dangerous sandy coastal shoals and coping with its capricious winds and currents. "They neither lose their way *nor have delays*" [author's emphasis]. In other words, this shipping guild was a rich and powerful organization that already had all the assets and resources necessary to carry out sea transport—resources that the state lacked!

Recruitment of these merchant shippers, Yinghe explained, would save shipping expenses (*zhuangchuanzhifei*), extra fees, and squeeze that the grain fleets were forced to pay during the innumerable stops and starts on the long canal trip, especially when relay shipping was used. Existing grain-transport funds could be used to cover the cost of shipping labor, rations, and porterage fees for sea transport. Officials also need not fear pirates on the northeast coast because the fleets of shallow-draft sand junks could navigate the sandy shoals close to shore and evade the larger deeper-draft pirate ships (*niaochuan*) from the southeastern coastal provinces.

Finally, not to put too fine a point on it, Yinghe maintained that the merchant shippers would "jump for joy" (*yueyo*) at the opportunity to ship government grain because the holds of their ships were generally empty on the northbound trip except for the mud dredged up from the Shanghai harbor that was used for ballast. They made their money on the southbound cargoes of soybean products that were in high demand as fertilizer for cotton production in the lower Yangzi delta region.[35] Yinghe argued that if the state offered beneficial terms, such as allowing them to use 30 percent of their cargo space for tax-free private commodities (70 percent for grain), the shippers would be most cooperative. Moreover, if they were shielded from extortion on the Shanghai and Tianjin docks, and were awarded "titles of respect and real and brevet ranks" as had been done in 1824 with Taiwan grain shippers, they would be even more enthusiastic.

In view of all of its advantages, why, Yinghe queried, was official opposition to sea transport so strong? Some of it, he argued, was due to ignorance of maritime issues. Officials tended to exaggerate the risks of storms on the northeast coast, not realizing that when unfavorable winds threatened the shipping out of Shanghai, merchant shippers waited in the Inner Ocean ports from Wusong to Shixiao at the eastern-most tip of Chongming Island before sailing.[36] Yet, he pointed out, these very same officials routinely dismissed the equally serious dangers to grain fleets on the Yangzi River near Dongting and Poyang Lakes and the fire hazards to ships and cargo on the crowded canal. The important

---

35   Johnson, ed., 1993, pp. 151–181; 1995, pp. 43–65; Zhang Zhongmin 1987, pp. 85–94; Zhang Zhongmin 2002, pp. 103–128.

36   JSHY 1:7b–8 (5.4.10); JSHY 12:2.

point for him was that the sea route was five times faster than the canal route (usually about 7 to 8 days, at most 10 days); it eliminated countless transaction and brokerage fees; and the shortness of the trip minimized the loss of grain from water damage and mold—a fact born out by the grain shipments from Taiwan in 1824.

But how would such a plan be organized? Yinghe sketched out several concrete steps that the government should take to organize an emergency sea-transport plan, even though at this early stage, he did not seem to fully understand its scale and complexity. He initially proposed that the Shanghai Intendant alone could make the recruitment arrangements by issuing a public notice explaining the terms and conditions of this state-private collaboration. In the notice, the intendant was to assure merchant shippers that the collaboration with the state was temporary and would not bind them into a long-term yearly arrangement. Yet, later, in the same memorial, Yinghe did acknowledge that the authority of the intendant was probably not great enough to direct this innovative experiment.

Yinghe was on firmer ground when he spelled out the terms and conditions of the recruitment deal because this governing tool had often been used to enlist private organizations to perform government tasks and because he was familiar with the intricacies of the grain-transport system. In addition to an allotment of wastage rice, each shipmaster, based on the amount of grain transported, should receive payment in silver, one-half of which would be paid in Shanghai and the other half in Tianjin after Zhili grain authorities officially received (*shou*) the grain. The government should also cover the cost of porterage labor (*jiaojia*) on the docks in both ports. Both parties would enter into a written mutual guarantee (*hubao*) and a voluntary bond (*ganjie*), spelling out the liabilities for accidents and loss. When loading was completed in Shanghai, each shipper would receive "a clear official receipt verifying the amount of grain loaded on his vessel to use as evidence" when he arrived in Tianjin and granary officials received the grain.[37]

The presentation of official documentation verifying the exact amount of each ship's grain load was common practice in canal transport, but it was doubly important for sea transport because this means of transport was new and its procedures were not spelled out in the administrative code governing grain transport, leaving Shanghai merchant shippers vulnerable to dockside extortion in Shanghai and Tianjin. Moreover, such documentation was essential in the eyes of officials like Yinghe (and merchant shippers too) because they generally expected trouble from entrenched Zhili grain-transport and granary

---

37   JSHY 1:10–b (5.4.10).

officials, especially the extra-bureaucratic grain brokers (*jingjiren*), who performed critical tasks, such as the inspection and bagging of arriving grain on the docks and the contracting of dock labor, porterage, and lighterage for the grain transfers from Tianjin to Tongzhou.[38] When brokers performed these jobs, they, as a matter of course, demanded extra exactions from shippers and labor organizations that reduced the latter's rightful wages. Yinghe also wanted to prevent low-level sub-bureaucratic functionaries from "discounting" (*kekou*) the wage payments made to shippers and keeping back part of the money to line their own pockets (*zhongbao*). If these corrupt practices were not eliminated, shippers might refuse to participate in sea transport.

To eliminate these various forms of corruption, Yinghe urged that Zhili grain authorities set up a supervisory framework that would intensify their dock-side supervision of the complex tasks connected to the grain transfers from sand junks to lighters in Tianjin. He proposed that a Granary Vice President[39] travel to Tianjin in order to personally oversee and monitor the official receipt of the grain to insure that *only officials*, not sub-bureaucratic functionaries, made the direct payments to merchant shippers from funds drawn from the Zhili provincial treasury and the Board of Revenue, eliminating the role of brokers and low-level clerks and runners.

Yinghe saw the *ad hoc* use of sea transport in 1825 as a test run. If its implementation were successful, the state could continue to "turn over more than a million *shi* [of southern rice] to merchant shippers in the future." Such a course of action was not, he emphasized, "a case of giving up strategic grain transport on the canal. Nor was it a policy that is contrary to what was right and customary."

In addition to recruiting Shanghai merchant shippers for sea transport, the second part of Yinghe's comprehensive plan proposed that "next year, we must temporarily discontinue grain transport on the canal. We should collect the grain taxes as usual, then divide them up, sending part by sea and commuting (*zhesi*) the remainder to fund a major water conservancy project that would *harness* [author's emphasis] and open up the Grand Canal–riverine hydraulic system in order to permanently benefit grain transport for the future."[40] In other words, harnessing the river meant not just carrying out the yearly repairs of dikes and revetments and the cycle of dredging riverbeds, the canal, the

38 JSHY 1:10–11 (5.4.10).

39 JSHY 1:13b (5.4.10). The Granary Superintendency was a department of the Board of Revenue, headed by two Granary Superintendents (*cangchangshilang* 倉場侍郎), one Manchu and one Chinese, holding the rank of vice president of the Board of Revenue, 2a). Mayers, [1899] 1966, no. 362.

40 JSHY 1:11–11b (5.4.10).

lake beds, and the various lock gates on the Shandong canal, but it also meant fundamental redesign and reconstruction of the junction facilities! Only canal closure in 1826 would provide the needed time for *"concentrated efforts to open and harness"* the canal-riverine network [author's emphasis]. Such *fundamental* conservancy work, he stressed, had been carried out during the Kangxi reign and had placed canal transport on a firm footing. Yinghe wanted to do the same for the Daoguang reign.[41]

He queried, why, in view of the dire conditions on the canal, hadn't officials from the Board of Works come up with similar restoration plans? He cited three reasons. They erroneously believed that closure would jeopardize capital grain supplies; the cost of such large-scale and complex projects would be exorbitant; and, moreover, such projects could not be contemplated while officials were struggling to respond to the on-going canal crisis.

Yinghe dismissed these reasons out of hand. Officials need not be "anxious" about granary supplies. The capital granaries would be filled to overflowing in 1826, he asserted, because of the regular shipments from Shandong and Henan provinces, the 1825 southern grain shipments (1.2 to 1.3 million *shi*) that had already crossed the junction, the continued purchase of husked rice from Fengtian and Henan, and not least, the 1 to 1.5 million *shi* of rice from the remaining Zhejiang, Jiangnan, Jiang'an, and Huguang fleets that would either be sent by sea or by relay shipping on the canal in 1825. Moreover, Yinghe predicted that the commutation of tax grain from Jiangsu and other southern provinces would yield a handsome seven to eight million taels, which, he argued, was enough to fund desperately needed hydraulic works.

The greatest worry, however, was, and would continue to be, the handling of monies during the commutation process itself. How would it be implemented so as to eliminate the corrupt manipulation of the grain-to-silver exchange ratio at the county level? Yinghe blithely dismissed this extremely vexing problem, explaining that in the autumn of 1825, governors and governors-general of the provinces designated for commutation should follow existing precedents that included determining the price of a *shi* of grain in their respective jurisdictions, then memorializing the emperor for approval, after which the provincial treasurers of each of the canal-zone provinces would notify all the various *zhouxian* officials of the official price, which these officials would collect and hand over to the provincial treasurer, who would, in turn, forward the funds to the work sites. These officials were warned against corruptly manipulating the price of grain and other forms of extortion.[42] As experienced as Yinghe was,

---

41   JSHY 1:11 (5.4.10).
42   JSHY 1:12–13 (5.4.10).

one can hardly imagine that he did not understand that commutation would unleash a torrent of corruption!

And what about labor unrest among unemployed grain-transport bannermen and boatmen that usually manned the grain fleets each year? Yinghe understood that officials were deeply troubled about this issue, so he carefully outlined how the income and prospects of such personnel should be managed by the state according to customary practice and the administrative code. The extra pay, or squeeze (*jintie*), that was normally exacted along with the tax grain levy should, he pointed out, be paid to the fleet bannermen, according to precedents for years when grain shipping was cut back. The other fleet labor, such as pole punters, helmsmen, and sailors, should be treated just as had those from Jiangsu and Zhejiang in Daoguang 2 (1822), when county magistrates at the various anchorages had given them travel money (*panfei*) of from 2,000 to 3,000 cash to return to their native places where they would enter into a security agreement with local officials that committed them to engage temporarily in agricultural work until grain shipping resumed.

When the 1825 fleets returned to their home anchorages, Yinghe advised that the governors and governors-general should apply these precedents in anchorage counties, whose fleets contained approximately a hundred grain boats, each with ten bannermen and boatmen. If each were given 3,000 cash, the cost for each county would amount to 3,000 taels. For those counties that would be commuting grain in 1826, he advised giving fleet personnel extra money for miscellaneous expenses to tide them over and help them find employment until canal shipping resumed in 1827, at which time they would be called back to work on the grain fleets.

In Yinghe's eyes, the long-term benefits of shutting down the canal in 1826 were significant. The savings in transport costs (*yunfei*) alone would total over 720,000 taels as well as saving 220,000 *shi* of wastage grain that otherwise would have been used to cover the cost of grain losses during canal transport. These savings would more than cover the costs of labor and shipping for sea transport. And, moreover, the funds from commuting the tax grain would enable the state to harness and dredge the hydraulic networks in both northern Jiangsu and Shandong. In light of the ability to fund these important hydraulic works, Yinghe urged that as soon as the 1825 transport was finished, the river-canal directors in Shandong and northern Jiangsu should prepare and quickly implement a comprehensive step-by-step conservancy plan "so that both canal and grain transport are benefitted for the long term."[43]

---

43   JSHY 1:13 (5.4.10).

At the end of the memorial, Yinghe identified another urgent problem that he anticipated might undermine his comprehensive plan—the shortage of bureaucratic resources. He asserted that officials faced two immediate tasks: (1) the hiring, loading, and shipment of the remaining 1825 tax grain on sea junks and (2) the completion of relay shipping from the Gaobao section of the canal to the Shandong border. How, he asked, were these tasks to be achieved with the current official personnel dedicated to grain transport in Liangjiang who were "up to their ears" in crisis management? These very officials "were presently stationed temporarily in Huai'an" at the junction to manage the crisis. "The acting governor-general has overall responsibility for the functioning of the canal-based grain-transport system; the Southern Canal Director has sole responsibility for canal and grain-transport matters at the junction; even more significant, the Grain Transport Director has overall responsibility for grain transport along the entire 1,000–2,000 miles of the canal, and, hitherto, he has taken custody of the last, tail-end grain fleet as it traveled to Tongzhou," to symbolize the completion of that year's transport cycle. Yet, he observed, "Now, because of the blockage from Gaobao to the Yellow River, the Grain Transport Director's 'voice' (*shengqi*), or authority, cannot be heard from Jiangnan to the Shandong border, nor further northward to Tongzhou. Even the Shandong Governor and Zhili Governor-General are separated from him and beyond his reach."[44]

Because of the breakdown of these lines of command, *the critical dredging of the canal in* northern Jiangsu around the junction and the convergence of grain junks and lighters at the Shandong-Zhili border had not yet been achieved. In other words, relay shipping of the cargoes from grain fleets stuck in the canal south of the Yellow River had ground to a halt. Worse yet, preparations for hiring merchant ships in Shanghai had not yet begun because the intendant and prefects [in the Shanghai area] *"do not dare do it on their own initiative"* [author's emphasis] because "it requires adapting to the times and making changes." As a result of this political paralysis, Yinghe urged the emperor to appoint "a skilled imperial agent" to galvanize the efforts of the various governors, governors-general, and directors to "plan and manage both the work at the sea port and along the entire canal route, investigating the myriad responsibilities and working out each and every detail of a plan so that it is both wise and workable."[45]

---

44   JSHY 1:13b (5.4.10).
45   Ibid.

4   The Significance of Yinghe's First Memorial

In summary, Yinghe's first memorial on sea transport marked the beginning of official dialogue on needed changes in Qing grain-transport traditions. It argued that closing the canal in 1826 would enable officials to reconstruct the junction hydraulic network in a fundamental way and that the savings from doing so would cover the costs of reconstruction as well as the recruitment of private merchant shippers on terms that "would give the shippers no cause for complaint." In other words, commuting the tax grain to currency "would provide a practical convenient plan that would safeguard grain transport in the future." The plan was "urgently" needed, and "although there are 10,000 difficulties to implementing it, it is extremely important to do so, and officials should not be biased against it." Echoing Cheng Hao's views about the benefits of change, Yinghe urged the Qing leadership to *"eliminate old precedents* and accord with current conditions in order to reap the benefits. If, instead, we fear difficulties and live in a fool's paradise, relying on the emperor's vast blessings alone, the problems will continue, and there will be no end to their negative consequences."[46] Late in the fifth month, those negative consequences became clearly apparent.

---

46   JSHY 1:14–14b (5.4.10).

CHAPTER 3

The Deepening Crisis and Yinghe's Second Memorial

1　The Emperor's Response

The Daoguang Emperor greeted Yinghe's proposed plan with enthusiasm, exclaiming: "Yinghe's comprehensive plan gets to the heart of the daunting challenges facing grain transport and the canal!" One must assume, however, that the emperor and his close advisers knew about it beforehand and hoped that it would spark official discussions and innovative planning, which the emperor's earlier order in the second month had failed to do (5.2.5). The emperor pointedly reminded canal-zone officials that they had ignored this earlier order "to deliberate carefully and collect a wide range of opinions about the feasibility of using the sea route for grain shipments from their respective jurisdictions." Additionally, they had dismissed his grave doubts about the utility of "Yellow River back-spills to cope with junction blockages." Yet, not one of them had come forward with an alternative, but, instead, had casually dismissed sea transport as "too difficult to put into practice and had focused single-mindedly on the crossing of grain boats, failing to recognize the importance of the looming crisis in conservancy work."[1]

The exasperated emperor strongly asserted that *both* grain transport *and* river defense (*hefang*) were equally important and that none of the short-term expedients, such as Yellow River back-spills and relay shipping would solve the core problem of the deterioration of the hydraulic infrastructure on the canal-riverine route north of the Yangzi River. He grimly warned them that "if we treat the immediate passage of grain fleets as the most urgent issue (*muqianjiwu*) and ignore the impending calamity in river work, then disasters in the future will be even greater."[2]

The emperor gave officials their due, recognizing that they had struggled to the utmost to "push this year's grain shipments northward" and were currently "organizing a plan for relay shipping so that the fleets will arrive at Tongzhou one after another." But, he queried, "What about the return of empty boats this year and what about next year's spring transport? Obviously, you will be

---

1　JSHY 1:3–b (5.4.2.); TJ/S 00005–6 (5.4.2).
2　JSHY 1:14b–15b (5.4.10); TJ/S 00079 (5.4.10).

forced to rely on relay shipping again and again!" Softening his tone somewhat, he acknowledged that canal officials were "motivated by extreme caution" in managing the empire's strategic grain reserves and that their ideas were "not without insight." Moreover, he agreed with them that one should not "rush in with reckless proposals and alter (*gengzhang*) established administrative practices." But, he insisted, times had changed, and canal conditions had unalterably changed for the worse during the present canal crisis. Officials were simply ignoring reality. They must treat the long-term consequences of canal deterioration as an important matter and "not be too conservative in following the letter of the law to find a solution (*shaoshi ju'ni*)."

This ability to see the larger picture, in the emperor's eyes, was what made Yinghe's proposal so useful. It sought an approach that was "both good for the long-term security of grain shipping and the defense of the canal, while, at the same time, providing a way to finance costly upgrades to the hydraulic infrastructure."[3] He sent copies of Yinghe's memorial to all high-level canalzone officials for "exhaustive discussion and planning," in order to figure out how "to benefit grain shipping and the canal and to do so without conservative bias (*chengjian*). Nor should officials resort to ineffective measures that only address the immediate problems that stare them in the face at the moment."[4]

2   The Deepening Crisis at the Junction

Meanwhile, by the early fifth month, conditions at the junction worsened markedly. The report that canal officials had closed Yuhuang lockgate on the twelfth day of the fifth month (5.5.12) had also indicated that lightered grain from the Gaobao section of the canal had not yet crossed the Yellow River, nor had important work on the junction dikes been completed.[5] Worse yet, much of the grain carried in the first 1,700 boats, that had already crossed the river, had failed to reach the Zhili-Shandong border, nor had the plan to channel Hongze Lake water through the Jiyun Dam into the canal near Gaobao been carried out. To finish these tasks, junction officials had requested an additional 1.2 million taels—which did not sit well with an emperor who was obsessed with retrenchment. Equally disturbing, thousands of lighterage personnel and canal workers were gathering at Qingjiangpu, creating crowding and unrest.[6]

---

3   JSHY 1:14b–15b (5.4.10); TJ/S 0080 (5.4.10).
4   TJ/S 00080 (5.4.10).
5   S 00141–144 (5.5.19).
6   S 00167–00168 (5.5.2); TJ/S 00181–82 (5.5.25); P 00201–00203 (5.5.28b).

In other words, timeworn schemes for coping with the junction disaster had broken down completely.[7] Things were at an impasse!

By the middle of the fifth month (5.5.19), the Daoguang Emperor was more than disenchanted with junction officials and their management of the crossing debacle. His ire was directed at Sun Yuting, the recently fired Liangjiang Governor-General, whom he ordered to stay at the junction and assist his replacement, Wei Yuanyu, the Grain Transport Director Yan Jian, and the Southern Canal Director Yan Lang.[8] Up to this point, the emperor had entreated them to cast aside the customary methods of coping with canal grain-transport disasters and to devise a comprehensive new plan that would both rebuild the hydraulic facilities at the junction in a fundamental way and organize a sea-transport capability. He had encouraged them to abandon the old ways and embark on a new path to stabilize grain transport, and he had reshuffled the same cast of officials into different posts. He later reflected that he had been "too lenient" in his criticisms and punishments of these officials, leaving them at the junction "to shirk their responsibilities."[9]

The only official who had been severely punished at the time of the disaster was Zhang Wenhao, the Southern Canal director, who was blamed "for leaving the Hongze Lake gates open too long during the crossing in late 1824, dissipating the clear water" needed for the spring crossing in early 1825.[10] Later, he also reflected that he should have followed the Board of Civil Office's recommendation to fired Sun Yuting on the spot, even though he "had served three emperors," because he had "done nothing but dither around after the disaster, failing to take needed action, and then groveling in fear of harsh punishments."[11] The emperor had also had enough of Wei Yuanyu's subservient refusal to propose a plan of his own, stating openly that he would only act on a specific order from the emperor himself, thereby forcing the emperor "to control from afar."

At this point, the emperor took Yinghe's suggestion that he dispatch a high-level official from outside Jiangsu to shake up the management of the junction crisis. He turned to his trusted Shandong Governor, Qishan, sending him first to investigate the worsening situation at the junction, then quickly appointing him to serve as Liangjiang Governor-General. He was ordered to "temporarily dwell at Qingjiangpu" to expedite the stalled relay-shipping scheme, to reconstruct the junction hydraulic system, and to investigate the prospects for

---

7   TJ/S 00053–54 (5.5.10); TJ/S 00131–132 (5.4.15); P 00131 (5.5.18); TJ/S 00141–142 (5.5.19); SL 1496–97; TJ/S 00167–168 (5.5.22); P 00201–203 (5.5.28).
8   TJ 4.11.24; P 00019 (5.1.5); S 00075 (5.2.7).
9   P 00201–00202 (5.5.28).
10   Leonard 1993, pp. 85–86.
11   P 00201–00202 (5.5.28).

sea transport.[12] This appointment, not only made Qishan arguably the most powerful governor-general in the realm, but it also cast him as a kind of special commissioner to resolve the canal crisis.

3   Intensification of Imperial Crisis Management and Yinghe's Second Memorial

Qishan's appointment marked the beginning of a new and more intensive imperial involvement in crisis management—one that emphasized the leadership of trusted Banner elites, who shared the imperial decision to change canal grain-transport management in a fundamental way. This growing imperial role can be seen in the language of the edicts addressed to the top officials at the junction leading up to 5.5.19. At first, the emperor was fairly subdued in his orders, offering suggestions to junction officials about what might be done, but, at the same time, indicating that he was unwilling to *undermine* their administrative decisions in the field, insisting that he trusted them and held no bias towards any one of them because of "merits or mistakes in the past." He would not second-guess their specific decisions, insisting that this approach "followed the way of the state's laws." Working together, emperor and officials could achieve the "greater good" for the state, but, because conditions at the junction had deteriorated so quickly in the late fifth month, he felt impelled to send in an energetic and loyal Banner elite to take charge.

Three days later, Yinghe sent his second, and much more assertive, memorial about the urgent need for sea transport and fundamental reconstruction of the canal junction.[13] He didn't beat around the bush! He made it clear that he and, by extension, the emperor's inner circle at the capital were ready to jettison old anachronistic regulations and customary practices in grain transport that stood in the way of his comprehensive plan. The Grand Canal must be closed in 1826 because the dynasty "can absolutely not make fundamental repairs to the junction hydraulic network if grain fleets continue to pass through it in 1826. Sea transport, thus, provides a way to ship the grain cargoes (*shimuqianzhijimu*). There is no other good policy, and there is broad support for it [among the emperor's inner circle] (*lun yishu qiantong*)."

Yinghe strongly challenged critics of his comprehensive plan. "Why do those in charge of grain transport [high-level civil and grain officials] oppose sea transport?" he queried. Their stated reason was the fear of ocean sailing

---

12   TJ/S 00143–00144 (5.5.19b), SL 1496–97; P 5.5.22b, SL 1500.
13   JSHY 1:16–22 (5.5.22).

and piracy and the fact that "banner" troops (*qiding*)[14] and low-level transport officials (*yunguan*) on the grain fleets have had no experience with the sea route, and they feared that they would not be able to perform their core responsibilities to escort, protect, and oversee the grain if it were carried on merchant ships. The actual unspoken reason, however, was that these officials did not want to be responsible for taking charge of an innovation in which "10,000 things could go wrong. If it were to fail, they would be blamed; they would be held responsible for the costs; and they would surely become the target of court criticism."[15]

Yinghe harshly criticized canal-zone officials for their cowardly failure to address the urgent canal and grain-transport problems. Their memorial reports from the second and third months in response to the emperor's call for solutions were "muddled and ambiguous" and "wholly without substantive words." Yet, in his view, it was precisely these very officials who should have been leading, rather than running away from the challenge of innovation. Governing depended on "the authority and judgment of the officials in charge (*jinshan juzai dangshizhe zhi quanheng*)." All officials knew that "administrative changes, or innovations, have advantages and disadvantages, and any official 'worth his salt' would use the advantages and eliminate the disadvantages."[16]

Yinghe demanded that officials address three urgent problems: (1) the excessive, year-round demand for labor in northern Jiangsu, (2) the extortion of grain-transport shippers, and (3) the need for a corruption-free plan for commuting tax grain in 1826. As to the first, the faltering grain-transport system placed unsustainable demands on labor in northern Jiangsu around the junction. The pressure was constant and unrelenting, and it included labor for boat tracking, cart haulage, and for relay shipping, in addition to that needed for the yearly round of dike reinforcement and dredging—tasks that over the years routinely spilled over into the summer growing season because of the slowing of the transport cycle due to silt shallows and blockages. Moreover, the disaster in the spring of 1825 dramatically expanded the need for labor to reconstruct the junction hydraulic facilities. These demands for labor, he opined, occurred year after year without end (*wudizhi*). The year 1825 was no exception. As he wrote his memorial late in the fifth month (5.5.22), he also noted that two million *shi* had yet to be relayed through the junction, and the completion of this

---

14   The term "*qiding*" is used to indicate the government grain personnel that were enrolled in the grain transport *weisuo* system, or *caobiao*, noted above.

15   JSHY 1:16b (5.5.22).

16   Ibid.

work required more funds and "another 10,000 laborers for pulling the carts and boats."[17]

Laboring conditions were, indeed, harsh around the junction. In conditions of intense heat, cold, and rain, laborers worked without stopping to the point of exhaustion, leaving no time to return to their fields to cultivate the land for their families' sustenance. These conditions of hardship and hunger had been exacerbated in the southeastern grain-producing regions, which had experienced bad harvests for several years, intensifying the burdens on area labor, which had the potential for causing incidents of collective violence against the regime.[18]

The second problem centered on systemic extortion of grain fleet officers and lighter owners on the docks and anchorages of the Grand Canal by yamen underlings and grain brokers. Shanghai merchant shippers and officials alike were acutely aware of the way that low-level grain fleet officers were routinely victimized by sub-bureaucratic personnel at the canal anchorages, who demanded extra fees and special payments to handle grain transfers. Merchant shippers thought that they too would be similarly coerced if they agreed to ship tax grain, and they feared that the terms of the sea-transport agreements negotiated in Jiangsu might not be honored in Tianjin. They, like petty grain fleet officials, felt timid and powerless in the presence of official underlings, and they anticipated that they would face such treatment at both the Shanghai and Tianjin docks if they agreed to collaborate in the sea-transport project.

The best solution for Shanghai, Yinghe suggested, would be the appointment of two "incorruptible and skilled" officials from outside the Shanghai area by the Liangjiang Governor-General and the Jiangsu Governor to organize the sea-transport operation in Shanghai. These outside appointees would have greater authority than the local intendant, who, Yinghe had acknowledged in the first memorial, would probably lack the authority to implement a major innovation like sea transport. Having no local conflicts of interest, the outside appointees would have the authority to work out the terms of the recruitment deal with the merchant shippers in careful detail, spelling out the amounts to be paid for both shipping and labor costs.

Once the terms were agreed upon, Yinghe envisioned that these same officials would then carefully oversee the inspection of the grain on the Shanghai docks; record the exact amount of grain loaded on each ship; and "issue a certificate to each boat owner as was normally done (*zhizhao rengzhao*)," verifying that amount. A copy of the certificate and a voluntary bond (*ganjie*) between

---

17   JSHY 1:17 (5.5.22).
18   Ibid.

each boat owner and the grain-transport authorities would be retained by these two officials, and, after loading was completed, they would personally carry these documents on shipboard when they escorted the grain by sea on sand junks to Tianjin.[19] Later, it was decided that these officials should travel overland apparently in order to safeguard the documents, *as well as the officials*, from the dangers of ocean sailing!

Similarly, Yinghe reiterated his proposal made in his first memorial that a Granary Vice President and another high-level official from the Board of Revenue be dispatched to Tianjin on the arrival of the merchant ships to "weigh and receive the grain (*duishou*)" and pay merchants directly on the basis of the documents made out in Shanghai as to the actual amount of grain carried in each ship. Yinghe insisted that "all aspects of transferring [loading and unloading] the grain and the payment of merchant shippers for shipping and porterage labor must be managed by 'one hand' (*yishou chengban*), thus focusing responsibility on these two high officials and their official deputies. Officials in the Board of Revenue entourage must "record the amount due to each merchant shipper and pay them *in person* [author's emphasis] to avoid the evil of embezzling even the smallest amount of the pay that they are rightfully due." This included the payments for porterage labor, "which, while paltry enough, were extremely vital to the porters."[20]

The official procedure for "weighing in the grain," it will be remembered, was extremely complex and included inspecting the grain for quality and possible damage during the shipment by sea; then the measuring, bagging, and unloading of the grain on the Tianjin docks; followed either by temporary storage on or near the docks before transferring it to lighters for final shipment to Tongzhou. Normally, this work was managed by extra-bureaucratic grain brokers and low-level sub-bureaucratic personnel, all of whom had special expertise in the handling of grain for the Grain Transport Administration in Zhili. These individuals were quasi-government officials and essential participants in the management of grain transfers, yet, because of a lack of careful official oversight, they routinely engaged in various forms of corruption: embezzlement, squeeze, and extortion, which had all been allowed to creep in over the years.

Yinghe asserted that corruption by sub- and extra-bureaucratic personnel was the single greatest obstacle to official recruitment of Shanghai merchant shippers, who, he maintainend, would not agree to recruitment without its elimination. Yinghe pointedly insisted that grain brokers must not be allowed

---

19   JSHY 1:17b–18 (5.5.22).
20   JSHY 1:18–18b (5.5.22).

to interfere in the inspection and unloading process, even though they were essential participants in it. As for the payment of porters, this task was shifted to the deputies of the two special appointees from the Board of Revenue, rather than yamen clerks. These changes marked a significant short-circuiting of the normal bureaucratic methods of handing of grain tribute in Tianjin, and they represent official acknowledgment of systemic corruption in this sector of the spare, thinly spread layer of imperial government—corruption that the merchants shippers were simply not willing to accept.

Their position had hardened earlier in the spring because the previous Governor of Jiangsu, Zhang Shicheng (1769–1830), had forced these shippers to stay in harbor at Shanghai in the event that the delayed 1825 shipments of tax grain would be sent by sea (which did not occur, as it turned out). This action caused shippers to lose their spring trading run to the northeast,[21] and they weren't prepared to take this kind of economic loss and official bullying again. Many ships had already left the harbor, or "disappeared," as a consequence, and officials had come to recognize the stark reality that the state had no alternative but to recruit these shippers if they were going to implement a sea-transport plan.

The third pressing problem facing sea-transport advocates was the fear among grain-transport personnel that canal closure, commutation, and sea transport portended the end of the Grain Transport Administration. These personnel included civilian and military officials, Bannermen fleet workers, as well as hired boatmen. This fear, according to Yinghe, was nonsense. The funds for transport, *yanglian*, salaries, and labor would still be paid, according to precedent, as had been done in earlier reigns. Alternatively, some of these personnel could be sent immediately to conservancy projects near the junction where the demand for labor "to harness the river" was great.

Yinghe insisted that sea transport was a necessary alternative to canal transport during periods when the canal was silted, and he reminded officials that the Ming dynasty had continued to use sea transport every three years, even after the resumption of canal transport in the Yongle reign (1403–1424). Ming officials had again called for sea transport in the late fifteenth and sixteenth centuries when Chinese coastal and foreign trade was expanding.[22] Similarly, during the Qing Yongzheng reign, the Fujianese scholar-official Lan Tingyuan, living at the center of Fujianese domestic and foreign trade and serving in local government posts in Guangdong, had asserted that grain transport by sea was

---

21   ECCP, pp. 499, 511.
22   Qiu Jun, Liang Menglong, and Wang Zongmu. DMB, pp. 1:249, 2:898, 1438–1441.

both safe and easy.[23] The issue had again been raised in the Qing Jiaqing reign, but officials had again rejected it as being "too expensive and difficult" because it required building a Qing "transport fleet, new governing institutions, and maritime infrastructure." Unlike the Yuan case, the Qing dynasty did not have a pool of "official maritime experts who understood ocean sailing and the dangers of the shallow coastal shoals" that lay along the northeastern coast.

Now in the early Daoguang reign, it was clear that the Qing leadership could recruit just such experts from the Shanghai Merchant Guild for the sea-transport experiment. The beauty of the recruitment tool was that it was temporary; it could be used at any time; and it was easy and cheap; but it also raised a key problem with sea transport. How could officials escort and protect the grain at sea, and how could liability for accidents and loss of cargo at sea be determined and resolved?

This issue was fairly easy to solve. As noted in both of Yinghe's memorials, the normal deployment of Qing marine fleets could be adjusted to coincide with the sailing of sand junks from Shanghai so that the marines could perform the escort and policing function. When the sand junks were loaded and poised to depart from Shanghai, the Liangjiang Governor-General and the Jiangsu Governor were to alert the naval commanders and marine battalions (*ying*) along the Jiangsu coast to patrol the offshore islands extending from Chenqian Island and Majishan near the Zhejiang border to the Shandong border.[24] At the same time, these two officials would also send word ahead to the three Shandong naval commands to proceed to Yingyoumen on the Jiangsu-Shangdong border to take over escort responsibilities when the grain fleets arrived in Shandong coastal waters. Later, these deployments were set out in much greater detail by the Shandong Governor, Wulong'a, in the tenth month (5.10.28) when planning for sea transport began in earnest.[25]

4   The Challenge of Commutation

The most vexing question for critics of Yinghe's plan was how should the government commute grain tax so "that neither officials nor the people were burdened?" Yinghe lashed out at officials who said the plan would cause hardship for the people, who, once having commuted the tax in 1826, would, thereafter, be unwilling to return to the practice of paying the grain tax in kind.

---

23   ECCP, pp. 440–441.
24   JSHY 1:20 (5.5.22); see also Maps in JSHY 12:1b, 8b, 3b.
25   JSHY 2:6–11b (5.10.28).

He impatiently reiterated the regulations for commutation in the Board of Revenue's code, which governed all aspects of grain transport.

In earlier cases, when commutation was required, prefectural, department, and county officials informed the people of the price of grain, mats, planks, and the amount of wastage allowance to cover losses. "The collection of grain tax in the form of money is set, according to a fixed price per *shi*, which is based on the monthly market price of grain as reported by local officials," and which is then fixed by the governor and provincial treasurer; the latter, thereupon, inform local officials of the fixed price in every county that will govern their implementation of commutation. "If anyone dares to take advantage of commutation to extort money, he will be punished immediately!"[26]

All of these provisions, Yinghe noted in exasperation, "are documented in the administrative code, and every provincial official knows them (*gesheng jiezhi*)." He went on to point out that there were many cases of commutation in the Shunzhi, Kangxi, Yongzheng, and Qianlong reigns, which they should examine in order to find an appropriate way to carry it out. Moreover, he pointed out, those departments and counties, located far from the canal anchorages, have always been allowed to pay the grain tax in currency," such as the counties of Qinghe, Funing Suqian, Taoyuan, Haizhou, Shuyang, Ganyu, and Jiading in Jiangsu; four counties in Anhui (Ningguo, Taiping, Jingde, and Yingshan); Lüxi in Jiangxi; three counties in Hubei (Tongshan, Danyang, and Tongcheng); and Xiangfu and other counties in Henan.[27]

From Yinghe's perspective, these provisions for commutation certainly "did not constitute anything new! (*feichuangshi*) There are, indeed, records of these issues in old cases at the Board of Revenue."[28] Therefore, it behooved them to consult these cases and devise a multifaceted plan to halt grain transport on the canal temporarily in 1826, in order to "harness the rivers and lakes; transport the tax grain from Jiangsu and Zhejiang by sea; ship the grain from Shandong and Henan as usual by canal; and *commute the remainder to currency to pay for hydraulic work on the rivers, canal, and lakes.*" Commutation had the very real advantage of avoiding the need for special tax levies to pay for conservancy work, thus, it "killed two birds with one stone."[29]

Once the provincial treasurers of the designated grain tax jurisdictions informed the people of the fixed price of grain, local officials could begin to implement commutation. Because Yinghe admitted that it might be somewhat

---

26   JSHY 1:20b–22 (5.5.22).
27   JSHY 1:20b (5.5.22).
28   JSHY 1:21b (5.5.22).
29   Ibid.

difficult to commute grain, he suggested that people should be given extra time from the tenth month of 1825 until the fourth month of 1826 to do so. However, if local officials used commutation as an excuse to extort money from the people, the governors-general and governors were to impeach them immediately, and the latter themselves were warned: "Do not allow private interests to interfere with devising a perfect plan to address the current emergency."[30]

5   Conclusions

While Yinghe's first memorial triggered the debate on sea transport in 1826 and made the case for recruiting the Shanghai Merchant Guild's skilled personnel, navigational expertise, and capital resources to carry it out, the second memorial, written late in the fifth month in the midst of the deepening crisis and the almost complete breakdown of the relay-shipping plan, marked the beginning of more intense imperial involvement in crisis management and the appointment of Qishan to manage post-crisis conditions at the junction. In this second memorial, Yinghe made scathing criticisms of high-level junction officials for failing to respond effectively to the crisis, and he forcefully challenged critics of his comprehensive plan, especially its use of tax-grain commutation, which he viewed as an excellent way to fund sea transport and crucial conservancy work on junction facilities. His approach to governance in both memorials emphasized the critical importance of skilled officials and their mastery of the administrative code, which he regarded as a reservoir of practical governing know-how. He argued that, armed with the administrative code, skilled imaginative officials could chart a new and innovative course of action to strengthen and perpetuate the strategically important grain-transport system.

---

30   Ibid., 1:22 (5.5.22).

CHAPTER 4

Qishan and Disaster Assessment in Jiangsu

1   Qishan's Mission

When Qishan was sent to Qingjiangpu to serve, first as a special investigator
(5.5.19) and then, three days later, as Liangjiang Governor-General (5.5.22),[1] he
was charged with a threefold mission.[2] First, and most immediate, he was to
expedite the northward passage of southern grain fleets through the damaged
canal-river junction, which had been blocked with silt and scattered flood de-
bris since the collapse of the Gaoyan Great Dike on the east side of Hongze
Lake in early 1825; second, he was to direct the rebuilding (if possible) of the
hydraulic facilities at the junction in a fundamental way by 1827 in order to
overcome the destructive effects of centuries of Yellow River siltation that
threatened the yearly canal shipments of tax grain to the capital; and finally,
he was to evaluate the feasibility of sea transport in 1826, and if it were possible, then to carefully supervise Tao Zhu's and He Changling's organization
and implementation of such a plan. Additionally, Qishan was to serve as the
eyes and ears of the emperor, checking on the veracity of official reports on the
state of the junction, relay shipping, and the progress of reconstruction work.

Qishan was a good choice. He was a rising star among Banner-elite officials, having distinguished himself as a judicial officer in the capital and then
as a judicial commissioner and governor in Henan and Shandong before his
appointment to Liangjiang. He went on to enjoy a long and remarkable official career until his death in 1854.[3] Yet among modern scholars, he is most
prominently known for his futile attempts to negotiate and resolve the conflict
with the Western powers during the Opium War (1839–1842) and his fateful
negotiation of the Chuanbi Treaty (1841). This narrow focus has obscured the
important role he played as a disciplined and effective judicial specialist and
provincial administrator before and after the Opium War.[4] Both the Jiaqing
and Daoguang emperors trusted and relied heavily on him for managing vexing problems, and even when he was punished for failures, he was quickly
pardoned and restored to high rank.

---

1   TJ/S 00143–144 (5.5.19); SL 1496–1497.
2   S 00141–142 (5.5.22); SL 1500.
3   ECCP, pp. 126–129, 224–25, 694.
4   Wei Xiumei 1993, pp. 463–503.

© KONINKLIJKE BRILL NV, LEIDEN, 2019 | DOI:10.1163/9789004384583_006

FIGURE 5
Qishan (1786–1854)

Qishan entered government service in 1806 at age 20 *sui*, claiming eligibility for official position, not through the examination system, but by virtue of his family's noble rank, bestowed for military service during the founding of the dynasty.[5] He was initially assigned to the Board of Punishments in 1808 and continued to serve there until 1814, starting as a second-class assistant secretary (*yuanwailang*) and rising to the position of senior secretary (*langzhong*) by 1812. His early days at the Board of Punishments were anything but easy. He was ridiculed by more senior officials because of his inexperience and inability to handle the complexities of legal documents and cases—an attitude that was, no doubt, shaped by his lack of examination status. To rectify this problem, he hired a clerk in the ministry to tutor him for three years until he mastered the intricacies of legal work. He became recognized as an outstanding

---

5 Mayer 1966, pp. 123–128. Noble rank was bestowed on Qishan's forebear, the Khalka Mongol Enggeder. ECCP, pp. 224–225, 694.

judicial examiner and one that later was often used by the Jiaqing Emperor to solve difficult legal cases both in the capital and provinces.[6] His training and experience in judicial affairs greatly influenced his diligent and uncompromising approach to official and fiscal accountability, public security, and water conservancy.

Qishan began his administrative career in the provinces in 1814 when he was assigned, first to the post of judicial commissioner (3a), then governor (1819; 2b) of Henan,[7] followed in 1821 by a four-year assignment as governor of Shandong. During these eleven years, he confronted daunting administrative challenges. Both provinces served as an important security buffer along the southern border of Zhili, the capital province, and both experienced dangerous water-control issues that required the careful management of the riverine and lake networks that fed, drained, and silted the Grand Canal. These networks were essential to the passage of thousands of government grain junks each year as well as commercial craft engaged in the north-south trade. Persistent flood disasters in these provinces created conditions of poverty, banditry, and rebellion, as well as chronic problems with tax arrears and official malfeasance.[8]

With characteristic energy and discipline, Qishan familiarized himself with conditions in Henan and Shandong, and he developed a reputation as a careful and rather fearless administrator who meticulously assessed the performance of his subordinates, especially those holding the positions of intendant and prefect—offices that he felt were key to effective provincial governance. With the advice of provincial treasurers and judges, he made sure that "difficult" administrative posts were filled by capable officials, and he often transferred officials to posts that were more appropriately aligned with their skills and dismissed those deemed incompetent.[9] He was zealous in his efforts to eliminate tax arrears and make officials, past and present, accountable for these arrears.[10] Finally, because of his concern for public security, Qishan vigorously investigated and punished acts of collective violence and undertook military reforms to keep the provincial military organization up to standard, which included filling the quotas of Green Standard soldiers, repairing old and constructing new military bases, and providing the troops with essential military equipment.

---

6   Wei 1993, p. 489.

7   Qishan, at age 34 *sui*, was the youngest governor in Qing service at the time. Wei 1993, pp. 465, 472.

8   Wei 1993, pp. 464–467, 478–80.

9   Ibid., pp. 475–476.

10   Wei 1993, pp. 472–475.

He approached all these governance issues with the disciplined and practical application of the administrative code.[11]

In Henan and Shandong, Qishan developed an important repertoire of skills crucial to the resolution of water-control emergencies, especially those affecting the Grand Canal corridor that extended northward through Shandong's fertile western plain from Tai'erzhuang on the Jiangsu border through the commercial hubs of Ji'ning *zhou*, Dongping *zhou*, Dongchang *fu*, Linqing *zhou*, and finally Dezhou on the Zhili border.[12] This low-lying plain was repeatedly plagued by heavy rainfall, flash floods, and meanders from local rivers, as well as from the Yellow River to the southwest. Qishan managed just such emergencies affecting the large and small Qing Rivers that flow westward into the canal, as well as the Wei River that flows eastward to the canal near Dongping Lake. He also faced major water-control troubles in Wucheng and Xiajin counties and the area near Dezhou on the canalized Wei River that served as the course of the Grand Canal north of Linqing and whose silt deposits and erratic water levels were a constant threat to canal communications.

Through these experiences, Qishan gained practical skills and lore about the purchase and inspection of construction materials, the closure of breaches in stone and earthen embankments, the dredging of the canal, the Yellow River, and the feeder lakes and streams entering the canal, which required the use of stone and stalk fascines and revetments. He made a point of carefully supervising canal-river officials in person at work sites, and he scrutinized their use of conservancy funds in order to guard against the embezzlement of monies allocated for the purchase of construction materials and the payment of conservancy laborers.[13] He also gained familiarity with the hiring of private lighterage organizations to transport government tax grain when silt shallows in the Grand Canal required the transfer of grain cargoes from government grain junks to these smaller, shallow-draft vessels.[14] It was during his service in Henan-Shandong that Qishan became convinced that ever-worsening canal-river conditions eventually would require the temporary of use of sea transport if the government were to continue to supply grain to the capital.[15]

Because water-control issues bearing on the canal and the Yellow River in Henan and Shandong were so closely linked, the governors of both provinces often worked together to resolve them. At the beginning of the Grand Canal

---

11   Leonard 2005, pp. 27–31.
12   This corridor lies between longitude 115° 50' and 117° 51'.
13   Wei 1993, pp. 463–503.
14   Leonard 1996, pp. 5–49.
15   JSHY 1:33 (5.6.22).

crisis in early 1825, for example, Qishan and Cheng Zulou, the current governor of Henan, collaborated in the recruitment of private lighters to relay the grain cargoes from stranded grain fleets at the canal–Yellow River junction in northern Jiangsu. Moreover, Qishan raised contributions amounting to 800,000 taels that he sent to Jiangsu to help defray the costs of reconstructing hydraulic facilities and implementing the relay-shipping plan. As a result, he was singled out for praise by the Daoguang Emperor for "looking beyond the boundaries of Shandong and assisting in the needs of the empire as a whole."[16]

When he arrived in Liangjiang to investigate conditions at the junction and then assumed the governor-generalship, Qishan had over a decade of experience with water-control emergencies and related disaster relief. This experience enabled him "to hit the ground running," so to speak, in northern Jiangsu, even though, at age 39 *sui*, he was the youngest of the current serving governors-general whose ages averaged approximately 60.[17] His views on sea transport reflected those of some court elites, such as Yinghe and the emperor himself, who thought that sea transport was the only viable means of perpetuating grain transport to the capital, given the irreversible silt barriers to canal transport.

Qishan was assisted in Qingjiangpu by the newly appointed Grain Transport Director Yan Jian (followed by Wei Yuanyu, then Muzhang'a) and Southern Canal–River Director Yan Lang in northern Jiangsu. He also relied on Jiangsu Governor Tao Zhu and Jiangsu Treasurer He Changling for the planning and supervision of sea transport in Jiangnan. Both of these officials were headquartered in Suzhou, located in the heart of the Jiangnan tax-grain jurisdictions and close to the port of Shanghai, from which sea transport would presumably originate, in the event that it were authorized. Qishan was the lynchpin of this group because he was experienced in canal-river management; he was also the highest-ranking official in Jiangsu; and he represented the political clout of the emperor and his inner circle of Banner-elite advisers.

2   Investigation in the Sixth Month (5.6.1–5.6.22)

Qishan's first report on arrival at Qingjiangpu (5.6.1) announced that he was about to embark on a careful investigation of what he called the "real conditions" at the junction in consultation with Yan Jian, the Grain Transport Director. What this meant on a practical level was that the two of them would

16   Leonard 1996, pp. 163–172; Wei 1993, p. 501.
17   Ibid.

conduct on-site investigations of the actual progress of reconstruction at junction work sites, jump start the stalled relay-shipping scheme, and monitor, on almost a daily basis, the changing water levels in Hongze Lake, the Yellow River, and the southern canal head leading to the Clear Passage (Map 2), in order to determine the likelihood of using the junction in 1825 and 1826. His memorial responded to explicit questions that the emperor had raised in an edict a week earlier (5.5.25): Had relay shipping resumed? Had the diversion of Hongze Lake water through the Jiyun Dam and the Shuangkong sluice into the canal near Gaobao been successful? Had the seasonal dredging around the junction begun? Could the returning empty grain boats cross through the junction and return to their home anchorages in the south? In response to these queries, Qishan reported what he had gleaned from his investigations thus far, and his assessment was grim: "The grain boats can't sail; the lake water is low; the Yellow River rises daily; and people are working to the point of exhaustion."[18]

By the middle of the month (5.6.17), he had gathered enough evidence to make a scathing critique of the former Liangjiang Governor-General Sun Yuting's fraudulent claims about the number of grain boats that had actually crossed through the junction thus far, the number of lighters currently available for relay shipping, the crossing conditions at Yuhuang dam, and the ability of returning empty grain boats to cross through the junction and return to their home anchorages in the autumn.[19] Qishan's mid-month exposé suggested that conditions at the junction were in chaos—far worse than had been reported by Sun. This news, of course, was also grim.

The emperor's anguish on receiving this report is palpable in his stark description of gridlock conditions at the junction: "The boats are jammed into the junction passages; the military boats cannot offload the grain cargoes to lighters; commercial vessels add to the crowding in the passageways, leaving no room for private grain-bearing craft to proceed northward; and the crowding also prevents dredging work and the southward crossing of returning empty grain boats." His patience at an end, the emperor immediately replaced the current Grain Transport Director with a trusted Banner elite, Muzhang'a.[20]

At the same time that Qishan was beginning his careful inquiry into conditions at the junction, Tao Zhu, having only recently arrived at his governor's post in Suzhou, submitted a highly critical analysis of commutation and canal

---

18   TJ/S 00181–182 (5.5.25); P (5.6.1) SL 1505.

19   P (5.6.17), SL 1519, 1520–1521. A day later, the emperor ordered Qishan and Tao Zhu to check the accuracy of the grain transport director's report on the successful completion of conservancy work on Lake Tai and his judgment about rewards and punishments for officials connected to this project. TJ (5.6.18), SL 1523.

20   P (5.6.17), SL 1520–1521; TJ (5.6.20).

closure as it applied to Jiangsu that directly challenged Yinghe's proposed comprehensive plan.[21] Although Tao acknowledged that Jiangsu province was the empire's economic pivot and that grain transport was critically important, he flat out rejected commutation of Jiangsu tax grain because poor harvests in 1825 would make it extremely difficult for the common people to pay the regular *diding* tax in silver, much less commute tax grain, especially in the more remote mountainous areas of the province and those far from riverine communications. He pointed out that the province's tax grain levy was two million *shi*; if it were commuted, it would yield two to three million taels. However, the fact was that local officials had great difficulty collecting the regular *diding* taxes, which took months of pressuring and punishing people to pay up. If officials were required to collect twice that amount, they would face resistance, and, what's more, the price of grain would drop and peasants would be hurt economically. Additionally, if part of the tax grain were to be collected in kind and the rest commuted, the difficulties of collection would multiply. Tao concluded that "while tax grain might be commuted in other provinces, it simply can not be done in Jiangsu."[22]

Tao also expressed strong opposition to the proposed canal closure in 1826. He correctly pointed out that if canal officials had taken this action in early 1825, immediately after the collapse of the Hongze Lake dikes, then it might have made sense because low water levels in the junction arteries would have facilitated the dredging work. But now in the sixth month, it was too late. The stonework on the dike was nearly completed, and clear water reserves in the lake were rising as was the level of the Yellow River. At this stage of the game, it was simply too late to discharge and divert lake water into the canal head and Clear Passage to scour them out. The same was also true, he asserted, of Weishan Lake in southwest Shandong province. Moreover, stopping traffic on the canal just to focus on reconstructing Yuhuang dam-gate, where canal boats crossed into the Yellow River, was also not a good idea. He argued that such a move would draw resources away from other sites where work could and should be pursued. Additionally, canal closure would strangle the flow of private trade to and from the north. "Southern trade goods could not be shipped north, nor northern goods to the south."

The best solution, in Tao's view, was to use both the canal and sea transport in 1826. "In the fall and winter of 1825, river officials should dredge deeply to facilitate the passage of empty grain boats returning south. Then, in the spring of 1826, when the water levels in the lake rise, grain fleets can pass through the

---

21 JSHY 1:26–30b (5.6.15).
22 Ibid., 1:26–28b (5.6.15).

junction *without* the use of Yellow River backspills" [author's emphasis]—a possibility which he must have realized was hardly likely, given the scale of destruction at the junction. At the same time, while these measures were undertaken, Shanghai officials "should begin to recruit private merchant ships to transport 1.5 million *shi* of Jiangnan grain by sea in two trips, with any remaining grain sent by canal." The use of both canal and sea transport, he argued, was the wisest plan because realistically, "there are probably not enough ocean-going boats to carry all the Jiangsu grain by sea; nor enough lake water to send it all by canal. Using both will surely ease the burden on the canal."[23]

Tao reminded the emperor "that sea transport is merely a temporary expedient. The first and fundamental priority was canal restoration so that, in the future, the canal will be open and clear; then all the grain can be sent by canal. Even if the canal is silted, the canal is the customary way (*yishi suoshiyou*)." On the other hand, in the event that the canal becomes completely silted, the government should construct granaries on the banks of the canal near Huai'an in order to store the grain until there is enough water for lighterage transport. Such granaries would be closer to the capital than the southern canal anchorages, and, moreover, the start-up costs of building them, although expensive, were no more so than the cost of other temporary shipping schemes used during crises. Tao seemed to view these canal-side granaries as a useful adjunct to relay shipping, but one that had the advantage of lasting a long time and helping to insure that at least some stored tax grain might reach the capital."[24]

The ideas expressed in this memorial are very significant because they reveal that Tao Zhu was not wholeheartedly in favor of Yinghe's comprehensive plan at the outset, and that he held the view that canal transport, even in a modified and less than optimal form, was preferable to sea transport. It remained, in his view, the "customary" way for shipping grain supplies to the capital—one that should not be replaced by sea transport.

Seven days after the arrival of Tao Zhu's negative report on commutation and canal closure (5.6.22), another important official, Cheng Hanzhang, the Governor of Zhejiang, closed the door on sending his province's tax grain by sea. He reported that conditions at the ports of Ningbo and Zhapu precluded the use of these ports for transferring grain to sea-going vessels. At Zhapu, a rock embankment reinforced by metal planks blocked access to the harbor from the canal, and although ocean boats could dock at Ningbo at the mouth of the Yong River, the lighters carrying tax grain from the grain districts would have "to transfer their loads across two rivers and three water gates to reach

---

23   JSHY 1:29b (5.6.15).
24   JSHY 1:29b–30 (5.6.15).

Ningpo, making the scheme far too expensive and difficult to implement."
Because of Cheng's report, the emperor ordered that neither sea transport nor
commutation in Zhejiang should be discussed further and that the province's
tax grain should be collected as usual and sent entirely by canal![25] That left
only the tax grain from the Jiangnan districts for sea transport.

These two reports by Tao and Cheng drastically narrowed the scope of
Yinghe's proposed comprehensive plan, and their circulation to other canal-
zone officials seems to have influenced the growing view among these officials
in the seventh month that they must prepare for canal shipments and/or storage of grain in their home provinces in 1826.

3   Qishan's Assessment of the "General Situation"

At this point in the debate, Qishan vigorously weighed in on other difficult
issues surrounding the comprehensive plan in the late sixth month (5.6.22).
With characteristic bluntness and caution, he asserted forcefully that until
investigations were completed and a host of facts were known, he "dare not"
make specific recommendations about sea transport, commutation, or canal
closure. Instead, he stated that he would only address the "*general situation*"
(*dagaiqingxing*) surrounding these difficult issues.[26] (He would not have
known about Cheng's memorial or the emperor's decision to leave Zhejiang
out of the sea-transport plan.)

He pointedly alluded to the emperor's angry denunciation of Wei Yuanyu
and other canal-zone officials, who earlier had failed to send responses to
Yinghe's comprehensive plan even though he, the emperor, had twice insisted
that they come up with "a concrete, corruption-free plan to address the canal–
grain-transport crisis." These same officials had also ignored the emperor's request for concrete information about conditions at the junction and the water
levels in Hongze Lake and the Yellow River that bore on the ability of returning
empty grain boats to cross through the junction and return to their home anchorages in the autumn. These questions also bore on the ability of grain-laden
fleets to sail north on the canal to the capital the following spring. And, as for
the sea-transport experiment (*shiban*), could it be done at all? The emperor
insisted that he, himself, had no bias about sea transport one way or the other,

---

25   TJ (5.6.22), SL 1524–1525.
26   JSHY 1:32 (5.6.22).

which, of course, flew in the face of his ardent pursuit of this option since the early fifth month (5.2.5).[27]

In response to these questions, Qishan insisted that it was premature to make judgments about these issues before his investigations were completed! He pledged to exert all his energies to figure out what courses of action could, or should, be taken on sea transport and commutation, but he reminded the emperor that regulations for both of these plans had yet to be formulated and would have to be carefully weighed. He refused to offer concrete suggestions on either issue, saying that he "would not dare to give advice recklessly (*maomei*)" before he had fully investigated these issues.

Yet, irrespective of the outcome of these investigations, he nonetheless asserted that the *priority* issue in northern Jiangsu was, and must continue to be, "harnessing the river." A plan for this work must be figured out *before* the grain-transport system was changed and reorganized. At present, he explained, "the Yellow River rises higher and higher each day! The clear water in Hongze Lake is not strong enough to resist the Yellow River current, and, therefore, it must not, under any circumstances, be released into the junction to aid transport."[28]

Moreover, before the empty fleets could return south in the autumn and load "the new grain the following spring," impenetrable silt blockages in a 100-mile (*li*) stretch of the Grand Canal from Gaoyou-Baoying to the junction had to be dredged out to a width of six to ten meters (two to three *zhang*) and a depth of about three-and-a-half meters (one *zhang*, five to six *cun*). Without this critical work, grain boats could not pass through the southern canal head and the Clear Passage. Not only would dredging expenses be costly, but, more importantly, as far as Qishan could ascertain, there was "*no official in the junction area who he felt confident could successfully shoulder this particular dredging task*" [author's emphasis], which suggests that he had already reviewed the abilities of the officials working near the junction and found them wanting, much as he had done when he had first arrived at his official post in Shandong years earlier. He summarized his view by underscoring the fact that "without controlling the river, we cannot carry out grain transport [by canal] (*shihebuzhizecaobuxing*)." At present, "there is no good policy except the temporary use of sea transport. I held this view earlier when I was Governor of Shandong province, and since arriving at my post in Liangjiang and visiting many places and discussing the matter with many people, I feel fairly confident that sea transport can be implemented."[29]

---

27   JSHY 1:32–b (5.6.22).
28   Ibid.
29   Ibid., 1:33 (5.6.22).

4   Qishan's Approach to Sea Transport

Qishan based this judgment on the report by Jiangsu Treasurer, He Changling, who had already made preliminary contacts with merchant shippers in Shanghai and had determined that two shipments of approximately 700,000 *shi* each might be transported by sea in sand junks from Shanghai, for a total of about 1.5 million *shi*. Yet facts had come to light on He's visit that cast doubt on the availability of these very sand junks. Qishan reported that "although the circumstances are not completely clear, it appears that when Jiangnan-area officials had been asked to inquire into the feasibility of sea transport earlier in the spring, they had commandeered the merchants' boats and kept them in the harbor in the event that sea transport were implemented later that spring." This approach had "led to corrupt abuses" and had kept merchant shippers from making their regular voyages to the northeastern ports for trade. As a result of these actions, "many of these shippers had subsequently left the harbor, and none had returned to anchor at Shanghai because they feared that they will be forced to stay. If vessels failed to return, there will be too few boats to ship the grain. Consequently, I cannot determine, at present, how much grain can be sent by sea, and if I did so, I might have to break my promise later."[30]

Qishan also had other concerns about sea transport. Because of his own lack of knowledge about navigation on the northeast coast, he feared that the risks of ocean sailing might cause delays and harm the cargoes. "When the ships sail north [to Tianjin], they depend on the southern winds, and when they return to Shanghai for the second load, they depend on the northern winds. Generally, these trips are made in the spring and summer when the direction of the winds and the weather can change rapidly. As a result, it is difficult for me to say for sure if the merchant shippers can make these trips without stopping and anchoring." If forced to anchor, the ships might be delayed and the rice cargoes might be damaged. "Grain," he averred, "is different from other commodities. It can't be kept in one place for a long time." Qishan felt compelled to discuss this matter with *"people who have knowledge about shipping grain by sea* because, again, I do not want to make unfounded judgments" [author's emphasis].

Qishan clearly felt at a loss when it came to making concrete planning decisions for a major innovation like sea transport. There were, in his estimation, too few high-level officials to manage these essential and time-consuming planning tasks. He pointed out that all the merchant ships are based in Shanghai, while "I am based temporarily at Qingjiangpu and cannot go to Shanghai and examine the situation in person. Previously, Tao Zhu had

---

30   Ibid., 1:33b.

traveled to Qingjiangpu to discuss merchant shipping matters with me, and he had reported that he had ordered the Jiangsu treasurer to go to the port in person to meet with local officials and prepare a plan for recruitment of merchant ships (*shefazhaolai*)—one that will not give rise to merchant fears of abuses or shipping delays."

Another urgent matter related to sea transport that required Qishan's prompt attention was the mobilization and payment of lighterage organizations to transport tax grain from the Jiangnan anchorages to Shanghai for transfer to waiting sand junks. The distances between these various anchorages and Shanghai varied, and officials needed to figure out quickly the terms and conditions for local private lighterage hire, so that Qishan and Tao Zhu could meet again to finalize a plan.

Added to the list of important issues connected to commutation that he "dare not decide on immediately," was the difficulty of collecting and commuting the Jiangsu grain tax levy, which was comparatively heavy compared to that of other provinces. He pointed out that officials and the people will be doubly burdened in 1826 if both the *diding* and commuted tax grain were collected in silver at the same time, and, if it were, he warned that he fully expected low-level officials and sub-bureaucratic clerks to conspire to reduce the value of the grain and increase the price of silver, not to mention their arbitrary misappropriation of these funds. Moreover, disagreeing again with Tao Zhu, he was unequivocal about one thing. His investigation of the damaged junction had convinced him that grain boats could absolutely not pass through Yuhuang lock-gate in 1826 (Map 4), irrespective of whether or not they collected all or part of the grain tax in kind.

He explained again that his highest priority was the completion of urgent water conservancy projects (*gonglin*), the cost of which would be great and unrelenting. He warned that it would be extremely dangerous to risk fiscal and labor exhaustion by forging ahead with all the projects at the same time. Instead, he counseled practicality. "We should adapt to circumstances in order to return to and prioritize practical measures and fund only essential projects (*quanbianbiguishiyongeryugongxu*)." Moreover, before they rushed ahead with sea transport, "we should first determine with the utmost accuracy" how much tax grain can be shipped by sea and how many sand junks can be recruited to carry it. Second, showing that he still hoped that commutation could be carried out, he urged that a realistic method of commuting (either by peasants or officials) should be devised that would assure the funding of crucial conservancy works.

He acknowledged that he disagreed with Tao Zhu who, during their previous face-to-face discussions, "had maintained that commuting the grain tax absolutely could not be done in Jiangsu," and that it might be necessary to store the grain in canal side granaries. Qishan, on the other hand, believed that commutation was essential to fund the projects for "harnessing the river," repairing the junction passageways, and rebuilding the Hongze Lake dikes. He did not want to give up on commutation, so he turned to both the Jiangsu and Jiangning treasurers to investigate further and try to find a corruption-free way to carry it out so that they might fix "the dire conditions at the confluence of the river, canal, and lake." In his view, the key to the success of such a plan—sea transport as well—was the leadership of bold skilled "officials who are committed to benefitting public affairs" (*quanzaibanliderenfangyugongshiyouji*).[31] He urged Tao Zhu and the two Liangjiang provincial treasurers "to exhaust themselves," in order to create a plan for commutation and to choose virtuous deputies to implement it. "We must not fear difficulties nor conceal problems, but rather strive to resolve the issues facing grain transport and the canal. Then, we can ease the emperor's arduous burdens."

Even if all of the sand junks returned to port, Qishan was apprehensive that there would be too few of them to ship the Jiangnan grain, and this shortage would surely intensify if the inland provinces also wanted to send their tax grain by sea. In the end, he added pessimistically, it might be impossible even to send Jiangsu grain by sea. He did not yet know at this time that Zhejiang could not send their tax grain by sea from the ports of Chapu and Ningpo, but, for the remaining four inland provinces (Anhui, Jiangxi, Hunan, and Hupei), he advised the emperor to order each of their provincial heads to prepare a plan for either commuting tax grain and/or storing it so that they could "avoid acting hastily in the midst of later unforeseen crises."

At this stage, it was still unclear whether or not the canal would be closed in 1826. This meant that Qishan and junction officials could not focus wholly on repairs and reconstruction, but had to be ready at a moment's notice to manage the southward crossing of grain fleets in the autumn of 1825 and the northward crossing of grain-filled fleets in the spring of 1826. To do so, they had no alternative but to check water levels in the lake and river constantly to determine if, how, and when they could manage these crossings. If the lake were too low compared to the river, then lake water could not be used to "aid the transport" through the junction, and Yellow River backspills would again clog and damage the junction passages. Technically speaking, if the lake water were high enough, it could be used to scour the junction passages as the fleets were crossed into the Yellow River through Yuhuang Dam. However, if the lake

---

31   JSHY 1:35b (5.6.22).

water were *too* high, it might again tear out the retaining walls on the lake's eastern perimeter and destroy the junction, as had been the case in early 1825.

Qishan sarcastically took aim at Grain Transport Director Wei Yuanyu's overly optimistic memorial earlier in the sixth month (5.6.6) about following the customary method of using lake water to cross the fleets in 1826. Wei had reported that "ten layers of rock slabs reinforcing the lake dikes, or 70 percent of the dam wall, had already been completed, and the lake levels had risen to a depth of 3.2 m (8 *chi* 8 *cun*)."[32] Wei predicted that another 3.6 m (1 *zhang*), would accumulate by the following spring, making it possible to use lake water to cross the fleets. Failing that, the lake water could at least be used to carry the fleets up the last sections of the Southern Canal head into the Clear Passage, at which point, Yuhuang Dam could be opened quickly and all the fleets pulled through on Yellow River backspills within a month's time. In other words, Wei was advocating more of the same old failed schemes.

Just as Qishan had exposed Sun Yuting's false report on the progress of relay shipping, he proceeded to discredit Wei Yuanyu by revealing the "real facts" on water levels, showing that lake water could not be used without risking another collapse of the Gaoyan Great Dike, resulting in staggering silt damage to the junction. He pointed out that he and the Canal director, Yan Lang, had gone to the work sites and investigated the matter of water levels, in person. The lake levels had already reached 3.9 m (1 *zhang* 1 *chi*). By interviewing low-level civil and military officials at the dike work sites, they discovered that usually when the lake reached 3.6 m (1 *zhang*), the lake water would pour over the Xin and Zhi sluice gates on the east side of the dike wall (Map 2), and it would be necessary to raise the height of the gates another 1.1 m (3 *chi*) with earthen reinforcements. But that was the extent of the hydrostatic pressure that these gates could withstand. Moreover, their local informants asserted that these levels did not even take account of the water entering the lake from the Huai River watershed each spring, causing the levels to rise another 6.1 m to 6.4 m (1 *zhang*, 7–8 *chi*). Lowly as these canal officials were, they nonetheless unflinchingly expressed their fears to Qishan and Yan that such high water levels could not be contained. The lake water would not only rip out the two gates, but would surely burst through the newly repaired dike because the mortar used between the stone slabs would not have had time to set in order to hold the dike wall firm.

In other words, even the normal seasonal rise in lake levels from the Huai River might cause the newly repaired wall to collapse again. Therefore, Qishan stated categorically that he "did not dare" to put aside these warnings by

---

32   TJ (5.6.6).

on-site canal officials and "willfully ignore" their advice. The situation of the lake was really dangerous in his view because, in the autumn, although the levels of Yellow River were normally 10.7 m (3 *zhang*), which was 0.6 m (1 *chi* 6 *cun*) lower than the lake, he did not dare accumulate another 5.4 to 5.7 m (1 *zhang*, 5–6 *chi*) in the lake. This meant that even the returning empty grain boats, which were light in weight, could probably not cross successfully without using Yellow backspills, and, in the spring of 1826, when the fleets were heavily laden with grain, they most certainly would require much more time, more lake water, and more backspills to cross through the silt shallows in the junction passageways. Yet, because of the fragility of the lake dikes and the possible need to release lake water if it were too high, Yellow River backspills would have to be used yet again to cross the fleets in the spring. This was another reason why Qishan believed that the canal should not be used in 1826.

Qishan was unequivocal. He simply was not prepared to advocate "the reckless method of using Yellow backspills again." He closed the memorial by saying that he had received great benevolence from the emperor, and therefore he "dared not cover up the facts of the real situation."[33] That was why he felt he could only address the "general situation facing the Qing leadership" as they evaluated the myriad problems of sea transport, commutation, and the reconstruction of the junction. Many of the facts about these issues had yet to be determined! Skilled dedicated officials were needed to make a series of decisions, including the regulations for sea transport in Shanghai, if and how commutation (peasant or official) might be carried out in the various southern canal-zone provinces, and whether junction passages could be rebuilt without closing down the canal in 1826.

In his reply on 5.6.28, the emperor carefully weighed and accepted Qishan's reasons for asserting that final decisions on sea transport and commutation must await further investigation. He also reported that Zhejiang Governor Cheng Hanzhang had advised that neither sea transport nor commutation could be implemented in Zhejiang, which seemed again to limit the implementation of Yinghe's comprehensive plan. Following Qishan's advice, the emperor again ordered the governors of Anhui, Jiangxi, and Huguang to assess whether or not they should commute or store tax grain in 1826 in their respective jurisdictions. Because either course of action hinged on whether or not grain could be sent by canal, he ordered them to consult with Qishan and Tao Zhu before sending grain by canal. Given all the imponderables that officials faced, the emperor was not very helpful or realistic when he exhorted them

---

33   JSHY 1:36 (5.6.22).

"not to vacillate, on the one hand, nor take risky actions, on the other," and, what's more, their plans should be "absolutely safe and useful."[34]

Reluctantly, the emperor seemed to accept Qishan's assessment that Yellow backspills could not be used in the spring of 1826, but, nonetheless, he ordered him and the Southern Canal director to continue to monitor the water levels in the lake and river with great care and attempt to find "a way to conserve water in the lake to resist the Yellow River" with an eye towards gradually "returning to the old way of aiding transport (*fujiuguijiyun*)." This edict suggests that the limited amount of grain that could be sent by sea and the difficulty of commutation seemed to dim the prospects for a major reconstruction of the canal, leaving them, once again, little alternative but to patch together more stopgap measures to transport grain through the junction.[35]

The next day (5.6.29), bowing to grim realities, the emperor ordered Qishan and Tao Zhu to proceed with sea transport, according to He's impending report on his visit to Shanghai, and to abandon Yinghe's proposal to close the canal and commute the tax grain to fund the works projects in 1826. Instead, he implored officials at the junction to focus on "the most immediate urgent problems as they unfolded."[36] This meant monitoring the water levels in both the river and lake and completing the most crucial conservancy projects. Both were key to managing the return crossing of empty grain fleets in the autumn of 1825, as well as the crossing of some or all of the fleets the following spring of 1826.

Even though the emperor had given up on commutation and canal closure by the end of the sixth month, memorial reports on these issues continued to flow into the capital during the seventh month from the governors-general and governors of the southern canal-zone provinces. Some recommended collection in kind as usual, then transport through the damaged junction (although no one knew for sure if this would be possible); others proposed collecting unhusked grain, commuting part of the levy, and/or storing the remainder

---

34   TJ (5.6.28).

35   A separate edict was sent to Qishan and Yan Lang the same day that ordered them to work together to find a way to cross the grain fleets in 1826 so that all the tax grain would arrive in Tongzhou (TJ 5.6.28, SL 1530), while two more responded to Qishan's plans to use private lighters to pick up grain at the south bank of the Yellow River and transfer it to returning empty grain fleets from Henan and Shandong for final shipment to Tongzhou (TJ 5.6.28). Additionally, he also proposed the similar use of returning empty grain fleets from Jiangnan-Huguang (TJ 5.6.28; SL 1528–1529). See Leonard 1996, pp. 163–69.

36   JSHY 1:30–b (5.6.29); SL 1531–32.

locally until 1827. Many of the proposals were hopelessly complicated and unworkable.[37]

The most practical plan was that proposed by Huguang Governor-General Li Hongbin (5.7.3), which reflected the practical experience that he had gleaned in 1814 when he had served as a deputy director of canal and river affairs in Henan-Shandong. Because both canal and sea transport would be used in 1826 and because it was inevitable that some kind of relay shipping would be necessary through the damaged sections of the canal from Gaoyou to the junction, Li proposed that those twenty to thirty grain fleets that had already delivered their cargoes to Tongzhou should return to the Yellow River to assist with the 1825 relay shipping scheme, where there was a shortage of vessels. Then, after delivering that grain, they should either return to anchorages on the Wei River outside Linqing gate, which served as the canal route in northern Shandong and Zhili as far as Tianjin, or they should anchor in the Shandong Canal, then again proceed south in the spring of 1826 to pick up grain cargoes waiting at the Yellow River–canal junction for transport to Tongzhou.

Revealing an understanding of the yearly dredging calendar, Li further urged that the dredging from Gaoyou to the junction be scheduled carefully, starting at the Gaoyou end in the winter (1825) and the first and second month of 1826 (February 7–April 6), and then completing the final sections along the southern canal head to the junction during the summer and fall of 1826.

Li also advised that "next year in late spring when the grain fleets approach the junction and water levels in Hongze Lake reach 3.6 m (1 *zhang*), the Jiyun sluice gate on the northeast side of the Gaoyan Great Dike should be opened and water channeled into the southern canal head so that the grain boats can again be pulled through the silt, the grain unloaded onto carts, then pulled over to anchorages on the south bank of the Yellow River." At that point, he explained, the fleets waiting in Shandong should return to the Yellow River and pick up and transport the waiting grain to Tongzhou. This approach would use clear lake water in a limited way along the southern canal head, while allowing canal workers "to block up, rebuild, and dredge" the junction passageways. Then, in the fall, these same fleets could proceed to their home anchorages and pick up the "new" grain for delivery in early 1827. Li Hongbin's proposal is noteworthy because it outlined a way to dredge a hopelessly silted canal and to

---

37   S 00065–67 (5.7.6); SL 1536–1537. S 00245–246 (5.7.3); SL 1549–1550; TJ (5.7.17); SL 1544.
      S 00219–220 (5.7.21).

overcome the shortage of available craft for relay shipping by using returning empty southern grain fleets.[38]

In the emperor's response to Li, he reported that Zhejiang could not ship by sea and that he had instructed Qishan to send a deputy to Shanghai to make arrangements for implementing sea transport with local officials and merchant shippers. As for commuting grain taxes, the emperor's opposition to this part of Yinghe's plan had hardened, and he agreed with Li's view that it "would cause corruption to grow like weeds." Not only was it "inconvenient for officials and local people alike, but it is contrary to the *proper institutions of government (shushubuchengzhengti)*" [author's emphasis]. He feared that "local officials and clerks would coerce both the merchants and the people." Therefore, depending on water levels of the lake and river in the spring of 1826, Li should collect the tax grain as usual, and if the canal were blocked, then he should store the grain and send it the following year.

In response to the other memorials, the emperor urged officials to "post proclamations with their various schemes so that the village people could see and hear them discussed." They should "not cover up the people's reactions and force them to go along blindly with plans that the officials favored."[39] When officials said that commutation would "stir up disturbances and cause an explosion of corruption," the emperor told them to collect and send grain taxes in the customary way because, as he often stated, "commutation by local officials does not accord with proper institutions of government" and was certain to spawn three corrupt practices: (1) local officials would coerce merchants and people when contracting for the purchase of grain; (2) government clerks would falsely report a lower than market price for grain; and (3) they would heap grain on the level-measuring tools (*pingse*) used when receiving grain.[40] Although he lamented the loss of funds for canal restoration that commutation would have provided, there were just too many "obstacles to its implementation (*zhi'aishenduo*)."[41]

At the end of the seventh month (5.7.23), the emperor again, but more strongly, reaffirmed that canal closure and commutation would not be implemented and that the remaining grain from Jiangsu as well as that from Zhejiang and the Yangzi provinces (Anhui, Jiangxi, and Huguang) would somehow be sent through the damaged canal junction. Equally disappointing was the fact that

---

38   S 00009–11 (5.7.3); SL 1534–1535. Li Hongbin was against peasant commutation, but instead wanted collection and payment of grain tax in kind, followed by *zhouxian* official sale of the grain. JSHY 1:54–55 (5.8.9).

39   S 00065–67 (5.7.6); SL 1536–1537.

40   TJ (5.7.17); SL 1544.

41   S 00219–220 (5.7.21).

canal restoration around the junction could not possibly be implemented on the scale hoped for without the funds from commutation. Sea transport was all that remained of Yinghe's ambitious comprehensive plan. The optimism of the early spring had vanished, and the emperor's only hope was that Qishan and Southern Canal Director Yan Lang, laboring at the junction, might figure out some way to move the stalled 1825 grain cargoes through the silt mess at the Southern Canal head *without* opening Yuhuang dam-gate and to do so again in 1826 if the junction were still blocked and disabled.[42]

Yet, even though the emperor accepted the fact that the canal would have to be used in 1826, he was still not reconciled to the idea of opening Yuhuang dam-gate and using Yellow backspills to cross the grain fleets. He asked in frustration, "If we were to do so, would this not be a case of causing the same dangerous conditions for the river, the lake, and the canal? What will be the outcome? How deep will the trouble go?" [Inter-linal insertion in the secret edict] "If such a move were again to cause disaster, is this not a case of making the same mistake twice?"[43]

As it turned out, against all odds, Qishan and others at the junction did figure out a way to cross the fleets in 1826 without Yellow River backspills. They left Yuhuang closed, allowing the river water to sweep eastward, scouring silt from the riverbed. They simultaneously introduced a limited amount of lake water into the canal from Jiyun dam on the northeast side of the lake dike to raise the water level in the canal from Gaobao to the junction (Map 2). This facilitated the passage of grain-filled lighters up to a point on the canal that was close to and parallel to the south bank of the Yellow River so that their cargoes could be pulled up and over the river embankment on carts, and transferred to waiting lighters and grain boats for shipment northward to the capital, with some traveling via Jining.[44]

This scheme also required that some of the regular fleets should remain anchored in the north, outside of Linqing on the Wei River, and also in northern Shandong in 1825 and 1826; and from there they would then make several trips back and forth from the Yellow River to Tongzhou. The reasons for anchoring the fleets in the north were twofold. First, Qishan feared that throngs of sailors from the great number of boats crowding around the junction might cause disturbances. Second, the water levels in Weishan Lake in southwest Shandong were 3 m low (9 *chi* 6 *cun*). If the various fleets were to return immediately to the junction in 1825, they would deplete the accumulated water in the lake. If

---

42   S 00245–246 (5.7.23); SL 1549–50.
43   Ibid.
44   JSHY 1:42–43 (5.7.22).

water levels were to fall to between a third and two meters (1 to 6 *chi*), "the lake water would be depleted for another seven years."

In other words, even if the junction were navigable, grain fleets would not be able to reach the junction because they could not navigate the canal adjacent to Weishan Lake in Shandong.[45] He urged therefore that the *first* group of fleets to arrive at Tongzhou from Jiangguang (Jiangxi-Huguang) be ordered to anchor in the canal just outside the Linqing gate. Only after Weishan Lake accumulated enough water, some of it from ice melt in the spring of 1826, should these fleets set sail for the junction to the south. He also informed the emperor that he had summoned Tao Zhu, the Jiangsu Governor, and the two Liangjiang treasurers to meet him in Nanjing (the area around Jingkou and Jiangning) to design a scheme for commuting tax grain in Jiangsu after all and to streamline further the grain transfers through the junction during the relay-shipping process.[46]

This complex memorial is important because it shows how up-in-the-air all the various plans for the 1826 canal crossings were throughout the whole of the seventh month. Would the returning fleets be anchored north of Linqing to save the water in Weishan Lake and avoid crowding near the junction? Would, on the other hand, some of them anchor in Jining or on the north bank of the Yellow River next to the canal junction? Could some of them, such as the Zhejiang fleets, return to their home anchorages so they could load the "new" tax grain in 1826?[47] The final definitive edict on the canal crossing was not sent down until late in the eighth month.[48]

In the face of all these problematic issues about canal transport, Qishan and officials at the junction soldiered on to finish relay shipping in 1825; they crossed some of the returning empty fleets at the junction in the autumn; and they anchored the rest of them north of the Yellow River from northern Jiangsu to the Zhili border so that they were poised to pick up grain cargoes in the spring of 1826.

5　　Conclusions

The debate on Yinghe's comprehensive plan (5.5.22–5.7.23) and the decision to drop commutation and canal closure in 1826 left the Qing leadership with only

---

45　JSHY 1:42 (5.7.22).
46　JSHY 1:43 (5.7.22), rescript dated 5.8.6.
47　Ibid.
48　S 00197–201 (5.8.28).

the option of the sea transport scheme. The debate had revealed that the emperor and his central allies were prepared to undertake an extraordinary multifaceted plan to restore the Grand Canal around the junction so that it could continue to serve as the primary route for shipping tax grain to the capital and, at the same time, institutionalize sea transport to provide a reliable back-up plan in times of canal dysfunction. Qishan, too, had come to Liangjiang predisposed to these plans, but his blunt refusal to make blanket judgments about them until he had made thorough investigations raised questions about their feasibility. However, it was the realistic assessments about commutation from field officials in the southern canal-zone provinces, especially Tao Zhu, Cheng Hanzhang, and Li Hongbin, that had dashed their hopes and made them face the hard realities "on the ground." This was precisely what the Qing decisional process—with its reliance on direct secret communications between emperor and high-level provincial officials—was designed to do.

Accepting these realities, the Qing leadership turned their organizational energies to crafting a "perfect" sea-transport plan for shipping Jiangnan grain from Shanghai harbor. Sea-transport planning was officially launched by the Daoguang Emperor's public announcement early in the eighth month (5.8.9) after two important memorial reports, discussed below, one by the Jiangsu Governor, Tao Zhu, the other by the censor, Xiong Yutai, cast it in a positive light.[49] The single-minded focus on sea transport, without the distractions of the myriad complexities of commutation and canal closure, surely contributed to the creation of unified and realistic guidelines and intensified official oversight of its implementation in Shanghai and Tianjin, which ultimately contributed to its success.

---

49   P 00087–88 (5.8.9).

CHAPTER 5

Stretching the Bureaucracy for Sea Transport

1   Administrative Obstacles to the Sea-Transport Experiment

Even though "harnessing the river," canal closure, and commutation had dominated discussions between the emperor and canal-zone officials during the sixth and seventh months of 1825, Qishan, nonetheless, began to lay the groundwork for sea transport soon after his arrival in Qingjiangpu at the end of the fifth month, taking two important steps. The first was to assess port conditions and determine the number and availability of sand junks for hire, or recruitment, in Shanghai and possibly Zhapu and Ningpo (Zhejiang) as well. Although he had supported the idea of sea transport when he was Governor of Shandong and viewed Yinghe's comprehensive plan in a positive light, Qishan displayed characteristic caution once he had arrived at Qingjiangpu, refusing to commit to sea transport until Tao Zhu and He Changling had completed their preliminary investigations of these two issues. The second major step was to determine how best to mobilize leadership resources to plan and oversee practical implementation of the sea-transport experiment. In other words, whom could the Qing leadership tap to create the plan and supervise its implementation so that dockside extortion could be eliminated—without which merchant shippers would not buy into the plan.

Qishan recognized that the three senior officials in Liangjiang—Tao Zhu, He Changling, and Qishan himself—could not, by themselves, create and implement such a plan while concurrently performing their regular duties of office. Moreover, these tasks had to be carried out in Shanghai, the loading port for Jiangnan grain. Because the work, especially the dockside supervision of grain transfers, would be performed at the sub-county level and was extremely labor-intensive, officials from intendants to "assistants" would have to intensify their personal direction of the transfers and payments. To carry out these tasks, Qishan created a temporary *ad hoc* organization, or bureau (*ju*), in Shanghai to write the regulations and oversee their implementation. Thus, the Qing leadership turned to two well-established tricks of the governing trade—recruitment and *ad hoc* bureaus—in order to implement this important innovation in strategic grain-transport practice.

© KONINKLIJKE BRILL NV, LEIDEN, 2019 | DOI:10.1163/9789004384583_007

2 Obstacles to Recruitment

Early in the sixth month, soon after arriving at his gubernatorial post in Suzhou, Tao Zhu traveled to Qingjiangpu to meet with Qishan and discuss the preliminary information gathered by He Changling about sand junk availability and recruitment during He's earlier fact-finding trip to Shanghai. Although Yinghe's two earlier memorials had indicated that merchant shippers in Shanghai would "jump for joy" at the prospect of shipping government tax grain in 1826, He's report seemed to indicate the contrary—that these sand junk owners were less than enthusiastic about recruitment and that, indeed, they were fleeing the port.[1]

The flight of the sand junks, noted above, had apparently been triggered by the arbitrary and coercive actions of Tao's predecessor as Jiangsu Governor, Zhang Shicheng, who, earlier in the year, when the possibility of sea transport of the 1825 tax grain was still under consideration, had "commandeered" all the sand junks then in the harbor in the event that they would be needed for grain transport. This caused great consternation among the junk owners, who, as a consequence, lost the chance to sail to the northeastern ports for the spring trading season.[2] In retaliation, they had begun surreptitiously to leave the harbor, one by one, and "disappeared at sea," and it was unclear if they would return to do the state's bidding at the end of the year. Reporting this bad news to the emperor late in the sixth month, Qishan asserted that until the question of ship availability were resolved, he "could not make any promises" about the number of these ships available for sea transport and, by extension, the amount of grain that might be shipped. Without these ships, sea transport would have to be abandoned.

The crisis of the "disappearing ships" highlighted the critical need—indeed, the imperative—to stamp out sub-bureaucratic extortion of private shippers if the Qing were to move ahead with sea transport. State recruitment deals and collaboration with private organizations were often undermined because officials used the notoriously corrupt sub-bureaucratic clerks and runners to interface with these organizations, mainly because of shortage of ranked officials. To clarify the availability of sand junks, Qishan immediately sent He Changling to Shanghai again to find out exactly how many ships might be recruited, an

---

1 JSHY 1:32–37 (5.6.22).
2 JSHY 1:36–37 (5.6.28).

issue whose resolution ultimately would require Governor Tao Zhu's personal intervention late in the seventh month (5.7.23), described below.[3] The terms of the agreement were ultimately contained in the regulations that were finalized in the ninth month, which carefully specified the procedures for inspecting and transferring the grain cargoes leaving the Jiangnan anchorages and Shanghai and then arriving in Tianjin.[4] They emphasized ways to streamline grain transfers at each stage, in order to minimize extortion and assure the timely departure of sand junks from Tianjin to the Manchurian ports and their subsequent return to Shanghai.[5]

Official coercion, exemplified by Zhang Shicheng's recent impressment of sand junks, as well as sub-bureaucratic extortion, in general, on the docks of port cities and canal anchorages, were well known to private sand junk operators. They asserted that sub-bureaucratic clerks, runners, and (in Zhili) grain brokers would surely take a cut out of their shipping fees in both Shanghai and Tianjin when tax grain was transferred to and from merchant hands.[6] The Qing leadership was also aware of the ubiquity of sub-bureaucratic corruption. There are numerous official and imperial references to the importance of streamlining these grain transfers in order to avoid just such corrupt practices that would hurt merchants economically: "We should not cause harm for merchants and must design regulations that expedite the work."[7] One might realistically view this issue as a conflict between the interests of sub-bureaucrats and those of private, extra-bureaucrats (in this case, sand junk operators)— one in which the latter ultimately prevailed because of the Qing state's overriding need for their vessels and the skilled mariners to sail them. It also reveals that the Qing leadership understood clearly that systemic sub-bureaucratic corruption, in general, took a toll on administrative efficiency that could and would undermine state-private recruitment deals.

Earlier in the spring, Yinghe had forewarned of the seriousness of this problem when he alluded to the need to protect merchants from extortion in Tianjin. "Merchant shippers," he explained, "fear that they will be treated just like Banner officers on the Grand-Canal grain fleets, who are constantly pressured to pay special fees."[8] They suspected that if they agreed to ship tax grain

---

3   JSHY 1:44–47 (5.7.23).

4   JSHY 1:62–70b (5.9.2).

5   JSHY 1:45–b (5.7.23). The procedures for Tianjin, outlined by Jiangsu officials, were later modified by Zhili officials to take account of special factors governing grain transport and storage in Zhili.

6   JSHY 1:10b (5.4.10); JSHY 1:45–b (5.7.23).

7   JSHY 1:34 (5.6.22).

8   JSHY 1:17b (5.5.22).

and then faced extortion and delays in Tianjin, they would be "afraid to protest to officials," in which case, they would lose the full amount of their agreed-upon shipping fees and the opportunity to trade in the Manchurian ports. In a word, merchant shippers wanted "protection" from sub-bureaucratic extortion if they were going to assist with sea transport. And this would require the creation of a special bureaucratic framework and procedures in which middle- and high-ranking officials and their assistants would be required to exercise far greater scrutiny and control over the interactions between corrupt sub-bureaucrats and private shippers. And this would be extremely difficult to achieve given the dearth of bureaucratic officials in the "paper thin" provincial bureaucratic structure.

Yinghe had also warned that merchants feared corruption in Shanghai as well. "Merchant shippers," he explained, "are not accustomed to dealing with either officials or clerks." Their lowly position relative to that of officials made them "timidly cringe" in their presence.[9] Even with the prospect of lucrative shipping fees, they remained fearful of recruitment and collaboration. To overcome their reluctance "to aid the state," Yinghe had sketched out some practical procedural protections for loading grain in Shanghai that were ultimately included in the regulations for sea transport.[10] In particular, he proposed that Shanghai officials participate in the planning and implementation of sea transport to maximize local knowledge, but that they should be carefully supervised by "one or two incorruptible and skilled outside officials," appointed by the Liangjiang Governor-General and Jiangsu Governor, and sent to Shanghai "to summon ship owners and work out corruption-free payment procedures and the exact rates of payment for shipping and labor costs, calculated per *shi* of grain, using the established government measuring tool (*hu*)."[11] Such outsiders would not be burdened by conflicts of interest that might influence local officials.

Yinghe had envisioned that, besides working out the details of the recruitment deal with merchants, these two special officials would draw up regulations with the help of local Shanghai officials, then continue to dwell in Shanghai to supervise the loading of grain at the docks on the Huangpu River in the spring of 1826, taking grain samples from each and every Jiangnan lighter transferring its load to sand junks and then issuing a document to each lighter and junk owner that specified the amount unloaded from one, then loaded onto the other, with a copy retained "in official hands to eliminate extortion."

---

9   JSHY 1:17b (5.5.22).
10   JSHY 1:17b–18b (5.5.22).
11   JSHY 1:17b–18b (5.5.22).

Yinghe explicitly argued against the use of yamen clerks and runners for these tasks.[12] After the loading was completed, he suggested that these two special officials accompany the sand junks to Tianjin, carrying the documents and samples with them for reference when Zhili officials examined the quantity and quality of the grain prior to officially receiving, or taking possession of it.[13] It was assumed that these special officials would serve as advocates for Shanghai merchant shippers and Jiangsu grain authorities in Tianjin.

To guard against extortion by entrenched grain authorities in Tianjin, Yinghe, it will be remembered, had also proposed sending two high-ranking officials—a Granary Vice President and another official from the Board of Revenue—to Tianjin in advance of the fleet's arrival, in order to prepare for receiving the grain, after which the merchants would no longer be held responsible for its condition. Only these two officials, he insisted, should be empowered to pay the merchants directly, based on the documents issued in Shanghai that spelled out the "actual amount of grain" measured and loaded there. He emphasized that "all aspects of loading, unloading, and dispersal of funds to shippers and porterage laborers must be controlled by bureaucratic officials with *no interference from grain brokers*"[14] [author's emphasis]. No one would to be allowed to extort even one cash-coin from the wages that were due to merchant shippers and porters. Yinghe asserted that these procedures would protect the economic interests of the merchants while they "served the public good." Therefore, even at this early stage of discussion, before the nitty-gritty of planning and implementation had begun, Yinghe clearly indicated that the needs of the merchants had to be met because the state could not implement sea transport without them.

Beside corruption, a third vexing problem that dogged and undermined sea-transport planning was the dearth of mid-level officials to take responsibility for writing the regulations and organizing sea transport. In the sixth and seventh months, the three highest officials in Liangjiang had undertaken the preliminary investigations of the progress of reconstruction at the junction work sites; they had also scrutinized the accuracy of earlier reports sent by junction officials on the state of the repairs; and, of course, assessed the initial availability of sand junks in the sixth and seventh months. But these investigations were just that—preliminary. They had been undertaken concurrently with

---

12   Ibid., 1:18.
13   As it turned out, the two officials traveled overland to Tianjin, probably to safeguard the grain samples and records from what they viewed as the dangers of ocean sailing.
14   JSHY 1:18 (5.5.22).

their other regular duties of office. The question was: who would perform the crucial follow-up tasks of writing the regulations and implementing the plan?

Qishan had already borne the lion's share of responsibility for decisions about the allocation of scarce bureaucratic resources for the myriad problems of junction restoration. But he had his limits, and he made those limits known, stating explicitly that he was constrained by being confined geographically to Qingjiangpu until relay shipping and canal reconstruction were completed, which might take several years. After touring the construction sites and consulting with officials in charge, he affirmed with a great deal of hesitancy that he could probably expedite the stalled relay-shipping scheme and canal reconstruction, although he was not completely sure—but he definitely could not repeatedly travel to Shanghai or Jiangnan to carry out planning and oversight functions for sea transport.[15]

Concurrency was also a difficulty for He Changling and Tao Zhu. Although many of the initial investigative trips to Shanghai had been undertaken by He Changling, Qishan asserted that he could not dwell in Shanghai indefinitely to manage sea transport because of the press of his regular duties as Provincial Treasurer in Suzhou.[16] Moreover, when the controversy over sand-junk impressment in Shanghai had arisen earlier and jeopardized the recruitment of merchant shippers, Tao Zhu himself had personally traveled to Shanghai to work out the terms of the recruitment deal in the late seventh month (5.7.23). But there were also limits to what Tao could do. In this particular instance, he was forced to leave Shanghai early before the recruitment deal was finalized, in order to serve as chief examiner for the provincial examinations in Jiangning (modern Nanjing). To complete these negotiations, he again sent He Changling to Shanghai, explaining, "With regard to all the other [sea-transport] issues, I will, as is customary, order the treasurer, He Changling, to go to Shanghai to take care of the various arrangements for merchant boats, porterage labor, and wastage rice, as well as to deliberate about sending military officers to escort the sand junk fleets and civil officials to witness the transfer of grain [in Tianjin]."[17] In short, Liangjiang's top three officials had been hard pressed to manage even the initial investigatory issues related to sea transport. Someone else was needed on the spot in Shanghai to draw up the regulations and implement them.

---

15   JSHY 1:33b–34 (5.6.22).
16   JSHY 1:39–b (5.6.22).
17   JSHY 1:45b–46 (5.7.23).

3   Qishan and the *ad hoc* Planning Cadre

After Tao Zhu was sent to work out the recruitment deal with merchant shippers, the arduous follow-up work of crafting and implementing a concrete plan
of action still remained to be done. The performance of these tasks required
skilled and disciplined bureaucratic officials to organize and administer this
innovation in Shanghai. Shanghai local officials would, of course, have been
expected to play an important role in drafting the sea-transport regulations
because of their grasp of local conditions.[18] Yet Qishan was highly critical of
these very officials, who, as a group, he judged, were "lethargic and mediocre
compared to those he had just left in Shandong." He questioned whether they
were up to the job of managing an innovation like sea transport, observing
that they seemed completely incapable of "carrying forward a plan of action
(*wangzhizhenzhe*)."

He immediately sacked the Shanghai county magistrate (Wu Nianzu) for
incompetence, and asked He Changling to appoint a replacement. Qishan
observed, however, that both the new magistrate and the recently appointed
Shanghai Intendant, Pan Gongchang, were mediocre in ability and not terribly
knowledgeable about local Shanghai conditions.[19] And he was in a quandary
about how to proceed because the new sea-transport plan was "experimental
and the planning had to be perfect"—planning that would require officials'
knowledge of local conditions as well as their ability to rally their subordinates
to "push action forward."[20]

What was needed at this crucial juncture, according to Qishan, was the
appointment of one or two reputable high-ranking officials from outside the
Shanghai region who possessed the "boldness and open-mindedness (*gong-
zheng minggan*)" to create an innovative sea-transport plan that would radi-
cally depart from previous grain-transport practice and "where there are no
precedents to follow (*wuchenglikexun*)." Every aspect of the plan, he commented, from the hiring of merchant ships to loading, transporting, and transferring
grain would be new and original (*shuzhuangshi*). "The regulations will have to
be clear and understandable so that local officials can easily implement them."
The outside official planners would, of course, have to take account of local
conditions and patterns of collaboration between bureaucratic, sub-bureaucratic, and extra-bureaucratic personnel in order to create a workable plan,
but their outsider status and dynamism, he hoped, would offset local conflicts

---

18   JSHY 1:32–37 (5.6.22).
19   JSHY 1:39–b (5.6.22).
20   Ibid., 1:39b (5.6.22).

of interests. In short, Qishan wanted creative problem-solvers with effective leadership skills.

At the end of the sixth month, drawing on ideas from Yinghe's second memorial, Qishan asked imperial permission to set up a temporary management bureau in Shanghai. He proposed sending two mid-ranking officials to the port "who are open-minded and bold" and who, in collaboration with local officials, local notables, and private merchant shipping and porterage organizations, would draw up the sea-transport plan and supervise its implementation.[21]

The two officials he proposed for this job had impressed him in Qingjiangpu—the Jiangsu provincial judge, Lin Zexu, together with Zou Xichun, a former Henan Canal intendant. Both had recently been sent to the junction to inspect and verify the adequacy of stonework repairs on Nianyu dike. On the completion of this task, Qishan asked permission to send them to Shanghai to mastermind the sea-transport plan.[22] Due to illness and the death of a parent, Lin did not continue in the project although he may have traveled to Shanghai once.

Thereafter, Zou and three mid-level Jiangsu officials: Susongtai Intendant Pan Gongchang, Susong Grain Intendant Song Huang, and Lin's replacement as judicial commissioner, Qing Shan, constituted the core of the new sea-transport management group. Qishan looked to Zou to provide the leadership energy, or dynamism (*dutong*), while the local officials would provide the Shanghai-Jiangnan local knowledge. All three worked closely with Zou to draw up the regulatory "boundaries" of the plan under He Changling's supervision, with Pan and Song "dwelling temporarily" in Shanghai to direct its implementation on the Shanghai docks in early 1826, assisted by an army of assistant and expectant officials. Collaborating together, they would craft an "excellent plan." Even though he had been skeptical of the abilities of local Shanghai officials, Qishan apparently thought that their "mediocrity" would be offset by the dynamic leadership of Zou. With workable new regulations in place, "local officials will have no difficulty implementing the plan."[23] After the departure of the sand junks in the spring of 1826, Pan, assisted by low-level unranked assistants (*zouza*), would carry the Shanghai records and grain samples overland to Tianjin.[24]

---

21   JSHY 1:39–40 (5.6.22).
22   JSHY 1:40b–41 (5.6.28).
23   JSHY 1:39b (5.6.22).
24   JSHY 4:20b (6.6.5); P 6.6.17 (00121–122).

4   Tao Zhu's Special Mission to Shanghai

While Qishan laid the groundwork for sea transport, Tao Zhu's report on his
successful mission to Shanghai (5.7.23) and an important memorial by the
censor, Xiong Yutai, (5.8.5) launched the planning stage.[25] The former regaled
the emperor's inner circle with the positive attributes of Shanghai's harbor facilities and the highlights of his successful recruitment negotiations with the
Merchant Shipping Guild. The latter proposed concrete measures to facilitate
the collaboration with merchant shippers. In response to these two reports,
the Daoguang Emperor announced in a public edict that planning for sea
transport from the port of Shanghai in 1826 would commence, and that there
would be no further discussion of commutation because of the corruption and
turmoil it would most certainly cause (5.8.9).[26]

Tao traveled personally to Shanghai late in the seventh month to straighten
out misunderstandings with merchant shippers over recruitment that the former Jiangsu Governor's coercive and corrupt treatment had triggered. Because
He Changling had failed to resolve these issues during his earlier trips in the
previous two months, Tao's rank and prestige as Jiangsu Governor gave him
the necessary authority to resolve them and work out a recruitment deal. He
also used the trip to investigate general conditions at the port and the state
of "water communications in the Susong area" along the Huangpu River from
the Jiangnan grain anchorages to the Shanghai docks and the Inner Ocean
(neiyang) ports of Wusong and Shixiao on the easternmost tip of Qiongming
Island, the departure point for sand junks traveling along the northeastern
coast.

While in Shanghai, Tao gathered first-hand reconnaissance about port conditions and navigational challenges encountered along the northeast coast
from a knowledgeable "mariner" in order to reassure Qing officials, who had
little direct experience with maritime administration, stating "that boats can
navigate smoothly from the Jiangnan grain anchorages to Shanghai" and northward by sea to Tianjin.[27] He explained that sand junks normally anchored
outside Shanghai's East Gate near the Merchant Shipping Guild, where the
Huangpu River is "from five to six li (about 3 km) wide." The distance from this
anchorage to Wusong where the Huangpu joins the Yangzi, he calculated, was
over 40 li (about 20 km). He reported that he had seen over 100 large and small
sand junks and had even boarded one of them, reporting that "in all cases, the

---

25   JSHY 1:48–52 (5.8.5).
26   TJ/P 5.8.9 (00087–00088).
27   JSHY 1:44–47 (5.7.23); JSHY 10:1b–2.

mast planks are strong, and the floor of the hold is level and in good repair. The large junks can carry from 1,400 to 1,500 *shi*; the medium ones 800 to 900 *shi*; and the small only 400 to 500 *shi*."

A licensed boat broker, or commission agent, (*chuanhu yahang*) accompanied Tao and explained that "these craft constantly ply the northeastern coastal waters, but when winter arrives, three days after the winter solstice, these vessels gather together in a convoy and return to Shanghai." The broker estimated that approximately 900 large and medium-sized junks would be required to transport 1.5 to 1.6 million *shi*, as well as wastage rice (*zhenghaomi*), in two successive trips to and from Tianjin. The broker stressed that Shanghai merchant shippers were extremely skilled mariners, who were accustomed to sailing around the sand barriers and silt threads (*lijianshaxian*) that extended out from the mouth of the silted Yellow River. They sailed with the seasonal winds and normally took no more that ten days, certainly no more than one month, and their losses never exceeded one or two percent of their cargoes.[28]

Tao went on to explain carefully why the merchant shippers were reluctant to agree to a recruitment deal, saying that "up until the present, they have never transported government tax grain, and their hearts are filled with fear that they will be delayed in Tianjin and fall victim to extortion [on the docks]." To calm their fears, Tao had "issued a public proclamation that summoned boat owners, helmsmen, and sailors to a meeting where I personally explained the recruitment plan, assuring them that they would be paid the customary shipping price (*jiayun*) and rations (*liang*) for their work, and that they would not face 'bitter' experiences on the docks." As soon as they arrived in Tianjin, they would be able "to unload without delay." Referencing the successful case of private Fujianese transport of Taiwan rice to Tianjin the previous year, he assured them that they too would be able to unload and leave Tianjin quickly and be rewarded by the Daoguang Emperor's benevolent bestowal of brevet ranks and titles.

On the practical side, Tao further assured them that if they agreed to take responsibility for grain transport, the "state will draw up a bond, or guarantee, that would be kept on file as evidence of the state's agreement to the merchant's terms and conditions (*qiejiecun'an*)." The agreement would also specify the amount to be paid to shippers for porterage labor and wastage rice, as well as the appointment of civil and military officials to accompany the grain on shipboard, guard the grain, and adjudicate matters related to accidents and loss of grain.

---

28   JSHY 1:45b (5.7.23).

The agreement would stipulate that the sand junk owners would be allowed to load goods for sale in Fengtian, but that they would also be required "to give the Shanghai magistrate and intendant a written undertaking that at the beginning of winter, they will return south to Shanghai without delay or loitering, and even if they returned late, they will still take responsibility for transporting grain." To be on the safe side, the shippers were advised "to go north early and return to Shanghai early." Finally, Tao assured them that "no one would impress their sand junks nor stir up trouble for them." With these assurances, the merchant shippers "all jumped for joy with enthusiasm for the chance to work for the public good," just as Yinghe had earlier predicted. When He Changling presented his final report on recruitment arrangements, Tao and Qishan would review it and jointly send a memorial for imperial comment.[29]

5   Xiong Yutai's Advice on Recruitment

While Tao had reported on conditions in Shanghai, Censor and Former Zhejiang Intendant Xiong Yutai sent an important memorial on Jiangsu regulations twelve days later (5.8.5). It contained six proposals that advised how best to guide the implementation of the recruitment deal. He warned that officials must do two things: first, they must empower private shippers to manage all the navigational tasks during the sea-transport operation and, second, they must eliminate sub-bureaucratic extortion of merchant shippers by streamlining grain transfers to private shippers at the Jiangnan anchorages and at the Shanghai and Tianjin docks. If these arrangements were made, Xiong argued, merchants would feel confident that they would receive full payment according to the terms of the recruitment agreement and that they would be able to depart quickly for Fengtian to trade—a trade that was the heart of their livelihood. His six proposals reveal a grasp of dockside realities at the ports of Shanghai and Tianjin, as well as the Jiangnan anchorages.

First, Xiong was a strong advocate of sea transport because, he argued, even if the arduous and expensive task of dredging silt blockages from the canal were completed, it would not necessarily make the canal navigable. He argued that the more grain that could be shipped by sea the better! The best ships for the project were those sand junks that were built and owned by wealthy households in Tongzhou and Haimen, which generally anchored at Wusong and engaged in the soybean trade. Their construction had apparently soared in recent years to more than 2,500 vessels; the larger junks could transport

---

29   JSHY 1:44–47 (5.7.23). Edict in response: 1:47 (5.8.29).

approximately 2,000 *shi* and the smaller ones about 1,000 *shi*. Collectively, these craft could carry a total of over two million shi in two trips in 1826.

He reported in greater detail than had been done earlier why sand-junk owners had been unwilling to ship tax grain because of the high-handed treatment they had received from the previous Jiangsu Governor, Zhang Shicheng, in the spring. At that time, as noted above, when it was thought that part of the 1825 tax grain might be shipped by sea, Zhang had ordered "the Shanghai intendant to commandeer the whole fleet and hold them in port for two months, during which time, sub-bureaucratic 'runners' (*chayiren*) had extorted money from them." Later, in the fifth month, Zhang again had ordered that these ships remain in port, and the extortion intensified. In both cases, Xiong commented, Zhang had failed to follow the custom of "issuing a public proclamation to inform them about the proposed recruitment." As a result, the merchant shippers were "anxious and fearful, so they left port and scattered to the four winds to hide." This had been the reason why Qishan had indicated earlier that there were too few sand junks available for sea transport.

Xiong was extremely critical of Zhang's treatment of merchant shippers who, in his view, were stalwart propertied households of Tongzhou and Haimen and important members of the Shanghai commercial community. "They have a common trade association (*huiguan*), employed licensed brokers (*yahang*), and have a customs station (*guankou*). They can be recruited easily because they are registered locally and have no other place to go." In other words, these merchant shippers were big-time operators and should not be pushed around. To work out aspects of the recruitment deal, he insisted that Jiangsu officials should "post a public proclamation about the proposed terms and conditions of recruitment, and they should make it known that the runners, who had extorted money from these shippers in early 1825, would be punished." Moreover, to sweeten the deal, he advised that merchant shippers, who "earnestly contribute to the public good," should be allowed to carry some commercial goods duty free and should also be given "an honorary tablet for their guildhall—all of this so that the interests of the government and the merchants would both be served."[30]

Secondly, Xiong emphasized that the best way to eliminate one major source of extortion was to streamline the grain transfers at the Jiangnan anchorages, Shanghai, and Tianjin. In Jiangnan, local officials should hire private lighters to transfer the grain to Shanghai, rather than use government grain fleets. This would eliminate extortion by fleet officers, who imposed expensive fees on local officials at the anchorages. These fees included a fleet fee (*xusuobangfei*),

---

30   JSHY 1:49b–50 (5.8.5).

a loading fee (*zhuangfei*) for every 1,000 *shi* loaded, even though a single boat could only carry 800 to 900 *shi*, and another illegal fee (*lougui*) for carrying grain from the anchorage granary to the boat hatchways (*chucangjincang*).[31]

Xiong fully understood why bannermen extorted these fees! They themselves would fall victim to extortion as they journeyed northward on the canal where countless grain deputies and low-level civil and military officials demanded gifts (*kuisong*) and fees in order to perform such tasks as opening sluices to raise the water level in the canal or opening up the lockgates (*tiliudazhafei*) to enable the boats to pass. The fees extorted from bannermen were "very expensive," but none more so than those imposed by Zhili grain brokers for inspecting and measuring grain and also the boat registration fee (*huahu*) collected from each Zhili lighter when it deposited its grain cargo at Tongzhou.

Xiong described this pattern of systemic extortion, saying: "The bannermen seize from the officials at the local anchorages, and officials turn around and seize from the people. It is the custom. Next year, if the government grain fleets are used to transport grain the short distance to Shanghai, we will again have the old problem of extortion (*jiuxusuo*)." The best way to prevent it, in Xiong's view, was "to order local officials at the anchorages to hire private lighters to manage the loading and delivery of grain to the seaport where grain officials can inspect the color, purity, and dryness of the rice, then order its transfer to waiting sand junks. By excluding government grain boats from the Jiangnan and Shanghai transfers, officials can save money and avoid trouble."[32]

Third, Xiong argued that merchants should be paid a fair price for shipping grain, and that price should include both the cost of porterage labor (*geifachuejia*) for loading and unloading grain and also a fair allocation of wastage rice to cover any grain losses during the voyage. He insisted that they pay merchants the same amount for portering rice as was normally paid for portering commercial goods, and the payments should be based on the number of *shi* portered. His greatest concern was to prevent "clerks, runners, and brokers" from taking a cut at each stage of the trip and to prevent the worst extortion that was perpetrated by Zhili grain brokers, who demanded gifts from fleet bannermen before they would unload and store the grain.

To prevent this unrelenting pattern of extortion, Xiong urged that incorruptible higher-level deputies be designated to make direct payments to shippers, as well as to porterage and lighterage organizations, thus keeping clerks, runners, and brokers out of the payment process. These officials would presumably manage *ad hoc* bureaus to do so. He also advocated the selection of

---

31   JSHY 1:48b (5.8.5).
32   JSHY 1:48–b (5.8.5).

"capable officials" to accompany the grain on board the sand junks to Tianjin. Similar to Yinghe's earlier proposal, Xiong suggested that when the grain junks arrive in Tianjin, there should be two high-level officials dispatched from the capital by the emperor to oversee the inspection of grain, its official receipt by Zhili grain authorities, and its transfer to lighters for the final trip to Tongzhou.

Fourth, Xiong argued forcefully that merchant shippers should be given total control over any and all operational and navigational issues because they, not officials, were the experts on such matters. "Do not hamper or obstruct them! They know how to look out for 'silt threads' (sand banks) and changing wind patterns at sea. For them, these issues are as clear as the palm of the hand. Because of their navigational skills, their losses are less than one percent. The helmsmen and sailors all have guarantors (baozai)." Xiong asserted that these shipping organizations were so reliable and trustworthy that people who did business with them "are never required to sign a shipping contract. Nor do they cheat or quibble."

For example, he explained, "In the winter when the north wind is dangerous, if by chance a ship runs aground and is forced to loosen the hatches and throw cargo overboard, they use commercial precedents to decide liability issues." Moreover, such accidents would be "extremely unlikely in the spring and summer—maybe one chance in a thousand." However, just to be on the safe side, officials "might draw up a voluntary agreement (ganjie), based on the precedents found in the Board of Revenue's Complete Book on Grain Transport related to wind and fire damage." In the case of accidents due to human failure, then restitution must be made "in order to underscore the importance of grain transport."[33]

The interests of merchant shippers were also at the heart of Xiong's fifth point, which sought to streamline the transfer of grain from the sand junks to lighters at Tianjin so that shippers could quickly sail on to Fengtian. Yet even if these transfers were streamlined, another problem might delay lighterage to the capital, and that was a severe shortage of these craft caused by the need to ship huge amounts of tax grain to Tongzhou in 1826. The grain included: (1) sea-transported grain; (2) beans and wheat from Fengtian; (3) canal shipments of 1826 grain; and (4) the 1825 grain that had been stored in Tianjin's Northern Granary the previous year.

He emphasized that lighters must be mobilized well ahead of time in late 1825 and sent to Tianjin "before the canal freezes over." This fleet of lighters should include 2,000 official lighters stationed at Yangcun, located in Zhili on the Northern Canal between Tianjin and Tongzhou, as well as 300 private and

---

33   JSHY 1:50b–51 (5.8.5).

300 government lighters from Shandong province. "They must be repaired and caulked after the 1825 shipping cycle to prevent leakage and water damage to the grain." Send them ahead to Tianjin "to anchor and wait" for the arrival of the sea-transported grain. "If there are too few lighters to transport the grain, then prepare to store approximately 400,000 *shi* in Tianjin's Northern Granary."[34]

The sixth and most deeply troubling issue would be finding employment for laid off grain-boat personnel: bannermen, private sailors, and pole punters. Xiong knew that regular fleet bannermen would be paid according to the regulations in the code for work-reduction years, but the problem was more difficult for hired laborers, who might "stir up trouble if they were not handled carefully." Moreover, the hire of private sailors differed from province to province. In Jiangxi and Huguang, the private sailors were "natives" of these provinces. "Each year when the grain boats are loaded, these sailors leave their homes and work on the boats; when the empty boats return at the end of the season, they return to their native places where they either depend on their families for support or they return to regular jobs." In other words, they still had a means of making a living, and there was no need to provide for them.

But this was not the case for the sailors from the Jiangnan and Zhejiang grain fleets "who were jobless vagrants from Shandong.[35] These people have no families to return to, and as soon as grain transport stops, they make trouble." Xiong recounted events earlier in the year when the canal disaster led to a transport stoppage, and these boat laborers were left with no income. "People in the area feared that these men would loiter around and stir up trouble, so the gentry and rich households raised enough money to give each of them a sum of 3,000 *wen*, and then officials ordered them to return to their native places where records still existed, and the plan worked well."[36] Yet, Xiong feared, there would be many more transport laborers who would be laid off in 1826. Even if they were sent back to their native places, "there will be few jobs for them and their lives will be difficult." These unemployed workers should, he urged—as did Yinghe—be sent to the work sites on the Grand Canal to dredge and repair the canal facilities, where at least they will be given food aid.

Xiong's proposals were extremely important for galvanizing sea-transport planning because he had outlined a practical way to drastically reduce systemic extortion by grain fleet officers during grain transfers at the Jiangnan anchorages and Shanghai by using local lighters. He also made it crystal clear that merchant shippers must be given operational control over coastal

---

34   JSHY 1:51 (5.8.5).
35   Kelley 1986, pp. 176–303.
36   JSHY 1:52–53 (5.8.5).

shipping in order to capitalize on their expertise and shipping resources. The emperor strongly agreed with Xiong's proposals "to eliminate extortion, recruit merchants voluntarily, and give merchant shippers equitable terms," and he forwarded Xiong's proposals to Qishan and Tao Zhu to guide their formulation of guidelines for sea transport. "Do not," he ordered, "under any circumstances, allow clerks and runners to extort money."[37]

Four days later, (5.8.9), the emperor announced publically that sea transport from Shanghai would be used in 1826 and that there would be no further consideration of commutation or canal closure.[38] Once this decision was made, the Jiangsu leadership began in earnest to formulate the regulations.

6   Conclusions

In the midst of the chaos and the investigations at the canal junction in the sixth and seventh months, Qishan played a critical role in laying the groundwork for sea transport by carefully assessing port facilities at Shanghai and by setting up an *ad hoc* bureau there for creating sea-transport regulations and for imposing strict implementation of the plan to eliminate extortion of private lighterage and sand junk shippers. His actions highlight his painstaking and critical investigatory work and his stubborn unwillingness to acquiesce to the three main components of Yinghe's comprehensive plan or his predecessors' dishonest and faulty projections about the functionality and feasibility of the traditional method for crossing grain boats at the canal–Yellow River junction. These were complex and difficult issues because of the precariousness of the water levels in the hydraulic passageways at the junction. He would not commit himself to courses of action unless investigations justified them. Even then, he maintained one could not be absolutely sure!

With Tao Zhu and He Changling's reports on port conditions in Shanghai and on recruitment, especially the former's report in late seventh month, Qishan felt fairly confident that sea transport could be implemented, but only with imaginative dynamic leadership from the outside at the head of a managerial bureau in Shanghai, which, in his view, would galvanize the efforts of "mediocre" local officials: the Shanghai magistrate, intendant, judicial commissioner and their "assistants" and would overcome any conflicts of interests with individuals and organizations in the Shanghai-Suzhou area. But dynamic

---

37   JSHY 1:52b–53 (5.8.5).
38   S 5.8.9 (00087–00088); JSHY 1:54–55 (5.8.9).

leadership had to be paired with a careful assessment of the administrative traditions embedded in the grain-transport code.

Xiong Yutai's forceful proposals (5.8.5) in support of sea transport and his positive assessment of the skills and resources of Shanghai merchant shippers to carry it out reinforced Tao Zhu's report and led to the imperial decision to implement sea transport in 1826 (5.8.9). Qishan then proceeded to hash out the regulations with Tao, He Changling, Yan Lang (Southern Canal Director), and Muzhang'a (Grain Transport Director) until the early ninth month when the proposals were sent to the emperor for comment (5.9.2).

The train of events in the sixth and seventh months, especially Qishan's investigations, made patently clear that high-ranking officials in Liangjiang could not manage sea transport—its planning and implementation—in Shanghai concurrently with their regular duties of office. Concurrency would not provide the density of bureaucratic oversight nor the effort needed to carry out such a major innovation in strategic grain-transport logistics at the county and sub-county level. Hence, the need to stretch the bureaucracy to include an *ad hoc* bureau in Shanghai and the recruitment of extra-bureaucratic sea-transport specialists, the Merchant Shipping Guild. The first would direct the work and disperse funds; the second would do the shipping. Qishan master-minded this "stretching."

CHAPTER 6

Sea-Transport Regulations and Coastal Defense

1   Sea-Transport Regulations

Crafting the sea-transport regulations for the Jiangsu part of the plan took place during the eighth month of 1825 in Shanghai. He Changling and Zou Xichuan had traveled to meet with the Susongtai Intendant, Pan Gongcheng, in Shanghai, where the three of them acted as the core of the emerging managerial bureau, "leading and energizing the Shanghai prefect and magistrate." They organized the hire of large- and medium-sized sand junks whose cargo capacity ranged from "several hundred to two thousand *shi* of grain," and they also enlisted the aid of the Zhejiang governor to mobilize local "egg boats (*danchuan*) and *sanbuxiang*" and convince their owners to pledge to ship grain cargoes from Shanghai the following spring. These craft, they reported, were similar in size and construction to sand junks, and their owners had long experience sailing the northeast coast.[1]

By the time that Qishan sent the memorial containing the Jiangsu regulations early in the ninth month (5.9.2), he reported that 1,000 sand junks had already returned to port. He noted that when they return again "in the winter, the Shanghai intendant and magistrate will formally hire them to transport 1.5 million *shi* of tax grain and wastage rice from the four prefectures of Suzhou, Songjiang, Changzhou, and Zhenzhou, and the independent department of Taicang, as well as some remaining grain from 1823 and 1824," while the Jiangsu tax grain jurisdictions north of the Yangzi River "would be sent, as was customary, via the Grand Canal (Jiangning, Yangzhou, Huai'an, Xuzhou, Tongzhou, and Haizhou).[2]

The six regulations worked out under the direction of Qishan, Tao Zhu, and Muzhang'a, the new Grain Transport Director, centered on those issues most problematic for implementing sea transport in Jiangsu, including lighterage transport from the Jiangnan canal anchorages to Shanghai, close official (not sub-bureaucratic) supervision of grain inspections, sampling, and transfers at these anchorages and the Shanghai docks. They included some recommendations for handling these issues at Tianjin and Tongzhou although

---

1   *danchuan* (蜑船) *sanbusiang* (三不像). JSHY 1:62b (5.9.2) As it turned out, these craft were not used.

2   Qishan's regulations. JSHY 1:62–70b (5.9.2).

these matters were the prerogatives of Zhili authorities, especially the Granary Superintendency.

The regulations also included measures for allocating wastage and salary rice and for determining grain loss liability in ways that benefited merchants, as well as for bestowing honorary ranks and brevet titles for merchant shippers that participated in the sea-transport project. Security concerns shaped measures that provided for marine patrols of the Jiangsu and Shandong coasts, the escort of grain-laden sand junks, and the appointment of two military officials to accompany the fleet. Security concerns also shaped the provisions for paying the Grand Canal grain-fleet personnel, who would be laid off due to canal closure. Except for the last, these were issues for which there were no precedents in the grain-transport code.

The most important regulation (Regulation 3) defined in detail the procedures for the "initial transfer of grain to hired lighters at the Jiangnan anchorages and then to sand junks in Shanghai. At the appointed time for loading the new rice, four intendant and prefect-level officials, aided by their assistants and unranked miscellaneous officials, would travel to the anchorages to carefully scrutinize the transfers." Official supervision was seen as the only way to eliminate extortion by sub-bureaucratic yamen underlings and banner officers from the regular grain fleets, and this provision, it will be recalled, was taken from Censor Xiong Yutai's memorial a month earlier (5.8.5).[3] These supervisory officials would examine the grain to see that it was "whole, clean, and of the correct amount." Under their watchful eyes, the grain would then be bagged in regulation ten-peck bags (huliang), weighed and received for loading onto the lighters bound for Shanghai, but not before these officials took a "one-dou sample of grain from each lighter, which would be placed in a square wooden container (mutong) marked with a seal that identified the place of origin of the grain and the transporting lighter.[4]

At Shanghai, after the grain was checked again and loaded on to sand junks, "assistants" of the intendant and prefect would carry the samples by land to Tianjin and wait for the arrival of the sand junks whereupon they would "petition the court to send a special deputy to the docks to inspect the samples." When the grain was approved and received by this official, "the merchant shippers would no longer bear any responsibility for the grain and could

---

3   JSHY 1:48–52 (5.8.5).

4   Regulation 3. JSHY 1:65–66 (5.9.2). A *dou* is a dry measure of 316 cubic inches, or a peck. A peck is ¼ of a bushel or 8 quarts. E-tu Zen Sun notes that 5 pecks equaled ½ of a *shi/dan*. CAT, 741–745. The amount of grain in a *dou* could vary from 5 to 10 pints (*sheng*). In this case, it must have indicated 6 or fewer pints because the wooden box for depositing rice samples held only 6 pints.

FIGURE 6   Inspection tag attached to grain bags

immediately depart for Guandong." This regulation was expanded in the mid-eleventh month to add higher-level officials to the delegation.

As soon as the grain was officially received in Tianjin, one or two special officials would direct the transfer of grain to waiting lighters for transport to Tongzhou. However, because Qishan, along with other Jiangsu officials, anticipated delays in Tianjin, he asked the Board of Revenue to fix a time limit for these inspections and transfers. A shortage of lighterage craft was the main reason that these officials expected transfer delays in Tianjin, but they were also deeply apprehensive of bureaucratic obstacles, such as extortion, on the docks. To insure the availability of lighters, Qishan requested that the Zhili Governor-General "hire lighters ahead of time and dispatch them to Tianjin's East Gate to wait for the arrival of the sand junks so that the grain transfers could be made quickly."[5]

Later, when the lighters arrived at the Stone Dam at Tongzhou, the northern terminus of the Grand Canal, and unloaded their grain for transfer to the capital granaries, officials from the two grain sub-prefects' office would make a variety of payments to lighterage and porterage organizations, as well as to banner escort troops—payments that were stipulated in the grain-transport code. These sums included payments of silver to each lighter for the boat price (*chuanjia*), rations (*fanmi*), small gifts, mats, wood, and money for tea and fruit for the trip from Tianjin to Tongzhou, as well as payments to grain brokers for performing various accounting services for the lighters. Similarly, the Tianjin intendant was required to pay for porterage food and labor for the transfers from the sand junks to lighters at the Tianjin docks as well as silver and rice for the bannermen escorting the lighters to Tongzhou. The only issue that was not resolved in Qishan's regulations was the cost of sand-junk porterage in Shanghai and Tianjin, which he suggested should be decided by officials at the granary yamen in Tianjin.

Much less wastage and salary rice was required for sea transport than for canal transport because it was much quicker and involved vastly fewer transfer costs than canal transport. Merchant shippers would be allocated only 120,000 *shi* for wastage—60,000 *shi* less than the 180,000 *shi* normally allocated for canal transport on the regular grain fleets. One *dou* (10 *sheng*, or 1 peck) would be allocated for each *shi* of white rice and 8 *sheng* for each *shi* of unhusked rice (regulation 1).[6]

Liability for grain loss, personal injury, and loss of life drew on both commercial practice and the grain-transport code with the facts of each case determined after each sand junk's arrival in Tianjin. From the merchant's point of view, if a ship encountered storms and the goods in the hold were loosened and damaged, the merchant would only be liable to pay compensation if the ship's mast was *not* broken. If the mast was broken, it would be considered an accident, and no compensation was due. In the case of grain loss due to mold, if the mast was not broken, the merchant shipper was required to pay compensation. If the mast was broken and there was loss of life or injury, the merchant was required to follow "the precedents in the grain-transport code for wrecked grain boats." In such cases, the merchant could avoid liability for grain loss, but was required to pay "sympathy compensation to the relatives of the injured or deceased." If there was not enough wastage rice to do so, then merchants were required to buy rice to make up the deficiency.[7]

---

6   Regulation 1. JSHY 1:64–b (5.9.2).
7   Regulation 2. JSHY 1:64b (5.9.2).

Maritime defense practices (Regulation 4) along the northeast coast were adjusted and adapted to protect and escort the sand junk fleets. The Governor-General of Liangjiang and the Governor of Shandong were ordered to inspect their respective coastal defenses prior to the departure of sand junks from Shanghai and to establish signal lights by night and flag signals by day to mark rocky coastal shoals. Immediately prior to the fleet's departure from Shanghai, Qishan would request the emperor to authorize the dispatch of the two military officers to travel with the sand junk fleet to guard the grain. Additionally, each coastal battalion would keep a watchful eye on the landward coastline and send patrol boats to escort and protect the sand junks in their respective jurisdictions.[8]

The regulations also specified the rewards and incentives that would be given to merchant shippers for participating in sea transport. This was particularly important after the trouble over recruitment caused by Zhang Shicheng's abusive treatment of shippers in early 1825. The bestowal of honorary brevet ranks (*jiangxu*), was based on the amount of grain transported by each shipper from Shanghai to Tianjin. Those who shipped less than 10,000 *shi*, would be rewarded with a votive inscription written on horizontal boards (*geibian'e*) by an intendant holding the brevet rank of provincial judge, or judicial commissioner (3a).[9] Officials of this brevet rank in Jiangsu were the intendants of Huai'an and Yangzhou prefectures and the Haizhou independent department, all of which jurisdictions were located north of the Yangzi River. Those who carried from 10,000 to 50,000 *shi* would be rewarded with honorary rank (*geiyuxian*). However, if any one of these individuals had already purchased the fifth-grade official title (*wupin*), he would be given another kind of reward. "After the unloading is completed and the Susong officials have completed their inspections, Jiangsu officials will make recommendations to the emperor for final determination of the rewards for merchant shippers." As an added incentive, merchants were also allowed to use 20 percent of a ship's cargo space to carry tax-free commercial goods destined for Tianjin, although their return load of beans from Fengtian would be subject to customs taxes in Shanghai.[10]

The sixth and final regulation provided extra hardship pay for grain fleet crews from Susongchangzhentai jurisdictions. The question of hardship pay and aid for laid-off grain-fleet crews had emerged early in the second month as a dangerous issue for the Qing leadership because they feared acts of collective violence if these crews were dismissed without pay. Moreover, once

---

8   JSHY 1:66 (5.9.2).
9   JSHY 1:66b (5.9.2). See BH 830; 838.
10   JSHY 1:66b (5.9.2).

relay shipping was organized, officials began to impress grain fleets that had made it through the junction earlier in the year to make extra trips back and forth from the junction to Tongzhou in 1825, and many more such trips were planned for 1826.

The Jiangnan fleets noted above had been the first to cross the Yellow River and deliver grain to Tongzhou in the spring of 1825. As junction conditions worsened, they were ordered to stay and wait in the north, then travel later in 1825 to pick up and transport the grain loads of the Jiangguang fleets (Jiangxi, Hunan, and Hubei) from the junction. These same fleets were again ordered to transport Zhejiang grain in 1826. Although the grain-transport code authorized extra pay to cover porterage food and labor for this extra work, officials recognized that the allowance was a paltry sum. To make matters worse in 1826, the new grain from these Jiangnan districts would be sent by sea so that fleet personnel would not receive their regular income, yet they would still be required to pay for repairs to their boats in the fall and winter of 1825–1826. To offset these heavy financial burdens, the sea-transport regulations authorized a higher rate of payment "for periods of work reduction," but not so for the Jiangbei fleets workers, "who had not done extra work."[11]

At the end of the proposed regulations, Qishan noted the inclusion of Censor Xiong Yutai's six suggestions for eliminating extortion of merchant shippers and private lighters at the anchorages, which included intendant-prefectural oversight of inspections and grain sampling, direct payment of merchant shippers in Shanghai, and oversight of grain transfers by special Zhili officials in Tianjin. Moreover, the merchant shippers were given complete navigational control over the sand junks during the journey to Tianjin, "just as grain fleet officials controlled canal transport," and the two senior military officials on the sand junk fleet were "to ensure that low-level military officers and soldiers from the coastal battalions did not interfere in navigational decisions."

Qishan ended the memorial by stating that he, Tao Zhu, and Muzhang'a had jointly discussed and agreed on all six regulations, as well as those issues raised by Xiong Yutai (5.8.5). The only issue they had left unresolved was how to pay for sand junk porterage in Shanghai, which, of course, was also not spelled out in the grain-transport code. They wanted to avoid having the state pay for it so they referred the matter to the two Liangjiang treasurers to find another source.

Interestingly, Qishan referred to the sea-transport regulations as "a general plan" (*daju*), not a detailed set of regulations.[12] He explained that he fully

---

11   JSHY 1:67–b (5.9.2).
12   JSHY 1:68 (5.9.2).

expected other issues to arise during the course of implementation, but he did not want to define regulations too specifically because to do so would force them to "follow the plan too closely" and would not give them the discretionary authority to deal quickly with unforeseen issues as they arose. This would, of course, also avoid referring each and every issue to the emperor for a decision, which could cause delays and inhibit their ability to act quickly to address problems.

The emperor's public edict (5.9.8) wholeheartedly endorsed Qishan's regulations, emphasizing the importance of having intendants and prefects check the grain loaded on each lighter, "one by one," at the Jiangnan anchorages and "of taking, labeling, and carrying grain samples to Shanghai and then Tianjin." Although the provisions for handling grain in Tianjin were less specific than those for Jiangnan and Shanghai, he did agree that a high-level deputy from the capital should receive the grain in Tianjin and that one or two additional special commissioners would be sent from the capital to supervise the grain transfers from sand junks to Zhili lighters for final transport to Tongzhou. Additionally, he urged that marine brigade commanders (*tizhen*) in Jiangsu, Shandong, and Zhili each send as many patrol boats and low-level military officers and soldiers as possible to "patrol, defend, and accompany the sand junks," while the two higher-level military officials would travel with and watch the merchants as they sailed to Tianjin."[13] However, the emperor seemed to balk at the idea of giving discretionary authority to Qishan, saying that plans should anticipate unforeseen problems so that there would be no need for such authority!

In conclusion, the regulations formulated by Qishan and high-level provincial officials in Jiangsu, not surprisingly, center on those issues of greatest concern to Jiangsu—issues that reinforced the recruitment bond with Shanghai merchant officials, maximized the direct managerial role of intendant and prefects (and their assistants) to eliminate extortion, protected Jiangnan grain *en route* to Tianjin, and that attempted to protect the interests of Jiangsu officials and merchant shippers in Tianjin when Zhili authorities officially received the grain. They could not, however, dictate the procedures for Tianjin although they tried to do so to a limited extent.

Further regulations for Jiangsu continued to be made in the autumn as problems unfolded. Most important among these were regulations suggested by Qishan in the middle of the eleventh month to amend the arrangements for lighterage shipment from the Jiangnan anchorages, for inspecting, loading, and escorting the sand junks to Tianjin, and for improving the hand-off of

---

13   JSHY 1:70b–72b (5.8.9); P 00075–77 (5.8.9). SL 1583–1584.

Jiangsu grain to Zhili grain authorities in Tianjin, as well as assigning responsibility for the costs of porterage, brokerage, and lighterage in Zhili.[14]

Qishan reviewed the status of grain collection as of 5.11.17, noting that collection had begun, according to regulations, in the eleventh month; the merchant boats were returning, one-by-one, to Shanghai; and, in the second and third months of 1826, sea shipments would begin. To clarify and amend the earlier Jiangsu regulations, five changes were made. First, grain-tax inspections were made the sole responsibility of the Jiangnan Grain Intendant, Song Huang, not the Susongtai Intendant, Pan Gongchang, and Qishan, therefore, ordered that Song, accompanied by Pan, inspect the grain, take the grain samples at the anchorages, and then oversee its transfer to the sand junks in Shanghai. As soon as the sand junks had all departed from Shanghai, Song and Pan were to send word to the special commissioner at the capital to proceed to Tianjin to inspect the sea-transported grain.

Because officials were fearful of ocean travel, it was decided that the grain intendant would not accompany the boats to Tianjin. Instead, a cadre of special "high officials," led by Zou Xichun, who headed the special bureau in charge of writing the regulations, was selected to travel by land to Tianjin with the samples and related documents. The cadre included two *daofu*-level officials (Qing Yu and Li Xiangji), the Taizhou Department Magistrate (Wang Youqing), and the Assistant Sub-prefect for managing grain in Suzhou prefecture (*guanliangtongpan*), Qing Ping. They were appointed "to serve as sub-managers (*bangban*) in charge of transferring grain [to lighters] in Tianjin." Each of these officials was allowed "to take along one low-level assistant."[15] This regulatory change gave more political clout to the Jiangsu delegation.

As soon as this group of officials arrived in Tianjin, they were to notify the Grand Council to send a special commissioner to supervise the inspection of the sea-transported grain and to compare the grain samples to it. Once this task was completed and the grain was turned over to waiting lighters, the Jiangsu officials were to return home and report on their work. They were specifically ordered *not* to accompany the grain to Tongzhou—a departure from grain-transport practice on the Grand Canal but similar to the treatment of Fujian merchants transporting Taiwanese grain to Tianjin in 1824.

Noting imperial approval of a special commissioner to oversee the inspection of grain in Tianjin, Jiangsu officials also urged that a granary vice president order the granary sub-prefect at Tongzhou to appoint and dispatch honest grain brokers and yamen functionaries (*jingjiliyi*) "to check the purity of the

---

14   JSHY 2:13–16b (5.11.17).
15   JSHY 2:14 (5.11.17).

grain, manage its transfer to lighters in Tianjin," and then escort the grain in the ligherage fleets to Tongzhou, just as the grain intendants normally did along the canal. However, they stipulated specifically that the grain need not be subjected again to an inspection in Tongzhou. In other words, once the imperial commissioner in Tianjin officially received the grain, the merchant shippers were no longer liable for grain damage or loss."[16]

Jiangsu officials also suggested a slight increase in wastage and ration rice for both merchant shippers and Zhili lighters, but they requested that this issue be decided by the Zhili Governor-General and a granary vice president, according to Zhili grain practices and precedents. These two officials were also to manage the payments for additional unforeseen expenses and miscellaneous payments to grain brokers sent to Tianjin and also for porterage labor. Jiangsu agreed to cover these costs at a rate of 4 *fen* of silver for each *shi* of grain, part of which would be taken from the 60,000 *shi* saved by sending the Jiangnan grain by sea and from other allocations generally paid to the bannermen on the Jiangnan grain fleets. Jiangsu would forward these monies to the Tianjin granary treasury to cover additional wastage and rations, which would, in turn, be advanced to the Tianjin intendant's treasury to help cover the cost of hiring Zhili lighters.[17]

These adjustments to the original Jiangsu regulations also clarified how the sand junk fleets would be policed and disciplined. As noted above, the original Jiangsu regulations had stipulated that two high-ranking military officials would be sent with the sand junk fleet to police the fleets and assist in any judicial inquiries that might arise over grain loss. The second memorial, however, stipulated specifically that a lieutenant colonel (*canjiang*) from the Chuansha battalion, Guan Tianpei, would travel on the first ship in the fleet; and a regimental colonel (*fujiang*) from the territorial regiment at Jingkou, Tang Panlong, would travel on the last ship, both of whom could be accompanied by several aides. At the same time, the sole responsibility for patrolling and policing the coast was vested in coastal marine units.[18] The added regulations, according to Qishan, clarified which officials bore responsibility for specific tasks and would prevent them from "making excuses and shirking responsibility."[19]

These amendments to the Jiangsu regulations reflect the input from Yinghe in the first Board of Revenue memorial (5.9.11) and Zhili Governor-General

---

16   JSHY 2:14–14b (5.11.17).
17   JSHY 2:15–16 (5.11.17).
18   JSHY 2:16b (5.11.17). The details about the Jiangsu and Shandong coastal defenses are contained in JSHY 1:58–61 (5.9.2) and JSHY 2:6–11b (5.10.28).
19   JSHY 2:15 (5.11.17).

Nayancheng's critical response to the Jiangsu recommendations sent two months later. Changes and adjustments continued to be made until the end of the twelfth month (5.12.27) when the fourth Board of Revenue memorial clarified the remaining outstanding issues about Zhili's handling of sea-transported grain.

2   Coastal Defense

Not surprisingly, the decision to use sea transport in 1826 had turned the Qing leadership's attention to the northeast coast and marine defenses along the Jiangsu and Shandong coastal perimeter. It had also led Censor Xiong Yutai to make a stinging criticism of these defenses three days after Tao Zhu's report on Shanghai, charging that weaknesses in defenses along the Shandong and Jiangsu coasts could jeopardize the safety of the sea-transport fleets in 1826 (5.7.26). He claimed that the marine units (*yingxun*) stationed along the coast were understaffed and that mandated repairs of equipment, coastal forts, and war junks had been neglected. The fault lay, he asserted, with low-ranking military officials (*yingbian*), who embezzled funds earmarked for the "major" and "minor" repairs of war ships,[20] They often allowed shoddy work and the use of inferior materials for these repairs. Finally, they made false reports about the actual number of ships built and the cost of repairs. Even though every coastal guard station was, in principle, required by statute to maintain a fixed number of soldiers and an adequate supply of equipment, the reality was really quite different. Officials and soldiers at these locations existed "in name only, and, as a consequence, no criminals were ever arrested."[21]

This state of affairs, Xiong argued, would spell danger for grain-bearing sand junks when they sailed among the many small islands from Wusong harbor to Chengshan Cape and Dengzhou on the Shandong coast. (Map 7) Although he noted that *current* conditions were generally stable along the coast of Shandong and northern Jiangsu, the same was not true of the Jiangnan coast where "mountainous sand" islands, such as Jinshan (盡山), Dayang (大洋), Xiaoyang (小洋), Maji (馬跡), and Hua'niao (花鳥), extended from the Lower Yangzi River near the Grand-Canal entrance to the Jiangsu-Zhejiang border. The tangle of small streams on these islands formed pathways into dense interiors that served as hideouts for bandits. He charged that the marine units

---

20   Qing warships and patrol boats were required to undergo minor repairs every three years; major repairs every six years; and total reconstruction every nine years.

21   TJ (5.7.26); SL 1553–1554.

stationed around Chuansha sub-prefecture (*ting*) and Wusong had achieved little success suppressing them because the guard stations were understaffed and poorly equipped.

Xiong strongly urged that the governors of both Liangjiang and Shandong order their respective naval commanders to inspect, repair, and rebuild all their warships and patrol boats and that brigade and battalion officials (*zhen-canyou*) prepare their troops to deal with coastal problems that might arise during the implementation of sea transport, such as preventing sand-junk boatmen from giving false reports about grain losses at sea. These warnings prompted the emperor to order Qishan and Wulong'a, Governor of Shandong, to investigate and strengthen coastal defenses and reorganize the regular seasonal pattern of naval patrols to assure the surveillance and protection of the sand-junk fleet the following spring.[22]

Qishan completed his investigation of Jiangsu coastal and riverine defenses early in the ninth month (5.9.2). At this stage of planning, it wasn't clear if military escort boats would accompany the sand junks to Tianjin or if military officials would actually travel on the sand junks. He carefully explained that the Jiangsu coast was policed by two principal marine brigades (*zhen*). The Susong brigade, comprised of four battalions (Wusong, Chuansha, Nanhui, and Ji), patrolled the south bank of the Yangzi delta from the port of Wusong to the Zhejiang border.[23] The Langyou 狼右 and Juegang 掘港 battalions of the Langshan 狼山 brigade patrolled the north bank of the Yangzi from Tongzhou to Rudong county on the coast north of Lüsi, the northernmost of Shanghai's customs stations. These two brigades joined forces to patrol the various sand bars and islands that lay scattered along the coast and delta, as far north as the Dasha sandbank, eastward from Qiongming Island to Sheshan Island, and south to the islands that lay off the Jiangnan coast (Tayang, Shaoyang, and Majisha), noted above.[24]

The Jiangsu marines used a variety of craft to patrol the coast and inland riverine waters, including warships, patrol boats (*shaochuan*), sampans (*shanban*), and "tiger" boats (*xiaochuan*). The pattern of yearly patrols had been fixed in Qianlong 46 (1781) and stipulated that inspection patrols be sent "to the Inner and Outer Seas" four times a year at the beginning of each season. The Board of War required that these craft be repaired on a fixed schedule every three, six, and nine years; in the last case, they were completely dismantled

---

22   JSHY 1:58–61 (5.9.2); JSHY 2:6–11b (5.10.28).

23   The Susong brigade used 94 warships and patrol boats, led by 11 officers and manned by 288 marines. Ibid.

24   *ZGLSDTJ*, Maps 16–17.

and rebuilt, at which time each marine unit reported to the Board of War on the completion of the work and the cost.

Generally, the funds for boat repairs were raised by the Salt and Susong intendants, as well as local officials, and they were normally paid directly to the shipbuilders so that low-level military officers did not have the chance to steal these funds. Qishan observed that these officers often did not work effectively and certainly were "not free of corruption," citing a recent example in 1824 when the Board of War refused to appropriate money for major repairs because of poor quality workmanship. As a result, the repairs had been stopped in May of 1825 and had not been resumed since.[25] Because of this, Qishan was reluctant to assert that there were currently enough ships to maintain the patrols in 1826, so he appropriated funds to complete the repair work. In general, he was fairly confident that if the brigade and battalion officers "do a good job leading the marines, they will be able to eliminate piracy and make conditions safe, and it would not be necessary to alter or expand the patrol regulations in 1826."[26]

Qishan's confidence in Jiangsu coastal defenses probably reflected his earlier investigation and improvement of the Jiangsu military when he had first arrived at Qingjiangpu, just as he had when appointed to the Shandong governorship.[27] He did not foresee any major problems if he kept a close eye on the marine commanders, checked up on their preparations for 1826, and impeached those who were slacking. He vowed that he would keep a particularly watchful eye on security preparations around Wusong harbor—the exit point for the grain junks leaving for Tianjin—that he regarded as "the most strategically important place."[28]

Over a month after Qishan had reported on Jiangsu's coastal defenses, Wulong'a, the newly appointed Governor of Shandong, reported on that province's naval resources, including its three main naval bases and coastal guard posts, carefully explaining the normative seasonal pattern of coastal patrolling as well as the changes he thought were necessary to protect the grain-bearing sand junks in 1826.[29] He traced the great distances that each of the three Shandong Naval Commands were required to patrol: (1) the 1,680 *li* (810 km) of the Southern Command (*nanxun*) from Yingyoumen on the Jiangsu-Shandong border to Matouzui; (2) the 390 *li* (190 km) of the Eastern command

25   JSHY 1:58b (5.9.2).
26   JSHY 1:60 (5.9.2).
27   Wei Xiumei 1994, pp. 135–160.
28   JSHY 1:60 (5.9.2).
29   JSHY 2:6b (5.10.28). See *ZGLSDTJ*, map 22–23.

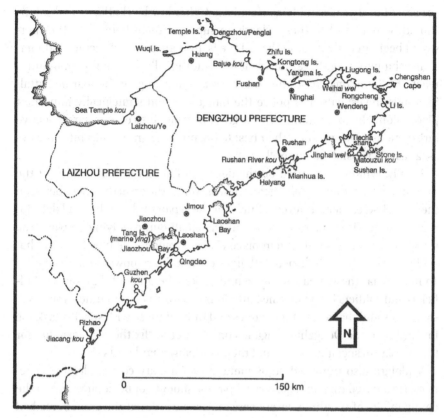

MAP 7   Shandong province

(*dongxun*) from Matouzui to Chengshan Cape); and (3) the 1,770 *li* (850 km) Northern Command (*beixun*) from the Cape to Xiaoshi Island in Ye County. He observed that navigation along the Southern Command was difficult because "there are no mountains or islands to serve as directional markers" until one approaches Laoshan Island 嶗山 in Mou county and Beichashan Island 北差山 in Wendeng county. Along this stretch, "if there is no wind, the boats must temporarily collect together and anchor" at Jiacankou 夾倉口 in Rizhao county or Guzhengkou 古鎮口 in Jiaozhou Bay, but further east, there were many more anchorage ports, such as Tang Island 唐島 in Jiaozhou Bay and Qingdao 青島 in Mou county, Mianhua Island in Haiyang county, and Rushankou 乳山口.

   In contrast, while there were numerous islands along the coast of the Eastern and Northern Commands (approximately 105) where it was easy to anchor, including Sushan Island 蘇山, Jinghai *wei* 靖海衛, Longkou 龍口, and Yayangyuchi 壓養魚池. "Twenty-five of the most strategically important of these islands are inhabited by lone transients and bandits," who were easily concealed in these island lairs. He advised "that low-level officers and troops should be deployed to these islands to suppress them before sea transport would begin in early 1826, so that all the islands are safe and secure, and merchant shippers need have no worries."[30] Additionally, before the grain junks reach the Shandong coast, the officers (*youji*) in charge of the marine battalions must investigate and police the dangerous and strategically important places along the route, and when the grain-bearing ships enter their respective jurisdictions, "they must try their best to organize the grain junks into convoys as far as it is possible to do so."[31]

Finally, Wulong'a reported on the deterioration and lack of staffing at the forts and beacon mounds along the coast as well as the great distances between them. He had earlier authorized funds for the repair of those that had deteriorated, but he also undertook to repair the small outposts lying between the forts and beacons, as well as to replace vital equipment, "item by item," so that soldiers would have the wherewithal to "exert military power and prestige."[32] To insure that these measures were undertaken, he ordered that low-level officials and soldiers in the marine battalions be apprised of their new escort assignments and that a list of the names and titles of those with specific tasks be forwarded to the Dengzhou brigade commander to "fix the responsibility for these tasks on specific officers and their company guard posts."[33]

Wulong'a also proposed adjustments to customary coastal defense practices. He advised that, in 1826, coastal patrols should not be deployed until the commanders of the three naval bases received word that the grain boats had left Shanghai. In other words, "there is no need to adhere to the customary calendar for departing from and returning to base."[34] Additionally, he advised that warships and patrol boats should "adopt the practice of sweeping back and forth, like shuttlecocks," in their respective jurisdictions and that their officers should attempt to escort the sand junks in convoy even though sailing conditions made it difficult to do so. In order to reinforce the coastal bases that he felt were understaffed, he proposed that soldiers from nearby land battalions (*lulugeying*) be dispatched to these bases, which would then free up "officers and ten or more soldiers from these bases to dwell temporarily and secretly on the islands to police them."[35] Finally, he urged that new coastal forts and beacon mounds be built to strengthen the perimeter of coastal bases

30   JSHY 2:7b–8 (5.10.25).
31   JSHY 2:8–8b (5.10.28).
32   JSHY 2:8b (5.10.28).
33   JSHY 2:9b–10 (5.10.28).
34   JSHY 2:9–9b (5.10.28).
35   JSHY 2:10b (5.10.28).

and that "soldiers from inland Wuding and Andong battalions near the Grand Canal in Yan*zhou*, be reassigned to these facilities.[36]

Wulong'a's memorial report on Shandong coastal defenses shows that he not only had already addressed many of the security issues raised in Censor Xiong Yutai's critique, but that he was prepared to carry out further adaptive changes that would intensify the province's ability to protect the grain fleets as they sailed by the many islands that dotted Shandong's eastern and northern coastal waters. Both he and Qishan made very matter-of-fact and practical assessments of and adjustments to coastal defenses in preparation for sea transport.[37] And from the vantage point of these Banner-elite officials, the state of these defenses in their respective provinces did not seem to be as problematic as Censor Xiong had warned.

3   Redrawing the Northeast Coastal Map

In marked contrast to these two reports, Tao Zhu painted the northeast coast in broad brush strokes to highlight the Chinese state's earlier historical experience with sea transport and, importantly, the dynamic role that Chinese mariners and traders had played in opening up this route in the Qing period and who could, as a consequence, play a vital role in the sea-transport project. Tao's assessment is extremely important because it linked the southern and northern parts of the coast into a single coastal highway. Because it emphasized the collaboration of the Qing state and commercial organizations in sea transport, it, in effect, showed the extended pattern of joint state-private management of the coastal ports of the four southeastern coastal provinces to those of the northeast coast.

Tao Zhu, it will be remembered, had begun his observations about the sea route during his important visit to Shanghai in the late seventh month (5.7.23) when he questioned "experienced mariners" about the nature of the route and the sturdiness of the sand junks that plied the northeast coastal waters. He then compared their accounts to those in the written administrative records of sea transport in earlier dynasties, in order "to find a good and direct route" to Tianjin. In the second month of 1826, he sent a memorial report (6.2.3) that included an introductory essay on the navigational challenges of the sea route, including route maps with explanatory notes, and an account of the navigational techniques that merchant shippers had developed over the years to

---

36   JSHY 2:11–11b (5.10.28).
37   JSHY 1:58–61 (5.9.2); 2:6–11b (5.10.28).

exploit the Shanghai-Fengtian soybean trade. This account appeared in the final *juan* of the newly compiled *Complete Record on Sea Transport*, published in 1826, shortly after the successful completion of sea transport.[38]

Tao Zhu's account of the route centered on the broad geographic sweep of the northeast coast and its hazards, and it has the feel of an eye-witness travel narrative, designed to enable readers to visualize the features of the coast, its dangerous reefs and sandbars, and the ocean expanses that separated coastal towns and guard posts that lined the coast. His assessment references two historical narratives to justify sea transport. The first placed the 1826 sea-transport venture into the context of the long history of government involvement in sea transport that dated back to antiquity, "when the *Yugong* recorded that the state had shipped tax revenues along the sea coast from Yangzhou to the Huai River estuary." Indeed, he noted, "the early empires of Qin and Han had used sea transport, although the exact routes they used are not clear from the historical record." But it was the Yuan and Ming use of sea transport that Tao looked to for the Qing model, especially the Yuan case, which had used sea transport for the longest period of time and had developed what he regarded as the best sea route, in contrast to the Ming, whose vessels had timidly hugged the coast, skirting the off-shore islands, and detoured around sandbars and shoals. The only difference he saw between the Yuan and Qing cases was that the latter used Wusong as the port of departure in the Yangzi estuary, rather than the Yuan port of Liuhe, which had since "silted up."[39]

The second and, from Tao's point of view, most important narrative that bore on the Qing case, was the history of the pioneering innovations of Chinese mariners and shippers who had developed the shipbuilding and navigational technology to master the challenges of coastal sailing, and, as a result, had developed the requisite skills and know-how to transport grain successfully by sea. It was a truism, Tao averred, that merchant shippers generally will exploit the opportunities for trade when they have the skill and technology to do so, "just as the tides wax and wane." The Kangxi Emperor had unleashed that innovative spirit by lifting the prohibitions of maritime trade in the early 1680s, after which sand junks began to sail the northeast coast from Shanghai to Tianjin and the ports of "Guandong, catching the southeast winds in the spring and summer when the sailing was particularly smooth."[40] By the 1820s,

---

38   JSHY 12:1–5b. This *juan* also includes detailed diagrams of sand junks, sample documents accompanying the grain cargoes, and lists of data on patterns of tides and winds affecting navigation on the northeast coast.

39   JSHY 12:1–1b.

40   JSHY 12:1, 5b.

Chinese merchant shippers were seasoned travelers who regarded sailing the northeast route as a commonplace.[41]

Tao underscored the navigational know-how and techniques of Chinese mariners. "Even though the ocean is vast and is without banks and boundaries," private seamen had mastered the northeast coastal route by using a variety of techniques, such as knotted ropes, weighted with lead sinkers, in order to calculate the water depth; they carefully observed the winds and tides; they noted the smells and changing color of the sea; and finally, they used the "compass to fine-tune" their course, especially when sailing far out to sea beyond sight of land. While he acknowledged that calculating distances at sea still remained extremely difficult, mariners had figured out these distances by extrapolating from the landward distances between county cities and guard stations on the coast that "faced the sea."[42] All these varied methods, in Tao's view, showed the resourcefulness of private mariners and merchant shippers.

Therefore, when silt blocked Grand Canal transport, it seemed obvious and prudent to Tao that the dynasty should turn to these mariners and merchant shippers to transport grain by sea even though sea transport represented a dramatic change in Qing grain-transport practice. Tao explicitly minimized these changes, asserting that "both sea and canal transport were merely two sides of the same coin." When canal shipping ground to a halt in 1825, the state responded, as it routinely did when faced with temporary administrative crises, by "establishing a bureau (ju) to manage it and sending [private] boats to sea."[43]

4 The Route

Tao Zhu, like most Qing officials in the early nineteenth century, viewed the northeast coast as one part of a bifurcated coastal periphery, divided from the southeast coast at Shanghai. Understandably, he saw it mainly in strategic geopolitical terms, not in commercial terms, reflecting the Qing emphasis on guarding the seaward approaches to the capital region. He conceptualized the route in three main parts that reflected the jurisdictional boundaries of the coastal *zhou* and *xian* and guard stations in each of the three provinces that lay between Shanghai and Tianjin.

---

41   JSHY 12:1b.
42   JSHY 12:1b–2.
43   JSHY 12:1.

The Jiangsu sector extended from Wusong in the Yangzi estuary to Yingyoumen in Haizhou Bay on the Jiangsu-Shandong border, but it also included a security zone that extended southward to the Zhejiang border and the island of Chenqian that marked the seaward approach to the Zhejiang port of Zhapu.[44] Tao's treatment of the northern Jiangsu coast stressed navigational challenges from the port of Wusong in the Yangzi estuary to Shixiao on the eastern tip of Chongming Island (Map 6) where "sand junks wait for favorable winds to carry them eastward out to sea" toward the uninhabited Sheshan Island where they then turn northward, carefully skirting dangerous reefs near the island.

As they sailed northward, Tao explained, sailors kept their eyes peeled for hidden sandbanks created by the silt discharge from the Yellow River and the labyrinth of rivers and canals that crossed the Xiahe region between the Grand Canal and the sea in northern Jiangsu and emptied into the sea. The largest were those that fanned out to the southeast from the mouth of the Yellow River to form a web of five large (and many more small) sandbanks. Finally, as ships approached the Jiangsu-Shandong border, they had to sail around the submerged and continually shifting Sandhead Mountain sandbar, lying east and north of Yunti Guan. This sand bar, Tao explained, was a dangerous moving obstacle formed by the silt that was carried by the convergence of different ocean tides. Pilots had to maneuver their ships with great care to avoid "easterly winds that might blow them back towards it."[45]

Strategic, navigational, and geographic conditions changed dramatically as ships sailed into Shandong coastal waters. From Rizhao county on the Jiangsu border, eastward along the south side of the peninsula to Iron Raft Mountain (Tiechashan 鐵槎山) and Horsehead Mouth (馬頭嘴) in Wendeng county (Map 7), coastal waters became deeper and greenish in hue. While this stretch of coast had fewer navigational obstacles, according to Tao, it was more difficult to navigate because there were fewer off-shore islands to serve as directional markers. Mariners had to rely heavily on the compass, depth measurements, and observations of the coastline; and, when faced with difficulties, found temporary anchorages at the commercial ports in Jiaozhou Bay. At the eastern end of the peninsula near Stone Island, off the coast of Rongcheng county, off-shore islands reappeared and served as markers to Chengshan Cape and then westward to Temple Island slightly west of Dengzhou/Penglai city on the

---

44   JSHY 12:1b–5b; CYQS 91:1–2; *ZGLSDTJ*, vol. 8, maps 22–23.

45   JSHY 12:3b.

FIGURE 7   Sand junks approaching Dagu Forts

north side of the peninsula. East of Temple Island lay treacherous reefs and the dangerous Long Mountain Peak sandbar.[46]

The third and final sector of the northeast coast extended from Sea Temple Island, the port of the Ye county capital, to the mouth of the Hai River on the Zhili coast—a route that lay well clear of the "yellow" muddy waters of the wide and shallow Zhili coastal shelf. Anchoring within sight of the Dagu Forts, ships waited for "a high tide before ascending the Hai River with the aid of trackers" for a distance of 215 *li* (103 km) to Tianjin, anchoring at the docks outside Tianjin's East Gate.[47] In contrast to Qishan and Wulong'a treatment of the northeast coast, Tao Zhu's narrative and maps incorporate historical and strategic images and catalog what he viewed as the most dangerous navigational challenges to sea transport, so that Qing officials would better understand the nature of the northeast coast and make concrete practical adjustments to existing coastal defenses to protect grain shipments. These adjustments became institutionalized when the grain-transport code was revised in 1845.[48]

---

46   JSHY 12:2b–4b.

47   JSHY 12:5–5b.

48   CYQS, *juan* 90–91.

5   Conclusions

The sea-transport experiment sparked an important review of coastal defenses and the northeast coast by Qishan, Wulong'a, and Tao Zhu—all of whom were intimately involved in the implementation of sea transport. Tao's treatment, however, was more broadly concerned with historical and strategic issues that linked sea transport to the long sweep of Chinese history and, significantly, to Qing maritime traditions developed by Chinese coastal and overseas traders in the four southeastern coastal provinces and characterized by state-merchant collaboration. His reports on the geography and navigational features of the northeast coast, not only informed the debates on sea transport, but broadened the Qing leadership's understanding of the whole coastline from the southeastern provinces to Manchuria, creating an image of a single coastal highway that had been used by merchant shippers since the Kangxi reign.

CHAPTER 7

Nayancheng and Regulations for Zhili

The final chapter of the sea-transport plan was written by Yinghe and Nayancheng, the Governor-General of Zhili, and, to a lesser extent, by Granary Vice President Bai Chun. These officials devised procedures for handling sea-transported grain in Zhili in 1826 that merged seamlessly with this province's long-established patterns of grain management. Zhili, the capital province, received huge amounts of tax grain each year from all of the eight canal-zone provinces as well as wheat and beans from Fengtian (Manchuria), and, now, in 1826, by sea from Jiangnan, and it had a complex bureaucratic organization for transferring and storing it that reached from the Zhili-Shandong border to the capital granaries at Tongzhou and Beijing. This organization included Zhili field officials as well as specialized grain-transport and granary officials stationed along the Northern Canal from the Shandong border to the Stone Dam at Tongzhou, as well as its extension along the Hai River to the sea. The bureaucratic, sub-bureaucratic, and extra-bureaucratic personnel that served this administrative behemoth were legion, and they had 150 years of codified tradition, precedents, and laws to guide their management. Because of the strategic significance of tax grain and the special role that Banner elites played in its management, changes to its administrative practices were complicated and heavily fraught.[1]

1   Governor-General Nayancheng

Adapting this huge grain-transport and storage system to sea transport was principally the task of Nayancheng (1764–1833), the Governor-General of Zhili and Concurrent Director of the Northern Canal. Compared to the relatively young Qishan, he had many years of experience as a high-ranking official and battle-scarred military commander. He had been appointed Zhili Governor-General in 1822 after returning from Shaanxi-Gansu where he had settled the unrest between Tibetans and Mongols in Kokonor. He was a skilled administrator, known for his ability to mediate and resolve conflicts both on the battlefield and in bureaucratic settings.

---

1   Leonard 1996, pp. 36–49.

© KONINKLIJKE BRILL NV, LEIDEN, 2019 | DOI:10.1163/9789004384583_009

FIGURE 8   Nayancheng (1764–1833)

Nayancheng was born in 1764 and was a Manchu of the Zhangjia clan and Plain White Banner. He was a grandson of the famous official and general, Agui (1717–1797), who had served earlier as a grand secretary and held the rank of duke. He passed the official exams at a young age (*xiucai* 1779; *juren* 1788; *jinshi* 1789), was assigned to the Hanlin as a bachelor, then compiler (1789–1790), and was then appointed to the Imperial Study in 1792. From 1794 to 1798, he served as a sub-chancellor in the Grand Secretariat, then on the Grand Council, and was later to head a number of central boards: Works (1799), Civil Appoints (1820), and Punishments (1821). Similar to Qishan, he was entrusted to carry out special investigations of military and civil officials in the provinces.[2]

However, his most noteworthy assignments were in Shaanxi-Gansu, Liangguang, and Turkestan where he served variously as governor-general, imperial commissioner, and military commander during the White Lotus Rebellion along the Shaanxi-Sichuan border (1799–1800, 1810); during the rebel Tiandihui and piracy suppression campaigns in Liangguang (1802, 1804–1806); during the Tianlijiao uprising in Zhili, Shandong, and Henan (1813–1814); and during the conflicts with Tibetans and Mongols in Kokonor and with Kokandians in Turkestan (1807–1809, 1822–1823, 1827–1828).[3]

---

2   ECCP, pp. 584–587.

3   Ibid. CHC 10, pt. 1, pp. 136–144, 360–373; Borei 2002, pp. 274–301; Murray 1987, pp. 99–118, 123–125, 137.

After the pacification of these groups, he distinguished himself by carrying out successful resettlement and rehabilitation plans in these locales. In the case of Guangdong after piracy suppression, he used pardons and rewards to reintegrate the pirates into their coastal communities, supported local militarization efforts, expanded the navy, and built up coastal defenses—constructing forts, ships, and coastal guard stations. After the suppression of the Tianlijiao rebellion in North China, he effected the careful demobilization of government troops and the resettlement of the region. After the cessation of hostilities between the Tibetans and Mongols in Kokonor from 1822 to 1823, he executed the Tibetan leaders and cut off military supplies to Tibet, then rehabilitated the Mongols, set up larger garrisons along the stretch of the Yellow River between the two warring groups, and carried out a demographic survey to keep track of the movements of Tibetans in the area.

After Muslim *khoja* unrest and the Kokandian invasions in Altishahr were pacified from 1825 to 1827, Nayancheng was dispatched to expand the Qing military presence in Eastern Turkestan, especially the oases communities in Altishahr, as well as rebuilding cities and forts and expanding irrigation and agricultural production in order to raise revenues to fund a greater Qing colonial presence in this region. He cracked down on the corrupt collusion between local *beg* officials and Qing military officers, imposed a trade embargo on Kokand, confiscated their land and possessions in Altishahr, then deported Kokandian residents and traders in Kashgar, after which he was rewarded with the appointment of Grand Guardian of the Heir Apparent. When unrest broke out again in Turkestan in 1830 due to the economic hardships imposed on Kokandians by his plan, Nayancheng was blamed for this, and, in 1831, he was stripped of all ranks and made a commoner although at his death in 1833, he was eulogized and given posthumous honors by the Daoguang Emperor. Overall, he had distinguished himself over the course of his career as an extremely effective civil and military organizer and administrator during the Jiaqing and early Daoguang reigns.

Having served as Zhili Governor-General and Concurrent Northern Canal Director in 1813 to 1816, when Nayancheng was again appointed to this post in 1825, he was familiar with the intricacies of canal transport and the mobilization of Zhili lighterage resources, and he brought this knowledge to bear on the planning for sea transport in late 1825. He had a lot of responsibilities to juggle and adjust for the plan to succeed, and he did so by asserting the prerogatives of the Zhili grain officials, who, in his view, thoroughly understood the logistical and managerial complexities of grain transport and storage issues in the capital province and who, he insisted, must be allowed to manage the handling of sea-transported grain according to long-established precedents.

The process of accommodation and reconciliation was not easy, and probably would not have been accomplished had it not been for the pressure that Yinghe brought to bear on him to complete the plan. The unfolding of the plan is captured, as noted earlier, in four key memorials[4] written by Yinghe and Board of Revenue officials after the Daoguang Emperor ordered the board to review and fine-tune Qishan's sea transport regulations and to complete the plan for receiving grain in Tianjin and its transfer to the capital granaries: "Determine and fix the number of days it will take to deliver and unload the grain tribute outside Tianjin's East Gate, and then report back to me."[5] Three days later on the eleventh day of the ninth month (5.9.11), Yinghe responded with the first of these memorials that began the process of adjusting the regulatory framework for handling the grain in Tianjin, welding the Jiangsu and Zhili plans into one seamless whole, and completing the last stages of planning for sea transport.[6]

These four memorials highlight the critical coordinating role of Yinghe and the Board of Revenue as they tried to take a firm hand with Zhili officials, led by Governor-General Nayancheng. Acting on the recommendations of Qishan that reflected Jiangsu provincial interests, Yinghe insisted that Zhili officials move swiftly and decisively to streamline the interface between the two provinces on the Tianjin docks, in order to eliminate extortion and speed the departure of sand junks so they could trade in Fengtian and return to Shanghai in time to pick up the second grain shipment. His leadership was critical in reconciling Zhili practice with the interests of Jiangsu grain authorities and Shanghai merchant shippers. Yet, at the same time, he also responded realistically and flexibly to Nayancheng's views about the complex realities of Zhili grain management and his defense of the critical role of both skilled and unskilled sub- and extra-bureaucratic personnel in the transfer and storage of tax grain.

2   Yinghe and the First Board of Revenue Memorial

Yinghe's primary goal in the first memorial was to create a streamlined procedure for handling the grain in Tianjin that assured that "the grain would be unloaded quickly," insisting that "the various managerial personnel" (*chengban'-geyuan*) in Tianjin, from the governor-general to low-level civil, grain-transport,

---

4   JSHY 2:1–4b (5.9.11); 2:32–37 (5.11.24); 2:39–53 (5.11.29); 2:56–71b (5.12.27).
5   JSHY 1:70b–72b (5.9.8); P 00075–77 (5.9.8).
6   JSHY 2:1–4b (5.9.11).

and military officials, "must prepare ahead of time to hire additional lighters and dock porters, and assemble peck-bushel measuring tools (*douhu*) . . . so that merchant ships can unload as soon as they arrive—the faster the better."[7]

This goal was not so easily achieved! There were, in Yinghe's view, three main obstacles to doing so, all of which posed daunting challenges. The first was logistical and centered on the mobilization and deployment of Zhili lighters, both government and private; the second was the preparation of temporary storage in Tianjin in the event of a shortage of lighterage craft to ship the grain directly to Tongzhou. The third was official extortion on the Tianjin docks, which, if not checked, would slow the unloading and transfer of grain to lighters, as well as the departure of sand junks from the port. Finally, it was necessary to provide security along the Hai River approach to the Tianjin docks from the sea, to nearby storage facilities, and along the entire canal route to Tongzhou.

Several thousand Zhili lighters, both government and private, were needed to transfer the huge amounts of tax grain that would converge on Zhili in 1826. These grain shipments included: (1) sea-transported grain; (2) "delayed" grain sent by canal that had arrived too late in the autumn (1825) to complete the trip to Tongzhou before the Grand Canal froze over and that was stored temporarily in canal-side granaries for final shipment by lighter to Tongzhou in the early spring of 1826; (3) the new 1826 tax grain, sent by Grand Canal relays (*panba-jieyun*) that would arrive in Zhili in the summer of 1826 at about the same time as the second sea shipments; and (4) bean and wheat shipments from Fengtian shipped by sea, then via the Hai River and Tianjin to the Northern Canal and Tongzhou.

Board of Revenue officials in the capital felt reasonably confident that there were enough Zhili lighters to complete the shipment of the delayed grain in the early spring of 1826 and then return quickly to the Tianjin docks to pick up the first sea shipments of approximately 800,000 *shi*, expected to arrive in the middle of the third lunar month. But they were not so confident about the availability of lighters for the second sea shipments that were expected to arrive later in the summer at Tianjin at about the same time as Grand Canal fleets would enter the Northern Canal in Zhili, both of which would require lighterage. The simultaneous convergence of sea- and canal-transported grain might, they thought, exceed the carrying capacity of available Zhili lighters, not to mention causing congestion in Tianjin harbor and exposing the grain cargoes to rain and accidents.

---

7 JSHY 2:1b, 3b (5.9.11).

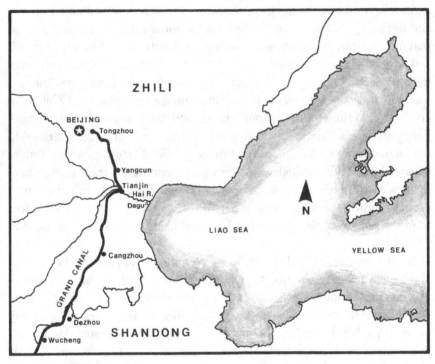

MAP 8   Zhili province

Yinghe argued that three initiatives were required immediately to assure the mobilization of the needed lighters. First, the Zhili Governor-General should immediately undertake the massive mobilization of government and private lighterage, directing Zhili grain-transport officials to repair the entire fleet of 2,500 government lighters that were regularly anchored at Yangcun, midway between Tianjin and Tongzhou."[8] More challenging was the hire of private lighters in the departmental and county canal ports along the Northern Canal from the Shandong-Zhili border to Tongzhou.

As was the case in Jiangsu, local county officials were customarily responsible for hiring lighters in the canal ports within their respective jurisdictions, after which provincial government would reimburse them for this expense. But because provincial officials often reneged on this obligation, leaving local officials to bear the costs alone, the latter were generally reluctant to hire local lighters, or if they did, they simply commandeered the craft without paying the owners, forcing shippers to wait for the provincial payments. As a consequence, neither local officials nor lighter owners were enthusiastic about

---

8   JSHY 2:39–52 (5.11.29).

undertaking government shipping work. Board of Revenue officials realized this fact, and they insisted that the Zhili Governor-General act immediately to pressure and cajole local officials to recruit these craft and to reimburse their owners promptly for doing so.

The second pressing task was the preparation of temporary storage shelters near the East Gate docks to protect the grain during the wait for lighters and during the bottlenecks that would undoubtedly occur as the shipment of sea-transported, "delayed," and canal-born grain overwhelmed the ability of grain officials to expedite lighterage shipments to Tongzhou. To protect grain during the various transfers in Tianjin, Yinghe argued that local officials in Tianjin should act quickly to prepare temporary storage for at least 100,000 to 200,000 *shi* at local temple grounds and prefectural and county granaries in the immediate Tianjin area, especially "the broad and spacious temple grounds near the East Gate. Spread wood planks and mats on the ground and fix leaking roofs in order to shelter the grain and keep it dry."[9]

Board of Revenue officials preferred local granaries in Tianjin over canal-side granaries that were controlled by the Grain Transport Administration because the former were closer to the Tianjin docks. When lighters became available, it would be easier to pick up the temporarily sheltered grain for the 145 kilometer trip to Tongzhou rather than use the Northern Granary on the outskirts of Tianjin, which was considered "too far away from the Tianjin docks and could only hold 400,000 *shi*." It was only to be used in an emergency as had been the case in 1824 to store 100,000 *shi* shipped by sea from Taiwan.[10] Yet, in the event that this granary might be needed, Yinghe ordered Zhili transport officials to immediately order "salt merchants to finish repairing the granary as was customary."

Yinghe and Board of Revenue planners urged officials in Tianjin to strive to transfer approximately 30,000 *shi* per day in 1826. This was the amount that "grain boats normally unloaded and transferred each day, in succession, at the Stone Dam in Tongzhou." Yet they cautioned Zhili officials that the "customary" process could not be used as a strict guide because "the sea-transport situation is different" from canal transport. The merchant ships at sea "are subject to the vagaries of wind and weather." They "wait to depart from Jiangsu until the seasonal winds are favorable." Moreover, they did not travel in fleet formation, like the canal boats, but set sail, one by one, and would, thus, arrive in Tianjin, one by one. Events encountered en route might also delay their arrival.

---

9   JSHY 2:2–b (5.9.11).
10   JSHY 2:2–3 (5.9.11).

In other words, Yinghe and his colleagues fully expected unforeseen events encountered at sea to affect the arrival of sand junks in Tianjin.

Board of Revenue officials initially thought that 2,500 government lighters, plus several hundred hired private lighters, could be mobilized to converge on the Tianjin docks in advance of the arrival of the first sea shipments. When they arrived, the grain could then be unloaded quickly onto the docks on the north bank of the Hai River and transferred to waiting lighters for direct shipment to Tongzhou. Any remaining grain could then be stored temporarily in local granaries while officials awaited the return of lighters from the first deliveries to Tongzhou.

These officials mistakenly thought that the need for temporary grain storage would be greatest later in the summer when both the second sea shipments and canal shipments converged on the Northern Canal and lighters would be in short supply. They advised Tianjin officials that, at that time, any remaining grain could initially be transported to nearby local granaries for storage, and if and when these were filled, the remainder should be taken to the Northern Granary.

Thirdly, during the frenzied period when "managerial personnel" in Tianjin sought to inspect, unload, transfer, and/or temporarily store grain, Yinghe and Board of Revenue officials worried that the security of the grain would be at risk, and they urged that the Zhili Governor-General order the Tianjin brigade commander (*zhenzongbing*) to deploy "low-level military officers and soldiers to patrol the Hai River from the sea to Tianjin and also to guard the docks, storage sites, and the assembled lighterage fleets to prevent theft and the 'mixing' of grain" [with water or sand to increase its volume in order to cover up theft]. These measures would help avoid congestion near the docks and assist civil officials "to hasten and push" the lighterage fleets on to Tongzhou.[11]

To work out the precise procedures for addressing logistical and security issues, Yinghe reiterated his call for the dispatch of a granary vice president and the Zhili provincial treasurer to work out these pressing issues jointly, and he also advised that when the sand junks actually arrived, the emperor should send an imperial commissioner to Tianjin to oversee the inspection and handling of grain during its transfer to ligherage fleets.

In Yinghe's eyes, the final and greatest obstacle to achieving the speedy transfer of sea-transported grain at Tianjin was extortion by customs officials and grain brokers at the East Gate Customs. He asserted that "slowing the departure [of the Shanghai ships] from Tianjin in order to force them to pay" will cause serious problems if not eliminated. He urged the emperor to order all

---

11   JSHY 2:2–3b (5.9.11).

customs officials to carry out inspections with dispatch and to forbid clerks (*lixu*) from extorting money in order "to speed up inspections." These changes had to be made, he explained, because, although merchant transport was more "unconventional and challenging" than either relay-shipping or regular canal transport, all three methods were plagued by extortion and delays caused by "grain brokers, clerks, and runners," who managed the low-level operational tasks of inspecting, unloading, and transferring grain. Zhili officials, he insisted, must not allow "the slightest bit of extortion and delay" because it would diminish "the merchants' zeal for acting for the public good (*jigong*)."[12]

The potential problems with sub-bureaucratic extortion on the Tianjin docks had been discussed earlier among Jiangsu officials when they designed the procedures for loading grain in Shanghai, but no specific measures had yet been worked out for Tianjin. Throughout their discussions, they became more and more convinced of the necessity of appointing high-ranking officials to supervise Zhili local and grain officials who were charged with carrying out the new plan in Tianjin, contrary to the previous practice of relying on clerks and runners. They felt that ranked officials and their assistants would be more effective in exerting discipline and control over the performance of low-level tasks. Zhili officials ultimately bowed to this pressure.

To direct sea-transport management in Tianjin, Board of Revenue officials, at Qishan's suggestion, proposed a temporary, three-tiered administrative structure that vested supervisory power in the hands of an imperial commissioner to insure the integrity of the inspection, unloading, and transfer of grain to either lighters or temporary grain-storage facilities. They urged the emperor to dispatch an imperial commissioner to Tianjin just as soon as word was received from Jiangsu that the last sand junk had set sail from the port of Shixiao on Chongming Island. The commissioner would be charged with the task of eliminating collusion between granary officials, their clerks, and grain brokers, which would, they hoped, defend the interests of Jiangsu officials and merchant shippers. In the event that merchants reported any "extortion," the imperial commissioner, not granary officials, would order "the arrest and punishment of corrupt officials."[13] Once grain cargoes were inspected, received, and unloaded, the imperial commissioner would then immediately authorize the payments due to each sand junk owner, after which each shipper was absolved of any further responsibility for the grain and was free to depart for the Manchurian ports to trade.

---

12 JSHY 2:3, 4b (5.9.11).
13 JSHY 2:3b–4 (5.9.11).

The second tier of the proposed management hierarchy consisted of a granary vice president and the Zhili provincial treasurer. The former was ordered to work jointly with the grain sub-prefect at Tongzhou "to select honest and diligent grain brokers" to travel to Tianjin to manage the unloading and transfer to lighters.[14] The treasurer, a field official in Tianjin, was charged with supervising the hiring and deployment of lighters and the preparation of temporary granaries in Tianjin. Later, he was also ordered to establish a third supervisory tier—a temporary general bureau (*zongju*) to be staffed by "assistants and unranked miscellaneous officials" to replace, monitor, and discipline sub-bureaucratic servitors (clerks and runners) and grain brokers. The bureau would make direct payments to sand junk owners, lighterage and porterage organizations, and then audit, record, and report on financial transactions between Zhili provincial government, grain-transport authorities, and Jiangsu province and, finally, forward these accounts to the Board of Revenue.

Revealing the complexity of sea-transport fiscal arrangements, Qishan had already affirmed the longstanding precedent that expenses for the transport of a province's tax grain should be paid by the province of the grain's origin—in this case Jiangsu. Jiangsu, therefore, was obligated to send the silver required to cover the cost of transporting Jiangsu grain to the "granary yamen in Tongzhou" after grain authorities in Tianjin had formally received it. "If the sea junks were to arrive in Tianjin before the Jiangsu silver, the Tongji Grain Transport Treasury and the Tianjin intendent's treasury were to advance the funds to the Granary yamen for allocation." When the Jiangsu silver arrived, Granary officials would then reimburse the two treasuries. Spelling out these arrangements precisely was seen as a way to "avoid delays" once the sea-transport plan was underway. The provincial treasurer, under the governor-general's watchful eye, was also responsible for coordinating the hiring and deployment of lighters back and forth from the Tianjin docks to Tongzhou, where the grain was finally unloaded at the Stone Embankment, the terminus of the Grand Canal.

It is clear from Yinghe's first memorial that the specific plans for receiving grain in Tianjin had to guarantee speed and careful treatment of merchants on whom the plan depended, and it also outlined some of the roles and responsibilities of Zhili field and grain officials in a three-tiered management structure, in order to achieve speed and eliminate extortion. He implored the emperor to pressure the Zhili Governor-General to get busy and "assess conditions and memorialize a plan for Zhili so that the the Board of Revenue could finalize its details."[15] His memorial was highly optimistic about the prospects

---

14   JSHY 2:3b (5.9.11).
15   JSHY 2:4b (5.9.11).

for sea transport, and it expressed the point of view of both the Inner Court and Liangjiang officials, led by Qishan, who insisted on the need for timely administrative actions and adjustments in Zhili in order to insure the success of the plan.

3   Nayancheng and Zhili Grain-Management Realities

The optimistic scenario spelled out in the first Board of Revenue memorial was dashed two months later when Governor-General Nayancheng forcefully asserted "the real facts" about Zhili transport management after consulting with Former Zhili Governor-General Jiang Youxian, Zhili Provincial Treasurer, Tu Zhishen, and Tianjin Intendant, Zheng Zhushen.[16] His detailed memorial corrected Yinghe's miscalculations about: (1) the total amount of grain to be transported by sea in 1826 (which did not include previously "held back" Jiangsu grain from 1823); (2) the number and availability of Zhili lighters for the transfer of sea-transported grain; (3) the projected calendar for grain arrivals in Zhili; and (4) the availability of temporary grain-storage facilities in Tianjin. The Jiangsu planners had simply got it wrong![17]

Correcting these mistakes, Nayancheng explained the facts about Zhili lighterage resources and Tianjin storage facilities, and he laid out an intricate logistical plan that coordinated their use. His plan relied heavily on customary practices and personnel, and it itemized the costs of each and every task that Zhili officials, sub-bureaucrats, and extra-bureaucrats would be required to perform, right down to the last cash coin paid to menials in the Tongzhou granary yards—costs that the Jiangnan grain districts, of course, were obligated to pay. His account of Zhili realities served as a rude awakening and a reality check for Liangjiang officials as well as for Yinghe and Board of Revenue officials, who had focused primarily on streamlining grain transfers to avoid extortion, not the technical demands of Zhili grain management.

Nayancheng's assessment reflected nearly 150 years of Zhili grain-transport lore and practice. Central to his plan was the use of government and private lighters (*guanbo, minbo*), which had played an essential role in this province's grain-transport system since its revival in the 1680s when the Kangxi Emperor had restored and expanded the hydraulic works in Zhili to facilitate grain transport. Canal engineers, at that time, had canalized the Wei and Bai rivers

---

16   JSHY 2:18–30b (5.11.22).

17   The reconciliation of these points of contention did not occur until 5.12.27. JSHY 2:18–30b (5.11.22).

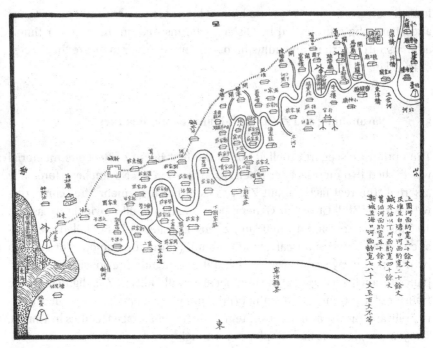

FIGURE 9   Hai River meanders from its mouth to Tianjin

to create the Northern Canal. To do so, they had dredged and diverted these and several other of the province's silt-laden rivers to converge on the Hai River near Tianjin and then flow directly to the sea, in an attempt to minimize the threat of floods and meanders that might obstruct canal transport. Silting was, however, to remain a constant problem, as can be seen in the illustration of Hai River meanders in 1825, as depicted in Tao Zhu's illustrated map of the Hai River from its mouth near the Dagu Forts to Tianjin.

4   Lighterage

Yet even with these earlier hydraulic projects, lighters were to remain an essential component of canal transport in Zhili because they could more easily navigate the heavily silted Northern Canal when water levels were low. From the beginning, a fleet of approximately 2,500 government lighters, as noted above, had been assembled and anchored at Yangcun on the canal, midway between Tianjin and Tongzhou. At the end of each transport cycle, these craft underwent "small repairs;" and after five or six years of hard service, they underwent major repairs so that they were ready for the next series of transport cycles.

When the demand for lighters was particularly acute, Zhili officials hired private, or "people's," lighters.[18]

Government lighters normally were used throughout the grain-transport season from the second to the tenth lunar month. In the spring (in the second month), they were used to ship what was called "delayed," or "interrupted" (*jue*) grain," to Tongzhou that had been unloaded and stored in canal-side granaries late the previous autumn to enable them to return to their home anchorages in time to repair their boats and collect the next year's tax grain, especially the late-arriving fleets from the middle Yangzi provinces. Then, in the third month, lighters were used to complete the transport of early-arriving grain fleets from Henan and Shandong that transferred their cargoes to government lighters at Yangcun, then returned to their home anchorages to pick up their second yearly shipment. Alternatively, these cargoes might be stored at canal anchorages on the Shandong-Zhili border. Lighters were also called on to ship special deliveries of beans and wheat arriving in Tianjin from Manchuria and, in 1824, rice from Taiwan.[19] During the slack season, government lighters were permitted to ship commercial goods, but if the needs of grain transport were particularly acute, the lighters could be called to service earlier, as was the case in 1825–1826, when they were alerted to be "at the ready" and stay close to their home anchorages.

To respond to increasing siltation of the canal and delays in the transport cycle, grain-transport authorities routinely began to deploy 200 to 300 government lighters from the Yangcun base to anchorages at the Wei River shallows on the Shandong-Zhili border, such as Gucheng and Jingzhou in Hejian prefecture, so that late-arriving fleets could offload their cargoes to waiting lighters for final shipment to Tongzhou.[20] If, however, the grain fleets arrived too late even for lighterage shipments, their cargoes were deposited in canal-side granaries at these border anchorages, and even at the Northern Granary on the outskirts of Tianjin.[21] Early the following spring, when the canal thawed, the delayed grain was quickly transported by lighter to Tongzhou before the first canal shipments from the south began to arrive. As silt deterioration of the Huaiyang and Shandong sections of the Grand Canal worsened in the mid-eighteenth century and grain fleets were slowed ever further, the demand for

---

18   Leonard 1996, pp. 75–77.
19   JSHY 2:18b–19 (5.11.22).
20   JSHY 2:19 (5.11.22).
21   The Northern Granary could hold from 400,000 to 500,000 *shi*, and Changlu salt merchants funded its repair. Government lighters generally picked up delayed grain from this granary in the second month.

lighters late in the season became even more acute.[22] When the province's fleet of lighters was insufficient to meet this demand, local officials from the departments and counties that lay astride the Northern Canal were ordered to hire private lighters to help out.[23]

Aware of the complicated pattern of lighterage use in Zhili during the yearly grain-transport cycle, Nayancheng laid out a careful strategy for meeting lighterage requirements in 1826—requirements that were determined by the amount of grain to be shipped and the arrival times of the various shipments converging on Zhili.[24] According to his assessments, "when the canal thaws in the second month," government lighters should ship several several thousand *shi* of delayed grain from Jiangxi and Huguang that had been stored temporarily in the Northern Granary in late 1825. In the third month, the first of two shipments of sea-transported grain (800,000 *shi*) would arrive in Tianjin, just as the first canal shipments arrived from Henan-Shandong (Hedong). Both required extensive lighterage. In the summer and autumn, beginning in the fourth month, the second shipment of sea-transported grain would arrive in Tianjin around the same time as the main shipments of new grain from the south arrived by canal. Many of these fleets might also transfer their cargoes to lighters at Yangcun, or, alternatively, might require lighterage from the Zhili-Shandong border if water levels in the canal were low or if it was too late in the season to insure the fleets' return to their home anchorages before the winter freeze.[25]

Both of the two seaborne shipments of 800,000 *shi* in the spring and summer would, according to Nayancheng, disrupt the customary shipment cycle in Zhili and increase the demand for lighters. He calculated that the total amount of sea-transported grain would equal approximately 1.6 million *shi*, not the 1.5 million calculated by Qishan and Yinghe, who had neglected to include an additional 100,000 *shi* that had been held back in the south the previous year for shipment in 1826.[26] Therefore, approximately 800,000 *shi* would need to be transported in each of two shipments—an amount that exceeded the carrying capacity of the entire Yangcun fleet! He explained that if each lighter carried 250 *shi*, then the entire Yangcun fleet could carry only approximately 500,000 *shi*, after wastage and food rice were deducted. *But the entire fleet* [2,500 craft] *would not be available* because 200 lighters were routinely deployed to

---

22   High demand for lighterage, naturally enough, took a toll on these craft and required careful yearly repairs and maintenance.

23   JSHY 2:21–22b (5.11.22).

24   JSHY 2:21–24 (5.11.22).

25   JSHY 2:20–22b (5.11.22).

26   He pointed out that the Jiangsu plan did not factor in this 100,000 *shi*.

anchorages on the Zhili-Shandong border and another 800 normally remained at Yangcun to transfer cargoes of the first-arriving Hedong fleets. This left only 1,500 government lighters available, which would account for only 375,000 *shi* for transport from Tianjin.[27]

To resolve the "crunch" in the spring when sea-transported grain arrived at Tianjin, Nayancheng asserted that it would be necessary to hire 500 private lighters and also commandeer 500 Hedong grain boats after they had transferred their first shipments at Yangcun. This would bring the total back to 2,500 craft. He explained that the 500 Hedong grain boats should first be used to ship the delayed grain stored in the Northern Granary to Tongzhou, thus emptying this storage facility in case it were needed to store the overflow from the second sea shipments expected to arrive later in the summer. That left approximately 2,000 lighters that could be sent directly to Tianjin to ship the sea-transported grain.[28] Yet, even this fleet of lighters could only ship 500,000 of the 800,000 *shi* arriving in the spring.[29] The remaining 300,000 *shi* would have to be stored immediately in temporary open-air bins built behind and adjacent to the docking area near Shangyuan Park, just southeast of Tianjin city. As soon as the lighters returned from Tongzhou, they could then load and transport the remaining stored grain. This scenario, however, would not work for the second shipment of 800,000 *shi* in the summer because the damp rainy weather would damage the grain if it were left in the open-air bins near the docks. Instead, Nayancheng proposed that lighters first ship 300,000 *shi* directly to the Northern Granary for safe storage, then return quickly to Tianjin to pick up the remaining 500,000 *shi* for direct shipment to Tongzhou.[30]

5   Storage Logistics

Nayancheng's plan also unambiguously corrected the Board of Reveue's mistaken assumptions about the availability of local government granaries and temple grounds in Tianjin for temporary storage and the role of the Northern Granary.[31] He argued that there were no such suitable local granaries sites in Tianjin. Instead, he explained in elaborate detail how temporary open-air storage bins would have to be constructed between Shang Yuan Park and the

---

27   JSHY 2:22b (5.11.22).
28   JSHY 2:21–b (5.11.22).
29   JSHY 2:26b (5.11.22).
30   JSHY 2:22b (5.11.12).
31   JSHY 2:42–43b; 46b–47 (5.11.29).

Dragon God Temple grounds immediately southeast of the docks to store as much as 300,000 *shi* of the first shipment. This area would have to be leveled and storage bins constructed with earthen walls of 100 *zhang* (320 m) in length and overhangs around and over each bin. Straw mats would have to be placed on the ground in the bins and also placed over the deposited grain, and then drainage ditches would have to be dug around each. Additionally, huts would have to be built to accommodate low-level officers and soldiers sent to police the area and guard against theft and who would also require the provision of food and salary.[32]

Nayancheng's intimate knowledge of the harbor docking area also enabled him to design a procedure to streamline the interface between the large sand junks and hundreds of small lighters along a distance of about 3 km, stretching from Shangyuan Park to the Shuang Temple, where arriving sand junks could line up and, one-by-one, unload and transfer grain directly either to waiting lighters or to the storage areas behind the docks. Although he observed that "normally each summer, hundreds of Jiangsu trading ships come to Tianjin and anchor from Shangyuan Park to the Dragon God Temple" near Tianjin's East Gate, this area, in his judgment, "is too narrow and congested with hundreds of lighters to allow the larger sand junks to maneuver." Instead, he advised that sand junks anchor in the more open areas of the harbor from Shangyuan Park southeastward to the Shuang Temple "where sand junks can go to one side to anchor, then unload one-by-one."[33] After the sand junks were unloaded, each fleet of 160 lighters could assemble further north near the Dragon God Temple to pick up the grain and proceed under escort to Tongzhou.[34]

Finally, Nayancheng proposed essential security measures to safeguard the grain cargoes from the time the sand junks arrived off the Zhili coast near the Dagu Forts until the grain was safely delivered to Tongzhou. This included, firstly, the guarding of the sand junks while they were pulled, or tracked, up the Hai River to Tianjin's East Gate; second, policing the storage grounds near the docks, noted above; and, finally, escorting and guarding the lighterage fleets from Tianjin to Tongzhou. During the first step, after local officials had hired the trackers, low-level military officials and soldiers from the guard stations along the river would be charged with "dividing up and spreading out along the river to hasten the boats" to the Tianjin docks. After the grain was unloaded and temporarily stored near the docks, troops would patrol the storage sites to prevent theft; finally, escort parties comprised of one civil official (from the Tianjin

---

32   JSHY 2:21b–22, 27b–28 (5.11.22).
33   JSHY 2:26b–27b (5.11.22).
34   JSHY 12:6b ff.

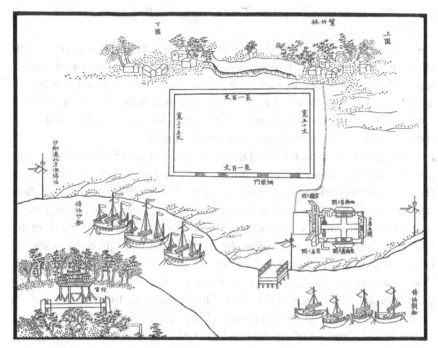

FIGURE 10   Storage area at Shangyuan Park

Intendant's office) and one military official with ten soldiers from the Tianjin brigade (*zhen*) would police each fleet during the trip to Tongzhou. The two officers would travel with the head boat of each fleet of ten vessels while the troops and a grain broker would guard and "care for" the grain."

This escort entourage was designed to put pressure on lighterage fleets "to proceed quickly and prevent them from stopping and going ashore, thus, risking theft and/or the mixing of the grain." Theft was to be reported to the civil and military escort officials who would send the accused to his home county for punishment. However, Zhili officials realized that wastage loss could not be avoided during grain transfers, so they advised escort officials "to protect honest lighter owners from broker extortion over issues of wastage loss."[35] When the fleet arrived at the Stone Dam in Tongzhou, the two escort officials would "report to the granary sub-prefect," and the escort broker would assist him in expediting the transfers from the ligherage fleets to the granary office.

---

35   JSHY 2:27b–28 (5.11.22).

6   The Performance of Low-Level Grain-Handing Tasks in Zhili

The unanswered question in all this was: how could Zhili civil and granary officials implement all the changes required to transfer sea-transported grain if sub- and extra-bureaucratic staff (clerks, runners, and grain brokers) were not used, as Qishan and Board of Revenue officials had insisted, in order to curb corruption? In other words, how could the work be done without a cohort of sub-bureaucratic and extra-bureaucratic underlings?

In Nayancheng's view, it did not make sense to reinvent the wheel and mandate changes in low-level Zhili grain-transport and storage practices without the use of clerks and runners, especially grain brokers.[36] He argued that Zhili officials should use the same institutional structures, regulations, and personnel that they customarily employed to ship delayed grain each spring from the Northern Granary. In other words, the Northern Granary precedents should continue to guide the transfers. The Granary sub-prefect at Tongzhou headed this management structure and was in charge of receiving and transferring grain from the grain fleets at the Stone Embankment to Tongzhou, as well as from other canal storage facilities where delayed grain was stored.

The actual direction of crucial low-level tasks, such as inspecting, bagging, and measuring grain, as well as engaging and paying porters and lighters, was the special responsibility of grain brokers, who were minimally supervised by deputies from the two granary sub-prefects' office. A sub-prefect, for example, would pick several grain brokers from a pool of approximately 150 attached to his office and send them to the Northern Granary "to measure and organize the transfer" of grain that had been temporarily stored there by late-arriving grain fleets the previous autumn. The practices established for the Northern Granary transfers should, Nayancheng asserted, serve as the norm for grain transfers from other canal anchorages and the port of Tianjin.[37]

The advantage of using these well-established procedures and practices was that they were "simple and focused responsibility in the hands of specific brokers (*guiyishoujingli*)."[38] He urged the emperor to order a Granary Vice President to apply these established precedents to sea transport. Select an official in the grain sub-prefect's office to appoint 50 to 60 "honest brokers from the pool of 125 who specifically manage the white rice granary. Order them to take 10-peck measurers and grain bags to Tianjin ahead of time." As soon as the sand junks arrived, the brokers should await the Imperial Commissioner's

---

36   JSHY 2:20 (5.11.22).
37   JSHY 2:18b (5.11.22).
38   JSHY 2:20 (5.11.22).

order to inspect, receive, and transfer the grain, as well as supervise the later pick-up of excess grain held in temporary bins close to the docks. These measures and the supervision by an imperial commissioner and his aides would, it was thought, keep the brokers honest and intensify the pressure on the two granary vice presidents, the sub-prefects, and grain brokers.

Nayancheng's only concession was to agree that key Tianjin field officials (the Tianjin intendant, prefect, and magistrates) should set up an *ad hoc* general bureau at the Dragon King Temple, close to the docks, to manage the tasks of paying porterage and lighterage organizations directly in order to eliminate "skimming" of these payments by brokers. These payments, made in silver, were based on the actual amount of grain that each lighter shipped during the transfers, and their payment in Tianjin was considered especially "convenient" for lighter owners who would not be required to return to their home counties to be paid.[39]

The bureau was to be staffed by two ranked assistants and their subordinates, as well as by several clerks and runners specifically assigned from the Tianjin county yamen. These personnel were charged with the usual bureau tasks of keeping fiscal records, auditing accounts, and sending fiscal reports to the provincial treasurer and on up the line to the Board of Revenue. But, in this particular case, they were also directed to manage the order and placement of lighters as they arrived in Tianjin and then to organize them into fleets of 100 boats, with each craft flying a banner that identified a boat's fleet, its number within the fleet, and the owner's name. Bureau officials would then direct each craft "to line up, side by side, in a row and wait." When the sand junks arrived and transferred the grain, "deputies of the grain sub-prefect will record the amount of each boat's load and issue a document to the boat owner." On the basis of that document, the bureau would then calculate and pay the boat owner 70 percent of the hiring price, ration silver, and the cost of porterage labor, with the remaining 30 percent to be paid at Tongzhou. During the course of this work, the Tianjin intendant, prefect, and county officials were directed to visit the bureau office unannounced to check on the bureau staff to insure the careful performance of these tasks; when the sea-transport project was completed, these same officials were to meet with bureau personnel to "make a report and send in accounts."[40]

All of these responsibilities associated with handling sea-transported grain, Nayancheng asserted, were time-consuming, complex, and burdensome, and their performance would require responsible officials "to dwell at the docks for

---

39   JSHY 2:29–30 (5.11.12).
40   JSHY 2:51b.

a long period of time to manage the general oversight of receipts and expenditures." This, he argued, local officials were unable to do *because of the press of their regular duties of office*! The establishment of the bureau would temporarily extend the reach of county government to the docks, and, at the very least, keep brokers out of the payment process, thereby eliminating a major source of extortion and facilitate the speedy departure of sand junks from Tianjin. On the whole, he deemed that these adaptive changes would not disrupt the normal performance of Zhili grain-transport practices.[41]

7   Calculating the Costs Down to the Last 1/100,000th of a Tael

Nayancheng itemized the expenses that Zhili would incur during the handling of sea-transported grain from its arrival until its final deposit in the capital granaries in mind-numbing detail.[42] It is not altogether surprising that he did so because the costs were substantial and would have to be paid from Jiangsu grain-transport funds. Although these details are difficult to wade through, they are very important for understanding the Qing leadership's attention to administrative detail and, thus, its ability to carry out major changes in a key strategic institution that were to be performed at the sub-county level with no established administrative regulations to guide them.

One of the most important fiscal tasks that Nayancheng and Zhili officials undertook was the determination of the differing pay rates for government lighters, the commandeered Henan-Shangdong grain fleets, and private lighters.[43] These different rates of pay depended on circumstances. Government lighters, for example, worked for the state during the yearly shipping cycle and were paid a hiring price (*gujia*) and ration silver for the five boatmen on each craft, and a surcharge for wastage, which inevitably occurred as grain was loaded, unloaded, and when accidents and/or theft occurred. The payments were calculated based on the distance and number of one-hundred-*shi* units of grain carried.[44]

During the slack season from the tenth to the third lunar month (roughly from October to February), when government lighters weren't engaged in grain-transport tasks, each lighter received 15 taels for basic food rations, which were

41   JSHY 2:29–30 (5.11.22).

42   JSHY 2:41–48 (5.11.29).

43   JSHY 2:19b, 22b–24 (5.11.22).

44   JSHY 2:41–45b (5.11.29).

generally raised from Changlu salt-merchant contributions (*juanna*).[45] During the second and third months as the canal thawed, these government lighters were allowed to supplement their incomes by engaging in private shipping before returning to government transport tasks in the fourth month when the yearly grain-tax shipments began to arrive by canal in Zhili. Even though these craft were called "government lighters" and were at the beck and call of the grain-transport authorities, they had a quasi-private status in the slack season unless there was a special need.

A special need was precisely the case in the early spring of 1825 when the destruction of the canal–Yellow River junction caused a slow-down of the entire transport cycle so that the last of the southern grain fleets had crossed the Yellow River only in the fifth month. As a result, the late-arriving Jiangxi-Huguang cargoes had been stored in the Northern Granary in the autumn, and government lighters would transfer this grain from the granary to Tongzhou immediately after the spring thaw in the second month of 1826. Then these lighters would be dispatched to transport the first sea shipments and the early-arriving tax grain from Henan-Shandong in the third and fourth months. In situations like this when the demand for lighters was high, government lighter owners were alerted that they might be called at a moment's notice, and while they were generally allowed to undertake private shipping jobs in the slack period, they were ordered to cut back on such jobs in early 1826 and "were not allowed to travel far" from their home anchorages.[46] The same conditions were applied to the 500 private lighters that were hired for service that year.

Because the Zhili plan for transferring sea-transported grain was so dependent on both government and private lighters, Nayancheng carefully worked out the payments for both groups, as well as for the commandeered Hedong grain fleets. The payments were calculated down to the last 1/100,000th of a tael and were based, as noted above, on precedents established for grain transfers from the Northern Granary to Tongzhou, a distance of 284 *li* (137 km). They included sums for hiring price, ration silver, a brokerage surcharge, as well as grain allotments, and the amounts were based on the number of one-hundred *shi* units of grain each vessel carried. The government lighters and commandeered Hedong fleets received roughly the same amount per vessel: 9 *taels* 5 *qian* 9 *fen* 7 *li* 3 *hao* and 9 *taels* 5 *qian* 9 *fen* 5 *li* 5 *hao*, respectively. In contrast, perhaps representing market prices, private lighters received approximately 3 taels more (12.6.4.4.8).[47] Moreover, because both private and

---

45   JSHY 2:24b (5.11.22).
46   Ibid.
47   JSHY 2:22b–24 (5.11.22); 2:43–44b (5.11.29).

government lighters traveled the added distance of 42 *li* (20 km) from Tianjin to the Northern Granary, they were paid an extra 10 percent.

Nayancheng estimated the total cost for transferring 1.6 million *shi* to be approximately 170,000 taels,[48] and he insisted that Jiangsu send this amount to the granary office "where the sub-prefect will allocate it to Tianjin local officials from the Tongji Treasury, "who will, in turn, change the money, then pay each lighter owner directly, based on the amount of grain he shipped, as measured by the level-peck measuring tool (*pinghu*)." In the event that the funds from Jiangsu did not arrive in a timely fashion and that the grain sub-prefect did not have enough funds to advance the money, then the Changlu Salt Treasury or the Tianjin Intendant's treasury should advance the money, which would be paid back when the funds arrived from Jiangsu. Such were the complicated and arcane details that marked the resolution of jurisdictional issues between Jiangsu and Zhili during the planning period!

Besides the payments for lighterage transport, special "waiting" payments were made to hired lighters to cover their costs from the time they were hired until they actually began transferring grain. Because the precise arrival dates of the two sea shipments were imprecise and because the lighters would have to be mobilized ahead of time, these craft would have a brief waiting period between the time they completed the transfer of stored grain at the Northern Granary and the arrival of the sand junks. If the sand junks were late, there were no precedents regarding the provision of food for boatmen, "who would have empty bellies" during the waiting period—a period that might last for ten days. Therefore, Nayancheng asserted, Zhili officials "must extend aid to the boatmen to avoid subjecting them to grief." The state should pay, he asserted, each of the five boatmen (master, helmsman, and three sailors) 5 *fen* per day for a total of 2 *qian* 5 *fen* per boat for the entire 10-day period, for a total additional cost of 7,000 to 8,000 taels.[49]

Bamboo mats were also needed to cover the floors of the open-air storage bins near the Tianjin docks and the Northern Granary bins. Interestingly, the cost of mats included the payments to sub-bureaucratic granary menials who managed the spreading of the mats. The customary cost of mats and menials prior to 1815 had been fixed at 100 taels of surcharge for every 10,000 *shi* of grain that was stored. This rate had been increased in Jiaqing 15 to 140 taels for each 10,000 *shi*. Because half of the total sea shipments, or 700,000 to 800,000 *shi*, would be temporarily stored at both locations during the transport process, Nayancheng estimated that 10,000 to 11,000 taels of surcharge allocations

---

48   Nayancheng based his calculations on the fact that 2,000 lighters could ship 500,000 *shi*, each carrying 250 *shi* per lighter.

49   JSHY 2:24b–26b (5.11.22).

would be required. In the past, these mat-menial surcharges had been paid from maritime customs revenues, but, in 1826, there were no surplus customs funds for this use because the private goods that sand junks were allowed to carry were duty free. Therefore, this was another charge that Jiangsu would be required to pay, as well as 5,000 taels for the construction of temporary storage bins on the docks and the huts for soldiers assigned to guard the grain.[50]

Finally, approximately 24,000 trackers would be needed to haul 1,600 sand junks the 180-*li* (87 km) route from the mouth of the Hai River to the Tianjin docks. Each boat required 15 trackers to pull it 50 *li* (24 km) per day over four days, and each tracker was allotted a daily ration wage of 80 *wen* (cash coin). The total cost for this operation would be approximately 8,000 taels.[51] All in all, Nayancheng estimated that "waiting," mats, preparation of storage facilities, and trackers would cost a total of 30,000 taels, over and above the cost of lighterage.

The Daoguang Emperor's response to Nayancheng's detailed logistical plan for incorporating sea-transported grain into Zhili's vast and complex grain transport and storage system was glowing. "He has organized a sufficient number of lighters to transfer the grain from Tianjin to Tongzhou, in order to insure that sand junks are unloaded quickly without crowding and delays and without causing grief and bitterness for the lighterage boatman. At the same time, he has coordinated temporary storage of grain near the port and at the Northern Granary with the lighterage process. He has done so in such a way that each official and underling has been given sole responsibility for a specific task, in order to expedite the plan and prevent corruption! Let the Board of Revenue examine and respond to each of the various provisions of the plan."[52] The board did, indeed, respond, wholeheartedly endorsing the entirety of Nayancheng's revision and expansion of the Jiangsu plan. Moreover, they strongly advised that he be given the authority to respond to unforeseen developments during the implementation of the plan.[53]

8   Conclusions

While Yinghe and Qishan had created the broad outlines of the sea-transport plan and the Jiangsu regulations, Nayancheng placed his mark on the plan as well, by vigorously imposing all the complex Zhili grain-management practices

---

50   JSHY 2:25, 27b–28 (5.11.22).

51   JSHY 2:26–27b (5.11.22).

52   JSHY 2:30b (5.11.25).

53   JSHY 2:39–52 (5.11.29).

that had evolved since the Kangxi reign and that would dominate its implementation in Zhili. Reflecting his gubernatorial experience in the northern strategic zone, he quickly and carefully crafted an amazingly detailed logistical plan that coordinated Zhili lighterage resources and storage facilities to manage the convergence and transfer of four categories of grain tax cargoes arriving in Zhili by sea and canal. Moreover, he devised a security network that protected grain shipments from the mouth of the Hai River on the Zhili coast to the docks at Tianjin's East Gate and onward to the Stone Dam at Tongzhou.[54]

Equally impressive was Nayancheng's affirmation of the temporary three-tiered supervisory system to "hasten" the grain transfers and eliminate extortion—a system that utilized long-established "tricks of the governing trade." The structure included an imperial commissioner at the top, Tianjin local and grain-transport officials at the second level, and a special *ad hoc* general bureau at the third level, staffed by specially appointed ranked assistants and unranked "miscellaneous" officials to supervise and discipline the bottom, or operational, level of personnel who performed the actual skilled and unskilled work of handling and protecting the grain: low-level civil and military officials, sub-bureaucratic servitors in the grain-transport and granary offices, and the notorious extra-bureaucratic grain brokers—the very people who were generally responsible for extortion and other forms of corruption.

Nayancheng maintained that these lowly government servitors possessed important skills that were essential to grain management, treating them as "quasi officials" when they were paid to perform government functions.[55] He was, however, willing to put a brake on extortion in two ways: first, by using an imperial commissioner to supervise the inspection and transfer of sea-transported grain from sand junks to lighters and, second, by creating a temporary bureau to pay lighterage and porterage organizations directly and to enforce discipline over sub-bureaucrats and extra-bureaucrats during the docking and loading of lighterage fleets—all in the interest of eliminating extortion and other forms of corruption. The crisis in imperial tax-grain transport in 1825–1826 required changes in institutions and bureaucratic practices, and Nayancheng had the experience and prestige to amend and adjust those practices in Zhili.

---

54   The transfers along the Inner Canal from the Stone Embankment to Datong Bridge and
       cart haulage from the bridge to the Beijing granaries were managed by Granary Vice
       President Bai Chun.
55   JSHY 2:63 (5.12.22).

CHAPTER 8

Bai Chun and Low-Level Grain Transfers and Storage in Zhili

1   The Role of Sub- and Extra-Bureaucratic Granary Personnel

Granary Vice President Bai Chun negotiated the final adjustments to Zhili's customary practices for handling sea-transported grain. These practices centered on the tasks performed by granary personnel, especially the extra-bureaucratic grain broker, in grain transfers from sand junks to lighters in Tianjin and the onward transport to Tongzhou.[1] In an eleven-point memorial, he argued that the sea-transport plan raised difficult issues for granary personnel that, in his view, would undermine the transfers, not to mention subjecting the much maligned grain brokers to unfair treatment.[2] He maintained that the use of an *ad hoc* bureau in Tianjin to pay sand junk shippers, porterage, and lighterage organizations directly would undermine the customary web of brokerage arrangements that bound Zhili grain transfers into a single network, and it would require the careful reassignment of brokerage functions and fees to assure the security and efficiency of grain transfers in 1826.

Bai Chun's memorial should be interpreted as the granary department's defense of its prerogatives in the face of attempts by the Board of Revenue and Qishan to speed the transfers in Tianjin and eliminate "excessive extortion" during these transfers. In this respect it is similar to Governor-General Nayancheng's defense of Zhili grain-shipping and storage logistics. The memorial is important because it reveals in great detail the indispensible role that brokers played in the granary superintendency's operations—a role that would be scarcely visible were it not for the memorial's explicit and detailed explanations of measures needed for implementing sea transport. It shows, once again, the dependence of the imperial state on extra-bureaucratic actors, like the grain brokers, to perform critical state functions, and it also underscores

---

1   Bai Chun was a member of the Bordered White Chinese Banner. He moved from the position of Vice Commander of this banner to acting Vice President of the Board of Civil Office in 1824, then the next year to the position of Vice President of the Granary Superintendency. See *Qingshikaojiazhu* 1986–1991, pp. 5993–5994.

2   JSHY 2:56–71 (5.12.27).

© KONINKLIJKE BRILL NV, LEIDEN, 2019 | DOI:10.1163/9789004384583_010

the use of the *ad hoc* bureau to stem corruption in the performance of low-level grain-management tasks.

2   Grain Brokerage

No group involved in the Zhili end of the sea-transport experiment caused more consternation than did the lowly grain brokers—extra-bureaucratic employees of the Granary Superintendency, who managed the transfer and storage of the yearly grain tax cargoes from the eight-province canal-zone.[3] Officers on the government grain fleets and lighterage boatmen hated them because they controlled porterage labor on the docks and could, as a consequence, "extort excessive fees" to unload and transfer grain.[4] Zhili and Liangjiang official planners saw brokers as "spoilers" who could derail the Zhili end of the sea-transport plan, so they acted decisively to ban any and all direct contacts between brokers and Shanghai merchant shippers on the Tianjin docks, and they created a temporary General Bureau (*zongju*), staffed by Tianjin assistants, to pay merchant shippers, porters, and lighterage boatmen directly in order to eliminate broker extortion and "skimming" of labor payments.

Yet no actor in the sea-transport drama was more crucial to its success than the broker who performed critical low-level organizational and managerial tasks—tasks on which the experiment depended. Zhili officials, especially those from the Granary Superintendency, recognized his importance, asserting that brokers had a "profound grasp of the care of grain and issues connected to the lighterage of grain."[5] They were "knowledgeable and experienced" in grading, measuring, and bagging it. Their close contractual links with porterage networks enabled them to mobilize labor organizations to transfer grain from boat to dock to granary.[6] While government officials openly and repeatedly disparaged them, yet each and every one of them knew that the broker was the ultimate "fixer" for the performance of myriad organizational tasks of low-level grain management because there were no other regular government staff to do them.

---

3   Leonard 2015, 420–439. The granary superintendency was a department of the Board of Revenue, headed by two officials called *cangchangshilang* 倉場侍郎, one Manchu and one Chinese, with the rank of Vice President of the Board of Revenue. BH, pp. 196–197; DOT, pp. 523–524; Mayers, 362; von Glahn 2016, pp. 268–69, 365.

4   JSHY 2:59b (5.12.27).

5   JSHY 2:62b (5.12.27).

6   JSHY 2:61b, 63 (5.12.27).

As a key manager of grain transfers, the broker contracted for and paid porterage and lighterage organizations to assist in the transfers. If he were inefficient in his work and slowed the entire process of inspection, unloading, and transfer, it would cause a ripple effect, leading to backups and delays down the line of grain fleets on the Zhili sector of the Grand Canal. When he intentionally slowed the transfers in order to extort excessive fees and skim wages, he also caused delays that were often blamed on grain-fleet Bannermen and/ or lighterage boatmen. In the eyes of sea-transport planners, in either case— inefficiency or extortion—brokers could jeopardize the speedy departure of Shanghai merchant shippers from Tianjin in 1826. These shippers, as noted earlier, were fully aware of these corrupt practices, and they refused to ship tax grain in 1826 unless officials could assure their speedy departure from Tianjin and the elimination of excessive brokerage fees.

The Zhili grain brokers worked hand and glove with the two grain sub-prefects (*zuoliangting*), their deputies, sub-bureaucrats, and menial servitors at the Granary Superintendency office at the Stone Dam in Tongzhou who inspected the incoming grain cargoes. The Granary Superindendency employed approximate 150 "official" grain brokers, who, with their underlings, managed the transfer and storage of yearly tax-grain shipments that arrived in Zhili. In theory, granary officials supervised the brokers when the grain fleets arrived at the Stone Dam in Tongzhou, in order to protect the "Bannermen" from excessive extortion. In practice, however, supervision by these officials was lax at best. There was, after all, a built-in conflict of interest in their relationship with brokers because they were so dependent on brokers for their performance of crucial transfer tasks.

Their oversight of brokers was even more lax at the canal anchorages near the Zhili-Shandong border and at Tianjin's Northern Granary where brokers and their assistants were sent to manage the transfers of delayed grain in the autumn and its onward transfer to Tongzhou in the spring without the grain sub-prefect's overseers. The same was true of managing the transfers of beans, wheat, and other grains that arrived by sea at the port of Tianjin. Moreover, as canal siltation worsened and canal transport was slowed by the need to transfer grain cargoes en route, the autumn storage at the Zhili canal anchorages increased, as did the use of brokers to manage it.

To cover the costs of these various service tasks, brokers were entitled to charge grain fleet officers and/or lighterage boatmen, three basic fees, which included an individual service fee (*ge'er*), ration silver (*fanmizhese*), and a surcharge (*jintie*) to cover the costs of arranging porterage and/or wastage rice. However, there was little to discourage brokers from charging extra fees

because oversight by granary officials was lax and because often these very officials and local field officials conspired with brokers in their extortion schemes.

To counter just such practices, sea-transport planners set up a new supervisory structure in Tianjin that removed the broker from direct contact with merchant shippers, forbidding him from "speaking a single word" to them, and that
oversaw the direct payment of sand junk shippers, lighterage organizations,
and porters, as noted above. The special oversight structure, first proposed by
Qishan, was headed by an Imperial Commissioner, his board secretaries, along
with Zhili, Jiangsu, and granary officials—all of whom were to "cooperate in
the joint and impartial (*gongtong*) inspection and formal receipt of the grain
when it arrived in Tianjin."[7]

A senior granary official, such as Bai Chun, fully understood the vital role
that grain brokers played in grain transfers. Without them, grain transfers and
shipments would grind to a halt. There was no one else in government employ
with the skills and expertise to do his job. When sea-transport planners sought
to eliminate the broker's direct interactions with merchant shippers, porters,
and lighter boatmen, it curtailed his ability to extort extra fees—this at the
very time when additional responsibilities for "escorting and caring for the
grain" en route to Tongzhou were increased.

Because of these changes, Bai Chun felt compelled to speak out in defense
of brokers. He had grudgingly accepted the Board of Revenue's measures to
streamline and, thus, speed, the inspections and transfers in Tianjin; but he
baulked at the assignment of escort duties to brokers during the trip from
Tianjin to Tongzhou, and he stressed the breadth of their responsibilities, their
expertise in handling grain, and the fact that they would be spread too thinly
to manage both the grain inspections at Tianjin and the escort duties on the
lighterage fleets to Tongzhou. Only 50 to 60 brokers would be sent specifically to manage the transfers from sand junks to the Tianjin docks; this was too
few to do both jobs. Bai acknowledged the importance of the new supervisory
measures and regulations that reflected the "Board of Revenue's attempt to
sympathize with the merchant shippers and protect them from extortion by
brokers."[8] However, there were, in his view, important technical issues associated with the handling of sea-transported rice that required the expertise of
brokers. "Steamy rice" was one such issue.

---

7   JSHY 2:56b (5.12.27).
8   JSHY 2:58 (5.12.27).

3   Brokers and the Inspection of Steamy Rice (*zhengzhao*)

How, Bai Chun asked, should they categorize and assign responsibility for what was termed "steamy" rice—rice that was neither clean and dry (*ganjie*), nor wet and rotten (*meibian*)—a condition that could be caused during sea shipment deep in the holds of sand junks.[9] If the rice was judged to be wet and rotten when it was unloaded in Tianjin, then merchant shippers, of course, were responsible to replace the damaged grain either from their allotted "wastage" grain or, if that weren't enough, by grain purchased on the open market.

If, however, the rice was moist and steamy at the time of its arrival in Tianjin, but not actually rotten, how, Bai Chun queried, should it be assessed, warning that once the grain was officially received by Zhili authorities and loaded on to lighters, it "would pass into the hands of grain brokers," and merchant shippers would no longer bear responsibility for it.[10] If the rice became wet and/or rotten in transit from Tianjin to Tongzhou, grain brokers and lighterage boatman might try to evade responsibility for it by asserting that it had become wet during the sea voyage, and then refuse to accept liability for it; or they might just as easily use this as a pretext for "smuggling and mixing the grain."

Steamy rice posed a technical problem that placed brokers and granary staff in a difficult position. Steamy rice might not be moldy when it arrived in Tianjin, but, nonetheless, it could not be called "dry and clean." Moreover, when sent to Tongzhou, it might or might not become rotten. If the steamy rice was declared to be rotten and moldy in Tianjin, the merchant shippers "would not accept nor be reconciled to this decision." If it was considered clean and pure in Tianjin, but on arrival in Tongzhou, it was judged to be wet and rotten and the broker and lighterage boatmen were forced to pay compensation, "they would not peacefully submit."[11]

Yinghe agreed that steamy rice presented a serious problem and, "in order to draw a clear line or boundary on such issues," he proposed that during the inspection in Tianjin, "besides the clean rice that is received according to regulations and the rotten rice that is replaced with wastage rice allocated to merchant shippers, inspectors should treat steamy rice as a special category and indicate as such when they prepared grain registers documenting each lighter's load for both the imperial commissioner supervising the inspections in Tianjin and for the granary sub-prefect in Tongzhou who would inspect the

---

9   JSHY 2:57b–59b (5.12.27).
10   Ibid., 2:57b (5.12.27).
11   Ibid., 2:58b (5.12.27).

grain when it arrived at the Stone Dam. Moreover, clean rice and steamy rice should absolutely not be mixed when loaded onto lighters.[12]

If, in Tongzhou, the amount of rice in a given lighter tallied with that noted in the sub-prefect's register, the dry rice should be put directly into storage. However, if a given lighter carried steamy rice that had become wet in transit, then it should be put out to dry in the open air. If it could not be air-dried and stored, then it was to be tossed out with no one blamed for the loss. However, if there was a shortage in the *total* amount of rice in a lighter, whether wet, steamy, or dry, "the broker who is in charge of overseeing the craft must make up the deficiency."[13] In this case, Yinghe's clarification of the status of steamy rice removed any ambiguity about responsibility for it and protected merchant shippers, brokers, and lighterage owners alike if it were too wet to dry in the open air.

Special measures were also adopted to help track steamy rice cargoes on lighters during the trip to Tongzhou.[14] To make each vessel easily identifiable en route, local officials and granary personnel were "to line-up the loaded lighters in order into fleets of ten craft with the name of each boat owner displayed; then issue each vessel a stamped bill of lading (*yinpiao*) that indicates *the amount and quality* of the boat's grain load" [author's emphasis]. Additionally, each boat "must mount a signal flag (*qihao*) and a bamboo shipping label (*qianshi*), which indicates the *quantity and quality* of the grain it carries, in order to help the various officials charged with 'escorting and hastening' the transport on the route to Tongzhou" [author's emphasis]. When the lighters arrived at the Stone Dam, the grain sub-prefect would then check his register against a boat's bill of lading to see if they tallied, respecting the amount and quality of the grain. Any discrepancies or any evidence of "stealing and mixing" would be investigated and punished, with both brokers and boat owners bearing the responsibility for shortages.

4   The Broker's Role in Grain Transfers

Bai Chun agreed to limit the broker's role in grain transfers on the Tianjin docks. They were only to be allowed to inspect the grain and "control the clever hands" of their assistants, who might manipulate the measurement of grain by heaping the standard grain measures and/or adjusting the amount of grain

---

12   Ibid., 2:59 (5.2.27).
13   JSHY 2:58b (5.12.27).
14   Ibid.

placed in each bag. Under no circumstances were brokers allowed to have direct contact with merchant shippers, nor to contract with or pay porterage
and lighterage organizations. Instead, these organizations, as well as brokers,
were all to be paid directly by ranked officials "acting as brokers (*junxiguan-
weijingji*)," who would staff the General Bureau set up in Tianjin for just this
purpose.[15]

Sea-transport planners agreed that brokerage problems would have to be
fixed in 1826. If government officials discovered that brokers had "confiscated,
obstructed, or extorted" or if someone "shouts out accusations" of broker malfeasance, the accused would be "arrested, placed in manacles, and sent back
to his home county for investigation and punishment." These restrictions on
brokers were necessary because, as the Board of Revenue reminded Bai Chun,
the use of merchant shippers for sea transport "is a case of using people's transport of government grain. Failure to reign in broker extortion will diminish the
merchant shippers' heart-felt zeal for the public good."

5   The Broker's Role in Escorting Lighterage Fleets

In Bai Chun's eyes, the most vexing issue regarding brokers was how to rede-
fine their role and responsibilities for escorting and protecting the grain during
lighterage transport from Tianjin to Tongzhou, given the fact that their responsibilities for contracting and paying lighterage and porterage organizations
were curtailed. He maintained that brokers had, in the past, played an important role in the careful handling of grain cargoes on Zhili lighterage fleets, and
this role was spelled out in earlier precedents for managing the transfers of
Fengtian rice, wheat, and soybeans at Tianjin, as well as delayed grain from
canal-side anchorages and the Northern Granary.

The grain cargoes at these locations were measured and received by local
officials and/or brokers dispatched from the granary sub-prefect's office in
Tongzhou. When the grain was shipped onward to Tongzhou, local officials
appointed an assistant magistrate and other deputies along with low-ranking
officers and soldiers to share responsibility for taking custody of and escorting
the grain.[16] These officials not only guarded and "hastened" its transport, but

---

15   JSHY 2:59b–6o (5.12.27).
16   The entourage for escorting the lighterage fleets with assistant officials and low-level mili-
      tary officials and soldiers was similar to that used to escort cargoes of monetary copper
      from southwest China to the metropolitan and provincial mints. See Kim (2006), pp. 1–15.

also played an important role in "resolving disputes between superiors and inferiors along the way."[17]

In 1826, these same officials would also bear the responsibility for carrying 30 percent of the wages for boatman and porters to the Stone Dam, 70 percent having already been paid by the General Bureau at the time of departure from Tianjin. The remaining 30 percent would be "wrapped up, guarded, and carried to the grain sub-prefect at Tongzhou," who would pay the boat owners, minus any deductions for grain losses. Bai evidently agreed that the escorts, headed by an assistant magistrate, would safeguard these funds, but he worried also that they might be slack in their oversight of the boatmen. If they failed "to keep an eye out for corruption by boatmen, they will be impeached and punished."[18]

The Board of Revenue fully agreed with Bai Chun and warned that "escort personnel must safeguard the funds that are due to the boat owners and porters. They must not abuse their power, but always act with justice." If, because "they hold the porterage funds in their hands, they arbitrarily skim these wages by even an 1/100,000th (*sihao*) of a tael, the case must be referred to the imperial commissioner to investigate and punish."[19] This indicates that the imperial commissioner in Tianjin was intended to function as a break on corruption by low-level escort officials as well as brokers during lighterage shipment to Tongzhou.

Brokers had customarily accompanied the ligherage fleets from various shipment sites, specifically to "look after, or care for, the grain." In this respect, they served in a capacity similar to that of grain boat bannermen who traveled with "their" grain cargoes after they were off-loaded to lighters due to silt blockages on the Grand Canal during the regular shipment cycle. However, Bai argued strongly against using brokers to escort lighterage fleets in 1826, stating that civil and military officials, not brokers, should bear the brunt of escort duties, noting that boat owners and porters recognized the power of these officials and "were rightfully fearful of them, believing that if there were corrupt practices, like smuggling and mixing grain, they (the boat owners and porters) would be blamed and punished." In other words, these escort officials had more political clout than extra-bureaucratic brokers and, thus, were more capable of controlling boatmen and porters although their power might equally embolden their underlings to engage in corrupt practices.[20]

---

17   JSHY 2:61b (5.12.27).
18   Ibid.
19   JSHY 2:67 (5.12.27).
20   JSHY 2:62 (5.12.27).

But there was a more serious problem with the practice of brokers sharing escort responsibilities in 1826. In Bai's view, it placed too much responsibility and potential blame on the cadre of 50 to 60 brokers sent by the granary sub-prefect to the Tianjin docks to inspect the incoming sea-transported grain. If some of them were also assigned to escort the ongoing succession of lighterage fleets to Tongzhou, they would be spread too thinly to do both tasks. The cadre of brokers, he argued, should remain in Tianjin to manage the inspection and porterage of grain because, as he reminded Yinghe, "after the lighters receive the grain in Tianjin, they proceed in succession for 300 *li* to Tongzhou, then return to Tianjin again and again to transport tens of thousands more *shi*." He argued that there were simply not enough brokers "to keep the boatmen and porters under control en route to Tongzhou, as well as to inspect all the incoming grain at Tianjin."[21]

Instead, he urged that the Zhili Governor-General send more assistants and low-ranking military personnel to take over security tasks, while "the brokers should appoint a trusted deputy to care for the grain on each fleet of 10 vessels during the journey to Tongzhou.[22] In this way, each category of escort personnel (civil, military, extra-bureaucratic) would have an advocate on the spot if problems arose. "If corrupt practices occur and the broker's men are responsible, then they must pay compensation for the lost grain. If the boatmen are the corrupt party, the head man (*touchuan*) of the said lighterage fleet (10 vessels) must divide up the responsibility among the fleet and guarantee payment for the lost grain, or if the head (*zongtouchuan*) of the entire convoy of 160 vessels is implicated, he must pay for the loss." Nonetheless, the main arbiters of these cases were required to be the assistants and military officers in charge of escorting. "They must act with fairness and justice at all times. They must see that neither the brokers' underlings nor the runners [of civil officials] confiscate the grain and then accuse the boatmen as a way to extort money."[23]

Bai contrasted the brokers' *shared* escort responsibilities en route to the Stone Dam with those they bore for the onward transport from the Stone Dam to the Datong Bridge on the Inner Canal in Tongzhou, where the broker was solely responsibility for the grain. "If shortages or wet rice occur on this part of the transfer, the broker must be investigated and punished."[24] Under no

---

21   JSHY 2:62b (5.12.27).

22   It appears that the broker and/or his assistant served as a custodian of the grain in transit much like the grain-boat Banner officials did when their cargoes were off-loaded to lighters.

23   JSHY 2:60–b (5.12.27).

24   JSHY 2:62b (5.12.27).

circumstances should they be allowed to trump up charges against lighters on the outer canal.

Board of Revenue officials and the governor-general flatly rejected Bai Chun's argument for reducing the broker's escort responsibilities during the trip to the Stone Dam. While they attached greater weight to the special role of civilian "assistants and military officials to conscientiously supervise and urge the lighterage fleets forward," they, nonetheless, insisted that brokers remain responsible specifically for the care of grain during lighterage shipments, just as was the case for delayed grain in years past and for Taiwan grain in 1824. "The broker's job (*jingjifuyi*) is to take care of transferred grain precisely because he has practical, down-to-earth understanding of all aspects of lighterage. Don't alter this practice with foolish schemes or make excuses for brokers!"[25]

Moreover, they intoned, when "brokers are paid extra ration silver to take charge of grain, they assume the role of government underlings (*zaiguanrenyi*) and must not conspire with boatmen in corrupt practices. Similarly, when boatmen are hired to take [sub-bureaucratic] responsibility for transporting government grain, they must not listen to or follow the corrupt practices of brokers or their aides. If either group commits such acts, they must pay compensation for the lost grain."[26] This passage is significant because it seems to suggest that when private, extra-bureaucratic entities, like lighterage organizations and grain brokers, agree to take responsibility and accept pay for performing government tasks, they, in effect, became sub-bureaucratic underlings.

6   Cart Haulage from Tongzhou to the Beijing Granaries

The final difficult issue raised by Bai Chun centered on the logistical challenges posed by cart transport from Datong Bridge to the Beijing granaries. The most easily managed of these challenges was congestion and crowding on the route through Zhaoyang Gate, the northern-most gate on the east side of Beijing. He explained that these conditions were caused by the convergence of carts from Datong Bridge with those carrying "tithing and salary rice" (*jiami, fengmi*) from four granaries that lay just outside the city walls. He suggested that crowding on this route could be reduced by adopting the plan used in 1822 when, due to road repairs, the Beijing Police Commandant had rerouted the carts carrying tithing and salary rice through the Dongzhi and Chongwen Gates.[27] The Board

---

25   JSHY 2:63 (5.12.27).
26   Ibid.
27   JSHY 2:63b–66 (5.12.27).

of Revenue agreed with this plan, stating that "at the appointed time, Yinghe should order the Police Commandant to send low-level civil and military officials to manage the diversion of tithing grain through these two gates."[28]

The more serious challenge on this route centered on the expense and availability of cart transport and porterage. At an earlier stage in sea-transport planning, Board of Revenue officials had worried that the convergence of various tax-grain shipments at Tongzhou's Datong Bridge would overwhelm cartage resources.[29] Zhili civil and grain officials really had no idea when, and in what order, these cargoes would arrive in Tongzhou, but they were aware of the fact that the cost of hiring carts and porters had skyrocketed in recent years due to a shortage of carts. Bai Chun cited a recent case in which the hire of 120 carts for hauling 20,000 *shi* of black beans had required the payment of much higher surcharges to cover these inflated costs.[30]

Besides the inflation of cart and porterage costs, another problem with cart haulage was the uncertainty of weather conditions. If weather conditions were good, 30,000 *shi* could be loaded and shipped per day on 120 carts from Datong Bridge to Beijing—the same amount transferred at the sites from the Stone Embankment to Datong Bridge. However, the daily work regimen was long and arduous, and was made the more so by rain and cold. When rain caused muddy conditions and slowed transport, only 10,000 to 20,000 *shi* could be loaded and shipped per day. Weather-related delays triggered a ripple effect that slowed the unloading of lighters and the rotation of grain bags all the way back to the Stone Dam.

If sixty more carts were hired, it would cost 4,500 taels for the cart-hiring price and the porterage surcharge. Sixty more carts in use would also require the purchase of 40,000 to 50,000 one-*shi* grain bags at a cost of 12,000 taels for a total of 16,500 taels. Even if more carts were hired, Bai Chun opined, there would be too few to manage the transfers in a streamlined way, especially if bad weather intervened. He concluded that the provision of more carts and bags would neither solve the problem of route congestion, nor the bitter daily working conditions for cart-men and porters because "the granaries are far away and the porters cannot work through the night [in bad weather]."[31]

Bai thought that the most cost-efficient approach would be to store the grain temporarily in various granaries along the route to Beijing and then

---

28   Ibid., 2:63b–64 (5.12.27).
29   As noted earlier, the tax grain for 1826 included the regular shipments by canal and delayed 1825 grain stored in the Northern Granary, as well as sea-transported rice and Fengtian beans, wheat, and millet entering the canal at Tianjin.
30   JSHY 2:64 (5.12.27).
31   JSHY 2:64b–65 (5.12.27).

finish moving it into the city when conditions permitted. "This will be cheaper and make it easier to control and discipline the porters." He calculated that "temporary storage near Beijing will cost 2 *fen* per *shi*; thus 400,000 *shi* will cost 8,000 taels," compared to 16,500 taels for more carts and bags. He urged that the registry office (*haofang*) of the local yamen find available temporary storage, but he warned, "Don't let the Datong Bridge Supervisor (*jiandu*) coerce the various granaries to provide space. Let the Tongji Treasury pay the granaries ahead of time, and when the work is finished, send in the accounts."[32]

The Board of Revenue was pleased with the plan because "public funds will be saved," and it ordered that "at the appointed time, send low-level civil and military officials from the Beijing Police Commandant's yamen to prevent cartmen and yamen underlings from taking advantage of the situation and stirring up corruption."[33]

7   Essential Equipment for Grain Transfers

Bai Chun and Board of Revenue officials were deeply concerned about the provision of high-quality equipment for measuring and transferring grain in 1826. This included one-*shi* grain bags and regulation-sized measuring tools (*hu*) for measuring, bagging, and transferring grain at Tianjin and Tongzhou.[34] Normally, a huge number of bags and measuring tools were used at each point in the transfers. During unloading, grain was measured and bagged, after which porters then carried the bags and dumped their contents into storage facilities or into the holds of grain boats or lighters for onward transport, thus leaving the bags in place for use for the next transfers. During the regular grain-transport cycle, this bagging procedure was also used each spring when tax grain at the various southern canal anchorages was conveyed to waiting grain fleets. If lighters were used at any later stage of the canal-transport process, the measuring and bagging was done again for each transfer.

The most critical need for grain bags was in Tongzhou where a total of 30,000 bags was used each day at each of six different locations on the Inner Canal to the Datong Bridge, in order to bag and porter grain, for a grand total of

---

32   Ibid., 2:65 (5.12.27).

33   JSHY 2:65b–66 (5.12.27).

34   When grain was loaded in Jiangnan and Shanghai, however, it was measured by what was called "a red measurer" (*honghu*). These measurers and the necessary hemp bags were supplied by the Jiangnan grain jurisdictions for the transfers to sand junks in Shanghai and for unloading these craft at the Tianjin docks. When this grain was portered to the Tianjin docks and/or lighterage fleets, the *hu* was used.

FIGURE 11   Grain bagging and dumping

180,000 bags: (1) the Stone Dam, (2) drop-off stations (*lohao; wohao*) near the Stone Dam, (3) the Inner Canal (*neihe*) leading to Datong Bridge, (4) Datong Bridge, (5) the various granaries [by cart], and then (6) back to the Stone Dam "to start all over again."[35]

After the grain fleets unloaded at the Stone Dam, the grain was measured and bagged under the watchful eye of the grain sub-prefect's deputies; however, brokers alone supervised its onward transfer to the various capital granaries. At each of these six sites on any given day during the yearly grain-transport cycle, 30,000 one-*shi* bags were used to measure, bag, and dump 30,000 *shi* of grain.[36] If there were a shortage of bags at a given site, for whatever reason, every place would experience delays; the transfers would stall; the grain would pile up; causing backups as far back as the Stone Dam.[37]

Because of the large amount of sea-transported grain to arrive in Tianjin in 1826, the Board of Revenue agreed to pay for an additional 50,000 bags and 100 new measurers (*hu*) for use at Tianjin, at a total cost of 12,000 taels, paid for with funds appropriated by the Grain Transport Administration's Tongji Treasury in Tianjin. Revealing the scrutiny of the smallest detail in the transfer process, the Granary sub-prefect was charged with arranging their production and directing his deputies to verify, one-by-one, that the bags and measurers

---

35   JSHY 2:60 (5.12.27).
36   This practice is shown in an illustration in Xu Yang [1759] 1988: "A picture of prosperity in old Suzhou" (*gusu fanhuatu*). Hong Kong: Commercial Press. [I am grateful to Nanny Kim for drawing my attention to this picture].
37   JSHY 2:60b (5.12.27).

were made according to specifications,[38] marking each bag and branding each measurer with an official seal.

Examining the budgetary details of the sea-transport plan with a fine-toothed comb, Bai highlighted costs that had either been entirely overlooked in earlier discussions or been incorrectly assigned for payment. The first was the cost of "scooping" baskets that porters used to fill the grain bags when they transferred the grain from the sand junks to the docks in Tianjin.[39] Normally, Banner fleet soldiers were responsible for this cost, according to the precedents established for offloading "delayed" grain at the Tianjin's Northern Granary, and Bai applied these precedents to transfers in Tianjin in 1826 when "scooping baskets will be needed for unloading sand junks, for carrying grain to temporary open-air storage bins, and then to lighters." He reminded the Board of Revenue officials, who had mistakenly ordered the Tianjin Intendant's treasury to pay for them, that these expenses "are the responsibility of the Jiangnan grain fleets. It is not an expenditure for Zhili."[40]

Besides the provision of bags and baskets, Bai Chun insisted that "private lighters must be in good condition and watertight so that they don't leak and damage the grain."[41] This concern about the condition of the private lighters hired by Zhili local field officials was also shared by Governor-General Nayancheng and Jiangsu officials, even though private lighters were generally understood to be in a better state of repair than government lighters. However, because virtually all private lighters in Zhili would be needed in 1826, Bai wanted to insure that each and every one of them was in good repair. To do so, he urged that the governor-general order the local officials, who had initially hired these craft, to verify that they were in tip-top condition. This, however, was not good enough for the Board of Revenue. They urged the emperor to order the governor-general to send additional officials to check again—in a sense, checking up on the checkers, and if local officials were remiss and slacking in their oversight, they were to be punished.[42]

---

38   The *hu* were made according to the specifications of the Board of Revenue's iron proto-type. See Sun 1961, 741–745.

39   JSHY 2:64–65 (5.12.27).

40   JSHY 2:67b (5.12.27).

41   Jiangnan officials had also requested private lighters for the transfers from the Susongchangtaichen tax-grain jurisdictions to Shanghai for the same reasons.

42   JSHY 2:61-b (5.12.27).

8   Terms, Conditions, and Pay for Lighterage Boatmen

A final issue that Bai Chun spelled out in careful detail concerned the terms and conditions of work for lighterage boatmen during transport to the Stone Dam.[43] Before departure from Tianjin, officials "will draw up a voluntary bond agreement (*ganjie*) that outlines the lighter's responsibility (*chenglan*) for the grain it carries to insure against shortages and/or wet rice when it arrives at the Stone Dam. If so, the boatmen are required to pay compensation to make up the losses. In cases of boatmen smuggling and adulterating to cover up theft en route, granary officials must guard against brokers and/or low-level escort officials joining in their plots." He noted that boatmen have skill in these corrupt practices, and if an investigation turns up evidence of corruption, they must pay and make up for the deficiency. He felt more sympathy for the cart haulers who endured bitter conditions: "These people are on their own, without family, and, as a consequence, should be paid ahead of time."[44]

Similar to the payments made to brokers, boatmen received three fees: (1) the boat hiring price, (2) ration silver, and (3) a surcharge for porterage and wastage, 70 percent of which the Tianjin General Bureau would pay directly to lighterage and porterage organizations at the point of departure from Tianjin. As noted above, the remaining 30 percent "will be wrapped up, sealed, and entrusted to escort officials to control and carry to the Stone Dam." If inspections at the dam showed no shortages or "mixing and wetting of grain," the boatmen would be paid the remaining 30 percent. If there were shortages, compensation would be paid from the remaining 30 percent. If some of the rice was wet, then a fee was deducted to cover the cost of "spreading it out for drying."[45] Bai Chun also explained that the headmen of each ten-boat fleet and/or the general headman in charge of the whole fleet, were often implicated in the corruption by boatmen, as noted above. If so, they were liable to pay compensation too—a provision that planners thought would "invoke fear in their hearts."[46]

---

43   See Nayancheng's regulations on "waiting." JSHY 2:24b–26b (5.12.27).
44   JSHY 2:66b (5.12.27).
45   JSHY 2:66–68 (5.12.27).
46   JSHY 2:66b (5.12.27).

9   Loose Ends

Bai Chun also urged that the fees paid to lighters and brokers be increased.[47] The prevailing fees had customarily been based on the transfer costs from the Northern Granary for each 100 *shi* of grain and included a fee for each boat's porterage costs (*bochuanjiao*), ration silver (*fanmizhese*) and silver for oil and caulking materials for boat repairs. When official lighters were used, the broker was only obliged to give each individual craft under his supervision one-half of his porterage and wastage surcharge, while the commandeered Shandong-Henan fleets were given the broker's entire surcharge. These lesser allocations for official lighters and grain junks perhaps reflect the fact that they were only transferring grain on the Northern Canal, not from Tianjin.

Bai Chun observed that when Governor-General Nayancheng had earlier reviewed the issue of increasing the boat and brokerage fees, he had argued that they should continue to use the Northern Granary precedents and drop any discussion of added fees, yet he had agreed to pay an added amount to cover the costs of traveling the additional 20 kilometers from Tianjin to the Northern Granary, which, when added to the 137 kilometers from the Northern Granary to Tongzhou, totaled approximately 150 kilometers. Bai also argued that brokers deserved more because of the extra burdensome escort responsibilities that they would perform during the trip from Tianjin to Tongzhou. At the point of departure from Tianjin, he pointed out, brokers are "divided and spread out along the canal bank all the way to Tongzhou, in order to look after (*zhaoliao*) the grain." They should be given greater wastage allotments "to show compassion" because grain would be lost during the transfers from sand junk to dock, to open-air storage bins, and to lighters in Tianjin. He also underscored, as noted above, that the payments for private lighters should be estimated and paid at the time [of departure from Tianjin] by the Tianjin General Bureau.[48]

The Board of Revenue agreed with Bai about the wisdom of increasing the fees given to brokers and lighterage shippers to cover the costs for the added distance from the Tianjin docks to Tongzhou, but they insisted that in the future, officials must return to the precedents for Northern Granary shipments of "delayed rice." In other words, "do not adduce a precedent from the 1826 case."[49]

---

47   JSHY 2:23 (5.11.22).
48   JSHY 2:68–69b (5.12.27). Other items that were normally paid to bannermen on the grain fleets that were also paid to sand junk operators, Zhili grain brokers, and lighterage shippers included sums for "fruit and tea" and for ritual funeral items.
49   JSHY 2:70b (5.12.27).

10   Conclusions

The issues addressed by Yinghe and the Board of Revenue in response to Bai Chun's memorial show the changes and adjustments that the sea-transport plan imposed on the administrative practices in the Granary Superintendency in 1826. First and foremost, it sheds light on the powerful role that Zhili grain brokers played in orchestrating the management of grain transfers at Tianjin, the Northern Canal anchorages, and at Tongzhou, even though their extra-bureaucratic position placed them at the margins of imperial government. Their powerful position resulted from the fact that the vertical reach of Qing government was limited and, by necessity, relied heavily on extra- or non-bureaucratic personnel, in this case, the broker, to carry out tasks on which the supply of strategic food grains depended—not just for the capital, but the whole of Zhili province, and the northern tier of provinces from Shandong westward to Xinjiang.

Brokerage lay at the nexus of contractual and recruitment ties between the state and private entities, and it played a central role in the operation of Qing imperial rule. In this case, it centered on critically important strategic grain supplies for the capital. It might, equally, apply to lesser issues, such as the Beijing government's use of private contractors to repair city walls.[50] In both cases—strategic and mundane—brokers organized and managed important government functions.

The resort to brokerage and different forms of state-private collaboration was ubiquitous throughout Qing imperial government. The practice prevented the vertical and horizontal expansion of the permanent structures of government. The practice was, of course, temporary and cheap, but it came with a price and that price was rampant corruption that was treated as a cost of governing in this fashion. On the upside, it allowed a certain degree of flexibility for undertaking governing innovations, but the collaborations could and did cause disruptions in governance and had to be handled with great care, which can be seen in both Nayancheng's and Bai Chun's careful attention to administrative detail in mobilizing lighters and managing the arcane details of grain-tax transfers and storage.

---

50   Moll-Murata 2015, pp. 233–262.

Conclusions

The sea-transport plan of 1826 as well as lock transport through the Grand Canal–Yellow River junction were imperial–Banner-elite enterprises from beginning to end. Initiated by the Daoguang Emperor in early 1825, the sea-transport plan was created and implemented by key Banner-elite officials. At the center in the capital, Yinghe, the emperor's fiscal adviser, laid out the broad outlines of the plan in the second and fourth months of 1825. The regulations for the Jiangnan part of the plan were crafted by Qishan in the eighth and ninth months. Qishan, a rising star in the Banner-elite ranks, was appointed to design and carry it out after the firing of Sun Yuting, a high-ranking and long-serving Chinese official who lacked the necessary political clout of this formidable young Banner elite. In fairness, no non-Banner-elite Chinese could have led the effort to create an innovation like sea transport that centered on a radical change in the management and transport of the imperium's strategic capital grain reserves. It was simply too highly charged an issue to be placed in the hands of a non-Banner-elite official.

Not surprisingly, the Zhili part of the enterprise was also directed by a prestigious Banner elite: the long-serving Nayancheng, Governor-General of Zhili province and concurrent Director of the Northern Grand Canal. His administrative and logistical expertise was crucial to making adaptive changes in grain management practices in Zhili, the capital province, where strategic food grains arrived by land, sea, and canal, and were transferred to the capital granaries from which Banner elites, officials, capital military units, and the general population were supplied. Yet these adaptive changes paled in comparison to the innovations directed by Qishan.

The actual implementation of sea transport was supervised in the field by high-level Jiangsu officials: Governor Tao Zhu and Financial Commissioner He Changling, who were assisted by Susong Intendant Pan Gongchang and Suzhou Grain Intendant Song Huang. These intendants played a key role in designing the regulatory guidelines, and they also personally "dwelled at the docks in Shanghai to verify and weigh the grain," after which they traveled overland to Tianjin to officially transfer Jiangsu grain to Zhili grain authorities and release Jiangsu funds to cover the costs of transporting the grain from Tianjin to the capital granaries in Tongzhou.[1]

While these two intendants were engaged in higher-level administrative tasks, two sub-prefects took over their regular duties of office, and assistants

---

1 JSHY 4:20–26 (6.6.5). P 00123–125 (6.6.17).

performed other critical lower-level tasks. Two assistant county magistrates took charge of policing the waters near the port of Shixiao on Chongming Island, "patrolling through the billowing waves to secure the harbor." Two other temporary officials—a probationary county magistrate and an expectant Lianghuai salt examiner—"traveled along the docks and river banks from Shanghai to Baoshan to oversee the transfer and loading of grain." The Baoshan county registrar (*zhubu*) helped to refine the guidelines of the plan and to conduct audits, and he also searched into the "records, correspondence, registers, and archives," in order to inform their work on sea transport. The commissioner of records (*jingli*) and various law secretaries (*liwen*) helped "to fine-tune the regulations, supervise the record-keeping during the implementation of sea transport, and evaluate the registers of ships and boats, grain loads, and boat personnel after the plan's completion," while extra-bureaucrats, such as "gentry, educated elites, and out-of-office officials worked in the interests of the public good." The flexible assignment of these little-known assistants was crucial to the success of sea transport because they imposed discipline and kept an accounting of the fiscal and personnel requirements of the plan, serving as a bridge between the regular bureaucracy and the extra-bureaucratic servitors who carried out the day-to-day implementation of the plan.[2] Both the first and second shipments from Shanghai to Tianjin arrived with hardly a hitch, the first leaving Shanghai during the first five days of the second month and the final shipments arriving in Tianjin by the mid-eighth month. Approximately, 1.6 million *shi* were delivered by over 1500 vessels, with only one ship lost at sea and two others meeting with accidents.[3]

There is much to see in the planning and execution of sea and lock transport that bears the hallmark of Qing leadership. The use of the secret decisional process, the dispatch of imperial commissioners, and the concurrent use of sitting provincial officials to perform additional tasks enabled the Qing to maximize the use of the regular bureaucracy, but, equally if not more important, was the use of special governing tools, or tricks of the governing trade, that enabled the Qing leadership to reach below the county and department levels and stretch into the sub-county sphere to address new and emerging problems. These tools, as noted above, included the strategic use of assistant managers to link the regular bureaucracy with sub- and extra-bureaucratic organizations, the recruitment and mobilization of extra-bureaucratic organizations with special skills and resources that the Qing state lacked, and the use of temporary *ad hoc* bureaus to manage low-level state-private enterprises. The use of

---

2   Ibid.

3   Leonard 1996, pp. 244–246.

these tools enabled the Qing to resist the permanent extension of bureaucratic governance, its costs, and the accompanying extortion of local economic organizations and interests, while, at the same time, to respond promptly and creatively to new and emerging challenges to imperial rule. When these challenges proved intractable and required permanent solutions, the temporary "fixes" were institutionalized in the code—as was the case for sea transport that was finally codified in 1845.

Overall, the sea-transport experiment reveals how the Qing dynasty used skilled Banner-elite officials, the administrative code, assistants, and *ad hoc* governing tools—recruitment and bureaus—in order to overcome the systemic thinness of the bureaucratic governing structure and to respond flexibly to crises and changing times. These tricks of the governing trade were fundamental to the success of the sea-transport effort just as they were with other important administrative innovations that enhanced the effectiveness of Qing rule. They highlight the linkage between crises, Banner-elite innovation, and the revision of the code—the process by which the Qing undertook important administrative adjustments and changes in governing practice.

Glossary

Bai Chun	百春
Bajiaokou	八角口
bangban	幫辦
Beiyang*xun*	北洋汛
bochuan	剝船
boyunfutong	剝運赴通
chayiren	差役人
chengcui	丞倅
chi	遲
Chongwenmen	崇文門
chuanzhang	船長
chuangshi	創始
chuangweiguantang	創為灌塘
danchuan	蜑船
Datong *qiao*	大通橋
Dongguan	東關
Dongyang*xun*	東洋汛
Dongzhimen	東直門
dutong	督同
fanmizhese	飯米折色
ganjie	甘結
Gaojiayan/*dadi*	高家堰/大堤
ge'er	個兒
gongzhengminggan	公正明幹
guanbo	官剝
guantangduyun	灌塘督運
guoji minsheng	國計民生
He Changling	賀長齡
houbuguan	侯補官
hu	斛
huliang	斛量
jingjiren	經紀人
jintie	津貼
ju	局
lijia	例價
Linhuang*yan*	齡黃堰
Linhu*di*	臨湖堤

Linqing	麟慶
Linqing*yan*	臨清堰
Maya	馬牙
maomei	冒昧
meibian	黴變
minchuan	民船
mulong	木龍
Muzhang'a	穆彰阿
Nayancheng	那彥成
panbajieyun	盤壩接運
panbo	盤剝
Pan Gongchang	潘恭常
Pan Xi'en	潘錫恩
Qishan	琦善
quanyibanli	權宜辦理
que	缺
shachuan	沙船
Shixiao	十效
shou	收
Shuqing*ba*	束清壩
Sun Yuting	孫玉庭
Susongchangtaizhen	蘇松常太鎮
tanghe	塘河
Tao Zhu	陶澍
wangzhizhenzhe	罔知振者
Wei Yuanyu	魏元煜
Wulong'a	武龍阿
Xiong Yutai	熊遇泰
Yan Jian	顏檢
Yan Lang	嚴烺
Yinghe	英和
yinhe	引河
Yuhuang*ba*	簎黃壩
zaiguanrenyi	在官人役
Zhang Shicheng	張師誠
zhaolai	招來
zhaoshang	招商
zhengzhao	蒸潮
Zou Xichun	鄒錫淳
zuoza	佐雜

References

Citations of Qing documents from the National Palace Museum, Taibei, include Public (P) and Secret (S) edicts from the Shangyudang fangben (Record books of ordinary Grand Council affairs) and Court letter drafts (TJ) from the Jiaobu tingjidang (Record books of court letter drafts). Citations for edicts include an abbreviation of the type of document, the Daoguang reign year, the lunar month, and day: S5.2.5 (Secret edict, Daoguang 5, lunar month 2, day 5). Some edicts and memorials also include the document's archival number. Citations of Qing documents from the *Jiangsu haiyang quan'an* (Complete records of Jiangsu sea transport; JSHY) include the abbreviation of the title of the collection, the *juan* and page numbers followed by the date (reign year, lunar month, and day) in parentheses: JSHY 1:1–14b (5.4.10). Other title abbreviations are listed in alphabetical order.

Amelung, Iwo. 2000. *Der Gelbe Fluss in Shandong (1185–1911). Uberschwemmungs-katastrophen und ihre Bewaltigung im China der spaten Qing-zeit.* Wiesbaden: Harassowitz.

Amelung, Iwo. 2005. "Preliminary observations on 'Regulations and precedents' (Hegong zeli) during the Qing dynasty." In Moll-Murata et al., eds., 285–305.

Antony, Robert J. 2002. "Subcounty officials, the state, and local communities in Guangdong province, 1644–1860." In Antony and Leonard, eds., 27–59.

Antony, Robert J. and Jane Kate Leonard, eds. 2002. *Dragons, tigers, and dogs. Qing crisis management and the boundaries of state power in late imperial China.* Ithaca: East Asian Program, Cornell University.

Bartlett, Beatrice S. 1990. *Monarchs and ministers. The Grand Council in mid-Qing China (1723–1820).* Berkeley: University of California Press.

Bastid, Marianne. 1985. "The structure and the financial institutions of the state in the late Qing." In Schram, ed., 51–79.

B.H. Brunnert, H.S. and V. V. Hagelstrom. 1912. *Present day political organization of China.* Trans. A. Beltchenko and E.E. Moran. Shanghai: Kelly and Walsh.

Chang, Michael G. 2007. *A court on horseback. The imperial touring and the construction of Qing rule (1680–1785).* Cambridge, MA: Harvard University Press.

CHC 10. *The Cambridge history of China.* Vol. 10. Late Ch'ing, 1800–1911. Pt. 1. John K. Fairbank and Denis Twitchett, eds. Cambridge: Cambridge University Press.

Chen, Hailian. 2016. Zinc for coin and brass: Bureaucrats, merchants, artisans, and mining laborers in Qing China, ca. 1680s–1830s. Ph.D. diss., Eberhard Karls University of Tübingen.

Cheng, Suiwai. 2008. *The price of rice. Market integration in eighteenth-century China.* Studies on East Asia, vol. 29. Bellingham, WA: Center for East Asian Studies, Western Washington University.

Chuan, Hansheng and Richard A. Kraus. 1975. *Mid-Ch'ing rice markets and trade: An essay in price history*. Cambridge, MA: East Asian Research Center, Harvard University.

CYQS. [*Qingding*] *Hubu caoyun quanshu* 欽定戶部漕運全書 (*Board of Revenue complete book on grain transport*). Comp. 1875; printed 1876. Cailing 載齡, comp. 96 *juan*. 1845 collection: 92 *juan*.

Dai, Yingcong. 2009. *The Sichuan frontier and Tibet. Imperial strategy in the early Qing*. Seattle: University of Washington Press.

DMB. Goodrich, L. Carrington and Fang Chaoying, eds. 1976. *Dictionary of Ming Biography, 1368–1644*. 2 vols. New York: Columbia University Press.

Dodgen, Randall A. 2001. *Controlling the dragon: Confucian engineers and the Yellow River in late imperial China (1835–1850)*. Honolulu: University of Hawaii Press.

DOT. Hucker, Charles O. 1985. *A dictionary of official titles in imperial China*. Stanford: Stanford University Press.

ECCP. Hummel, Arthur W., ed. [1943–1944] 1967. *Eminent Chinese of the Qing period, 1644–1912*. 2 vols. in one. Washington, DC: U.S. Government Printing Office. Reprint. Taibei: Chengwen.

Elliott, Mark C. 2001. *The Manchu way. The eight banners and ethnic identity in late imperial China*. Stanford: Stanford University Press.

Elvin, Mark. 1977. "Market towns and waterways: The county of Shanghai from 1480 to 1910." In Skinner, ed., *The city in late imperial China*. Stanford: Stanford University Press, 441–473.

Elvin, Mark and Liu Ts'ui-jung, eds. 1998. *Sediments of time. Environment and society in China*. Cambridge: Cambridge University Press.

Elvin, Mark and Su Ninghu, eds. 1998. "Action at a distance. The influence of the Yellow River on Hangzhou Bay since A.D. 1000." In Elvin and Liu, eds., 344–407.

Guy, R. Kent. 2010. *Qing governors and their provinces: The evolution of territorial administration in China, 1644–1796*. Seattle: University of Washington Press.

Herman, John E. 1997. "Empire in the southwest: Early Qing reforms in the native chieftain system." *Journal of Asian Studies* 56, 1: 47–74.

Hinton, Harold C. 1970. *The grain tribute system of China (1945–1911)*. Cambridge, MA: East Asian Research Center, Harvard University.

Hirzel, Thomas and Nanny Kim, eds. 2008. *Metals, monies, and markets in early modern societies: East Asian and global perspectives*. Monies, Markets, and Finance in China, vol. 1. Berlin: Lit Verlag.

Hou, Chi-ming and Tzong-shian Yu, eds. 1979. *Modern Chinese Economic History*. Taibei: Institute of Economics, Academia Sinica.

Hsu, Immanuel. 2000. *The rise of modern China*. 6th ed. New York: Oxford University Press.

Hu Ch'ang-tu. 1954–55. "The Yellow River Administration in the Ch'ing dynasty." *Far Eastern Quarterly* 14: 505–513.

Huang, Guosheng 黃國盛. 2000. *Yapianzhanzhengqiande dongnanshenghaiguan* 鴉片戰爭前的東南四省海關 (The maritime customs in the four southeastern coastal provinces in the pre-Opium War period). Fuzhou: Fujianrenminchubanshe.

Huang Pengnian 黃彭年 (Qing). [N.d.] 1994. *Jifufanchazhi* 畿輔梵刹志 (Records of Buddhist Monastery in the capital). Taibei: Zongqingtuchubanzongsi. Portrait of the Daoguang Emperor in court dress, No. 24, image 256.

HYHK. See Linqing 1841.

Johnson, Linda Cooke, ed. 1993. *Cities of Jiangnan in the late imperial China.* SUNY Series in Chinese Local History. Albany, NY: State University of New York Press.

Johnson, Linda Cooke. 1993. "Shanghai. An emerging Jiangnan port, 1683–1840." In Johnson, ed., 131–181.

JSHY. He Changling 賀長齡 and Tao Zhu 陶澍, eds. 1826. *Jiangsu haiyun quan'an* 江蘇海運全案 (Complete records on Jiangsu sea transport). N.p. 12 *juan*.

JSWB. He Changling 賀長齡, ed. [1826] 1965. *Huangchao jingshi wenbian* 皇朝經世文編 (Essays on statecraft in the Qing dynasty). Wei Yuan 魏源, comp. 120 *juan*. Reprint. Taibei: Shijie.

Kaske, Elisabeth. 2008. "The price of an office. Veniality, the individual, and the state in 19th century China." In Hirzel and Kim, eds., 281–308.

Kaske, Elisabeth. 2015. "Silver, copper, rice, and debt. Monetary policy and office selling in China during the Taiping Rebellion." In Leonard and Theobald, eds., 345–397.

Kelley, David E. 1982. "Temples and fleets: The Luo Sect and boatmen's associations in the eighteenth century." *Modern Asian Studies* 8, 3: 361–91.

Kelley, David E. 1986. Sect and society. The evolution of the Luo Sect among Qing dynasty grain tribute boatmen, 1700–1850. Ph.D. diss., Harvard University.

Kim, Nanny. 2008. "Copper transports out of Yunnan, ca. 1750–1850: Preliminary discussion of transport technologies, natural difficulties, and environmental change in a southwestern highland area." In Hirzel and Kim, eds., 191–220.

Kim, Nanny. 2009. "River control, merchant philanthropy, and environmental change in nineteenth-century China, 1805–1840." *Journal of the Economic and Social History of the Orient* 52.4–5: 660–694.

Kim, Nanny. 2012. *Mountain rivers, mountain roads: Transport in the southwest of Qing China, 1700–1850.* Leiden: Brill.

Leonard, Jane Kate. 1992. "The state's resources and the people's livelihood (*guojiminsheng*): The Daoguang Emperor's dilemmas about Grand Canal restoration, 1825." In Leonard and Watt, eds., 47–73.

Leonard, Jane Kate. 1996. *Controlling from Afar. The Daoguang Emperor's Management of the Grand Canal crisis, 1824–1826.* Ann Arbor: Center for Chinese Studies, The University of Michigan.

Leonard, Jane Kate. 2002. "Negotiating across the boundaries of state power: Organizing the 1826 sea transport experiment." In Antony and Leonard, eds., 183–211.

Leonard, Jane Kate. 2004. "Coastal merchant allies in the 1826 sea transport experiment." In Wang and Ngu, eds., 271–286.

Leonard, Jane Kate. 2005. "Introduction: General reflections on regulations and precedents (*zeli*)." In Moll-Murata et al., eds., 27–31.

Leonard, Jane Kate. 2005. "Timeliness and innovation: The 1845 revision of the *Complete Book on Grain Transport* (Caoyun quanshu)." In Moll-Murata et al., eds., 449–464.

Leonard, Jane Kate. 2006. "The Qing strategic highway on the northeast coast." In Schottenhammer and Ptak, eds., 27–39.

Leonard, Jane Kate. 2015. "The Fixers: The role of the Zhili grain brokers in the 1826 sea transport experiment." In Leonard and Theobald, eds., 420–438.

Leonard, Jane Kate and Ulrich Theobald, eds. 2015. *Money in Asia (1200–1900): Small currencies in social and political contexts.* Monies, Markets, and Finance in East Asia, 1600–1900. General editor: Hans Ulrich Vogel, vol. 6. Leiden: Brill.

Leonard, Jane Kate and John R. Watt, eds. 1992. *To achieve security and wealth. The Qing imperial state and the economy, 1644–1911.* Cornell East Asia Series, no. 56. Ithaca, NY: East Asia Program, Cornell University.

Li, Wenzhi 李文治. 1948. "Qingdaituntianyucaoyun" 清代屯田與漕運 (Military agricultural land and grain transport in the Qing periods). In *Zhongguojindaishiluncong* 中國近代史論叢 (Discussion of modern Chinese history). 2d series, vol. 3. Taibei: Zhengzhong.

Li, Wenzhi. 1989. "Qing Daoguanghougaigecaozhiyi" 清道光侯改革漕制議 (Late Qing Daoguang reign reforms of the grain transport system). 中國經濟史研究 (Chinese Economic History Research) 1: 24–44.

Li, Wenzhi and Jiang, Taixin 江太新. 1995. *Qingdaicaoyun* 清代漕運 (Grain tax transport in the Qing period). Beijing: Zhonghua.

Lin, Manhoung. 1991. "Two social theories revealed: Statecraft controversies over China's monetary crisis, 1808–1854." *Late Imperial China* 12: 1–35.

Linqing 麟慶. 1836. *Hegongqijutushuo* 河工器具圖說 (Illustrations and explanations of water conservancy tools). 4 *juan.* Shanghai: Commercial Press.

Linqing. [1841] 1969. *Huangyunhekou gujintushuo* 黃運河口古今圖說 (Historical maps and explanations of the topography of the Yellow River-Grand Canal junction, past and present). 337 pp. Reprint. Taibei: Wenhai.

Linqing. [1879] 1984. *Hongxueyinyuantuji* 鴻雪因緣圖記 (Illustrated diary of travels). 3 vols. Reprint. Beijing: Guji.

Liu, Kuangjing 劉廣京. 1991. *Jingshisixiangyuxinxingqiye* 經世思想與新興企業 (Jingshi thought and modern enterprise). Taibei: Lianjingchubanshe.

Lo, Jungpang. 1955. "The emergence of China as a sea power during the late Sung and Yuan periods." *Far Eastern Quarterly* 14.4: 489–504.

Lufrano, Richard. 2013. "Minding the minders. Overseeing the brokerage system in Qing China." *Late Imperial China* 34, 1 (June): 67–107.

Ma, Shibo 馬士鉢 and Yu Boming 于伯銘. 1992. *Daoguangchuan* 道光傳 (Biography of the Daoguang Emperor). Shenyang: Liaoning jiaoyu.

Marks, Robert B. 1991. "Rice prices, food supply, and market structure in eighteenth-century South China." *Late Imperial China* 12, 2: 64–116.

Mayers, William Frederick. [1897] 1966. *The Chinese government. A manual of Chinese titles, categorically arranged and explained, with an appendix.* 3d edition. Reprint. Taibei: Chengwen.

Metzger, Thomas. 1973. *The internal organization of the Ch'ing bureaucracy: Legal, normative, and commercialization aspects.* Harvard Studies in East Asian Law, no. 7. Cambridge, MA: Harvard University Press.

Millward, James. 1998. *Beyond the pass. Economy, ethnicity, and empire in Qing Central Asia.* Stanford: Stanford University Press.

Moll-Murata, Christine, Song Jiangze, and Hans Ulrich Vogel, eds. 2005. *Chinese handicraft regulations of the Qing dynasty. Theory and application.* Munich: Iudicum.

Moll-Murata, Christine and Song Jiangze. 2002. "Notes on Qing dynasty 'handicraft regulations and precedents' (*jiangzuo zeli*), with special focus on regulations on materials, working time, prices, and wages." *Late Imperial China* 23, 2: 87–120.

Needham, Joseph. 1971. *Science and civilization in China.* 4 vols. Cambridge: Cambridge University Press, vol. 4, pt. 3, 211–378 (hydraulics).

Ni, Yuping 倪玉平. 2005. *Qingdai caoliang haiyun yu shehuibianqian* 清代漕粮海運與社會變迁 (Sea transport of grain tax and social change in the Qing period). Shanghai: Shanghai shudian chubanshe.

Peng, Yunhe 彭云鶴. 1995. *Ming Qing caoyun* 明清漕運 (The history of grain tax transport in the Ming and Qing periods). Beijing: Beijing Academy of Social Sciences.

Perdue, Peter C. 2005. *China marches west. The Qing conquest of Central Asia.* Cambridge, MA: Belknap Press for Harvard University.

Perdue, Peter C. 1992. "The Qing state and the Gansu grain market, 1739–1864." In Rawski and Li, eds., 100–125.

Playfair, G.M.H. [1910] 1965. *The cities and towns of China. A geographical dictionary.* 2d ed. Shanghai: Kelley and Walsh. Reprint. Taibei: Jingwen.

Playfair, G.M.H. 1875. "The grain transport system of China. Notes and statistics taken from the 'Ta Ching Hui Tien'." *China Review* 3, 6: 354–364.

Polachek, James M. 1976. Literati groups and literati politics in early nineteenth-century China. Ph.D. diss., University of California, Berkeley.

QDHCZ. [1937] 1969. *Qingdai hechenzhuan* 清代河臣傳 (Biographies of canal-river officials in the Qing dynasty). Comp. Wang Huzhen and Wu Weizu. Nanjing: Chinese Engineering Society. Reprint. Taibei: Wenhai.

Qingdai zhuanji congkan 清代傳記叢刊 (Compendium of Qing biographies). Zhou Junfu, ed. Taibei: Mingwen, 1986.

Qingdai wenxianzhuanbaozhuangaorenmingsoyin 清代文獻傳包傳稿人名索引 (Name index of biographical drafts of the Qing dynasty). Guoligugongbowuyuan. Taibei: 1986.

Qinghe [Jiangsu] *xianzhi* (Gazetteer of Qinghe county). 1855. Lu Yitong and Wu Tang, comps. 24 *juan*; 1 head *juan*. 8 ce in one box. Harvard Yenching Library: 3205/3232.86.

Rawski, Thomas G. and Lillian Li, eds. 1992. *Chinese history in economic perspective.* Berkeley: University of California Press.

Rowe, William T. 2018. *Speaking of profit. Bao Shicheng and reform in nineteenth-century China.* Cambridge, MA: Harvard University Asia Center, Harvard-Yenching Institute Monograph Series.

Schottenhammer, Angela and Roderich Ptak, eds. 2006. *The perception of maritime space in traditional Chinese sources.* Wiesbaden: Harrassowitz Verlag.

Schram, Stuart, ed. 1985. *The scope of state power in China.* New York: St. Martin's Press.

Scroll map of Chinese coast. British Museum. Department of Maps, Map 162.0.3. N.d. London: British Museum.

Skinner, G. William, ed. 1977. *The city in late imperial China.* Stanford: Stanford University Press.

Sun, E-tu Zen. 1962–1963. "The Board of Revenue in nineteenth-century China." *Harvard Journal of Asiatic Studies* 24: 175–227.

Sun, E-tu Zen. 1968. "Ch'ing government and the mineral industries before 1800." *Journal of Asian Studies* 24, 4: 835–845.

Sun, E-tu Zen. 1971. "The transportation of Yunnan copper to Peking in the Ch'ing period." *Journal of Oriental Studies* 9: 132–142.

Sun, E-tu Zen. 1992. "The Finance Ministry (Hubu) and its relationship to the economy in Qing times." In Leonard and Watt, eds., 9–20.

Theobald, Ulrich. 2013. *War, finance, and logistics in the late imperial China. A study of the second Jinchuan campaign (1771–1776).* Leiden: Brill.

von Glahn, Richard. 1996. *Fountains of fortune: Money and monetary policy in China, 1000–1700.* Berkeley: University of California Press.

von Glahn, Richard. 2016. *The economic history of China from antiquity to the nineteenth century.* Cambridge: Cambridge University Press.

von Glahn, Richard. 1996. "Myth and reality of China's seventeenth-century monetary crisis." *Journal of Economic History* 56, 2: 429–454.

Vogel, Hans Ulrich. 1987. "Chinese central monetary policy, 1644–1800." *Late Imperial China* 8, 2: 1–52.

Wang Gung-wu and Ng Chin-keong. 2004. *Maritime China in transition, 1750–1850.* Wiesbaden: Harrassowitz.

Wang Yeh-chien. 1973. *Land taxation in imperial China, 1750–1911*. Cambridge, MA: Harvard University Press.

Wang, Yeh-chien. 1979. "Evolution of the Chinese monetary system, 1644–1850." In Hou and Yu, eds., 425–452.

Wang Yeh-chien. 1992. "Secular trends in rice prices in the Yangzi delta, 1638–1935." In Rawski and Li, eds., 35–68.

Watt, John R. 1975. *The district magistrate in late imperial China*. New York: Columbia University Press.

Wei Xiumei 魏 秀梅. 1985. *Tao Zhuzai Jiangnan* 陶澍在江南 (Tao Zhu in Jiangnan). Monograph no. 51. Institute of Modern History, Academia Sinica (Taibei).

Wei Xiumei. 1993. "Qishanzai Yulu dezhengji, 1814–1829" 琦善在豫魯的政績 (Qishan's political-administrative achievements in Henan and Shandong, 1814–1829). *Bulletin of the Institute of Modern History*, Academia Sinica (Taibei) 22, 1: 463–503 (June).

Wei Xiumei. 1994. "Qishanzai Liangjiangdezhengji, 1825–1827" 琦善在兩江的政績 (Qishan's political-administrative achievements in Liangjiang, 1825–1827). *Bulletin of the Institute of Modern History, Academia Sinica* (Taibei), 23: 135–160.

Will, Pierre-Etienne. 1990. *Bureaucracy and famine in eighteenth-century China*. Trans. Elborg Forster. Stanford: Stanford University.

Will, Pierre-Etienne and R. Bin Wong with James Lee. 1991. *Nourish the people. The state civilian granary system in China, 1650–1850*. Ann Arbor: Center for Chinese Studies, University of Michigan.

Worcester, G.R.G. 1971. *The junks and sampans of the Yangtze*. Annapolis: Naval Institute Press.

Wu, Silas H.L. 1970. *Communication and imperial control in China. Evolution of the palace memorial system, 1693–1734*. Cambridge, MA: Harvard University Press.

Xu, Yang 徐揚. [1759] 2008. *Gusufanhuatu* 姑蘇繁華圖 (The splendor of old Suzhou). Yang Dongsheng, ed. Tianjin: Tianjin renminmeishuchubanshe.

Zelin, Madeleine. 1984. *The magistrate's tael. Rationalizing fiscal reform in eighteenth-century Ch'ing China*. Berkeley: University of California Press.

Zhang, Zhongmin 張忠民. 1990. *Shanghai: Cong kaifa zouxiang kaifang, 1368–1842* 上海從開發走相開放 (Shanghai: From its development to its opening, 1368–1842). Kunming: Yunnan People's Press.

Zhang, Zhongmin. 1996. *Qianjindai zhongguoshehuideshangrenziben yu shehuizaishengchan* 前近代中國社會的商人資本與社會在生產 (Early modern Chinese merchant capitalism and social development). Shanghai: Shanghai Academy of Social Sciences.

Zhang, Zhongmin. 2002. "The civil role of sojourner and trade associations in Shanghai during the Qing period." In Antony and Leonard, eds., 103–128.

ZGLSDTJ. Zhongguolishidituji 中國歷史地土集 (Historical atlas of China). 1992. Tan Qixiang, ed. 8 vols. (Qing) vol. 8. Taibei: Hsiaoyuan.

Zhao, Gang. 2013. *The Qing opening to the ocean: Chinese maritime policies, 1684–1757*. Honolulu: University of Hawai'i Press.

Zhejiang haiyunquan'an 浙江海運全案 (Compilation on sea transport of tribute grain from Zhejiang province). Compiled by Ma Xinyi. First comp. 1853; supplement 1854; new 1867. 20 *juan*.

Zhou, Wu and Xu Kaiming. 1992. *Tao Zhulun* (A discussion of Tao Zhu). Changsha: Fouli.

Index

Printed in the United States
By Bookmasters